PARENTAL
ADVISORY
EXPLICIT LYRICS

STANDING OVATION FOR *ALPHA COUPLES*

"You slayed it! ... #RelationshipGoals"
—Lisa Leslie, 4x Olympic Gold Medalist & 3x WNBA MVP

"This book hits the most pressing challenges that face the modern marriage: dual professions, financial management, shortage of time, and work-life balance. Only read if you're willing to set aside all excuses and start living an extraordinary life."
—Sarah Rosnick, Senior Manager at Facebook

"Calling this book a marriage book is a misnomer. More than relationships, *Alpha Couples* is a business leadership book for power couples. The lessons about money management, personal assistants, and goal setting are applicable to all entrepreneurs, whether single or married. *Alpha Couples* is a book about alpha males and females together transcending all to live their best life in every possible way!"
—Alonzo Ford, Managing Director at AMG CRE Capital

"Practical, powerful, and personal. *Alpha Couples* is filled with plenty of tips and advice. Robert shows that marriages are far more complicated in real life than movies would have us believe. Even if readers do not agree with all of the principles, I am convinced that at some point in the book, they will be touched."
—Kelly Biggs, Principal at WSI Digital Marketing

"A great book for any couple, to include LGBTQ+ partners. I love this book because it is a guide for relationships and business. I was able to start using the tools in this book in my small business right away and see an increase in sales. If you want to be an Alpha Couple now or with a future partner, this is the book you have to read."
—Emilyrose Furman, Founder of Do I Look Gay Yet?

"Robert and Zaira give us an inside look at how entrepreneurial couples manage their careers, businesses, finances, and marriage. They don't gloss over any of the challenges of entrepreneurship or marriage. They are open and introspective, inspiring readers to achieve more. Well done!"
—Brian Retherford, Proprietor at Claudine Wines

"As both a mental health professional who sees and treats people every day, who are wading through relationship troubles, as well as a business owner myself, it was refreshing to read about a successful relationship that has included individual personal growth and career goals while also ensuring the growth of the relationship. This books gives couples a plan that sets them up for success. Highly recommend!"
—Anne Smith, Licensed Mental Health Counselor

"I don't think this is solely a relationship book. *Alpha Couples* is, at its heart, a book about leadership. Leadership surely starts at home. Robert's passion to improve himself and others is an inspiration, and *Alpha Couples* adds even more to an already humble but impactful pursuit."
—Chaveso 'Chevy' Cook, Executive Director of the nonprofit MilitaryMentors

"*Alpha Couples* is as insightful as it is interesting. Whether you're looking to empower yourself or your relationship, this is the perfect book for anyone. The Solano's have helped me and my significant other through things we thought we couldn't get through. They helped repair and strengthen our relationship and I couldn't be more grateful. This book is an inspiring read that you won't be able to put down. So do yourself a favor and become an Alpha Couple."
—Nicole Sager, Florida State College

"Finally, a book for modern couples! Robert and Zaira expose how Alpha Couples have always existed in nature and they disrupt everything we've been told about traditional marriage roles. If you are married, and especially if you are an entrepreneur, this book will speak to your soul."
—Jennifer Gore-Cuthbert, CEO of Atlanta Personal Injury Law Group Gore

"Fascinating and enlightening. This is one of those books that make you better, educated, happier, confident, and much more if you read this with a very open mind. Robert offers great insight into the dynamics between a power couple—dual careers, joint finances, time management—and shows how professional couples can partner together to foster communication, happiness, and partnership. I haven't read a better reason to be hopeful that professional couples can have two successful careers and a very happy marriage."
—Dr. Hise Gibson, Academy Professor at the United States Military Academy

"*Alpha Couples* is not only engaging and fun to read but it is full of real-life examples and challenges that successful couples face. The best part is that the solutions and insights will help you look at your own lives and situations with a fresh perspective. Whether you are in the corporate world or an entrepreneur, *Alpha Couples* is a must read!"
—Nadia Huda, Marketing Executive at DEKRA and
Investor of F45 Training Pasadena

"All couples have been there. You hit days when the pressure of work, family, everything else seems overwhelming. Days when you question why you are working so hard and why you can't seem to spend more time with the family. I know; I've been there. *Alpha Couples* addresses real issues professionals face and shares practical tips and solutions to many of life's current challenges. Robert and Zaira share a fresh perspective on marriage and personal growth. They show how couples, especially entrepreneur couples, can balance their business, family, finances, and happiness to build an amazing life!"
—Kristen David, Author of Uplevel Your Business, Uplevel Your Life!

ALPHA COUPLES

BUILD A POWERFUL MARRIAGE *Like a Boss*

ROBERT SOLANO FEAT. ZAIRA SOLANO

Names and details of some individuals have been changed to preserve their privacy. The opinions in this book are the authors' and do not represent any other organization. This book is intended for information only. Neither the authors nor the publishers are offering specific relationship, financial, or legal advice. Readers are encouraged to seek professional marriage counseling, financial advice, accounting, or legal advice when required.

This book is independently published by Alpha Couples LLC.
For more information about book sales, speaking engagements, or marriage coaching, visit www.alphacouplesthrive.com.

Library of Congress Cataloging Information available upon request.

First Hardcover Edition
Version 1.00, August 4th, 2020
Printed in the United States

Cover Design by Andrew Bell
Cover Photo by Vadim Davydov

Produced and Edited by Raab & Co. | www.Raabandco.com

ISBN: 978-1-7353468-0-9
www.alphacouplesbook.com

To my beautiful bride, Zaira,
Your love, energy, and spirit inspire me. I hope that
I will always be the man that you deserve.

Te amo todos los siempres,

Robert

Tracks

INTRO

FORWARD

"Best foot first just in case." —Beyoncé

In 2018, I was coaching a small group of million-dollar-plus law firm owners. Zaira Solano was one of four CEOs that I regularly met with. Once a quarter, we all gathered at my home for a daylong intensive session. Throughout the day, we would tackle business strategies to double their revenue. After her husband, Robert, joined us for a coaching session, I had to stop allowing spouses in our tactical workshops.

Zaira asked if Robert could join us, and though the request was uncommon, Robert *did* occasionally help her with the law firm. I didn't think much of it. My chef prepared us breakfast and then we went to the boardroom, where we began discussing sales, marketing, staffing, and stuff like that.

About two hours into the meeting, the topic of children came up. Within a few minutes, everyone was crying.

It began when Zaira shared her challenges about the right timing to get pregnant while also trying to fix issues in her law firm. In a room full of business owners, we all knew exactly how Zaira and Robert felt. As a business owner and mother who wanted a family, a successful business, *and* a great marriage, I was especially sympathetic to Zaira and Robert's story.

One of my businesses is helping entrepreneurs like Zaira and Robert build and grow their businesses. After coaching thousands of law firm owners over the past decade, it is easy to help them with marketing, sales, staffing, finances, and the other aspects of a business. But helping someone to maintain a good relationship and a successful business at the same time is hard. This is probably why most marriage counselors focus strictly on relationships and most coaches focus only on business. The truth is, however, that the intersection of marriage and business is the area where most of us actually live. We can't fully separate them.

In many instances, our relationships, especially our marriages, are even more important for the success of our businesses than any part of the business plan. The same is true if you are a corporate executive, doctor, policeman, or lawyer. The same is true whether you work directly with your spouse or not. Our marriages play a huge part in the success of our businesses, careers, and overall happiness and joy. Starting and growing a successful business is a lot of work. If a business owner doesn't have good support from their spouse, either the marriage or the business is doomed.

In *Alpha Couples*, Robert and Zaira take us on a beautiful journey through an ambitious professional couple's trials, tribulations, and lessons learned. They show us the challenges of balancing a corporate career with an entrepreneurial career, they offer great insight from other successful couples, and they teach us how to be successful in finances, in time management, and with each other.

Now, if a business owner asks to bring their spouse to one of our sessions, I allocate a little extra time, I bring a box of tissues, and I'm prepared for the conversation to go deeper than business strategy. In actuality, I love it when a couple each takes interest in a business because it is those couples—who share goals and desires in both their personal *and* professional realms—that are most likely to grow exponentially and achieve their goals. Robert and Zaira are an example of just such a couple.

Alpha Couples is a beautiful testament to the power of love.

Saludos,

Alejandra Leibovich
Cofounder of How to Manage a Small Law Firm

Alejandra Leibovich is an award-winning entrepreneur, animator, author, apps & games developer, and sandwich lover. Leibovich, a.k.a. Aleloop, is the cofounder of How to Manage a Small Law Firm. She uses her creativity in a wide range of fields because "why do just one thing when there are so many cool things to do!" Originally from Argentina, Leibovich has been living in the US for the better half of her life, but still takes pride in her thick Argentinian accent. You can usually find her doing something fun and interesting. Visit aleloop.com to know more about her.

INTRO

WHY I LOVE YOU

"Ooh, I love you so, but why I love you, I'll never know."
—Jay-Z

I realized Robert may be "the one" on our third date, when he cooked a three-course meal served on Vera Wang china. The evening began with an invite to his condo for dinner. As I sat at his kitchen island and drank a glass of wine, he seasoned the chicken cutlets, boiled pasta, stirred his homemade tomato sauce, and prepared a caprese antipasto. I watched him closely as Andrea Bocelli played softly in the background. It was like watching Bobby Flay on *Iron Chef*. He moved fast, he had different pans cooking at the same time, and it was clear he was experienced in the kitchen. He drained the pasta and served it on beautifully ornate plates. I never thought I'd find a man with his cooking skills and such a sexy choice of china.

His dining room was the balcony of his eighteenth-floor condo, which had a perfect view of Peachtree Street from Midtown to Downtown Atlanta. Over dinner, we laughed a lot, talked about our past, and talked about the future. We drank an Oregon pinot noir, which Robert explained was an up-and-coming wine region, as we enjoyed the spring evening breeze. It was natural and easy.

As the night progressed, I took a bathroom break and came back out to Robert strumming his guitar. I immediately thought, *He's really trying to hit that.*

He pulled out every trick! He played a few strings of classical Spanish guitar as I swayed back and forth. *Is this man real? He studied at the top military academy of the world. He's getting his master's in rocket science. He's gorgeous and into fitness. He can cook and has a clean, beautiful home. He has goals and is a family guy... Maybe I will let him hit that.*

This was the beginning of the fairy tale but it's not the everyday tale. If our marriage looks easy, that was never on purpose. In this book, we share our journey and how we fight for our marriage and for ourselves as individuals.

When I say fight, I mean not letting any circumstance, person, thing, or ourselves stand in the way of what we want.

We want extraordinary everything—marriage, career, relationships, experiences, and children. We agree that no one will hand it to us nor will it magically happen. To achieve the extraordinary, it requires intentional effort day in and day out. It requires the courage to be honest with yourself about what you really want and the same courage to go for it. It requires resilience to endure the pain, stress, and failure during your journey to your goals. It requires the ability to shift and change direction when things are not developing as planned or when you realize the plan is not going to work. It requires guts!

Robert has incredible discipline and I credit him for intentionally pushing us to grow as an Alpha Couple. Robert is the anchor and I'm the balloon—we balance each other. When I made the decision that I wanted more for myself than the life I was living, he joined me on my journey, and it transformed into our journey. Robert challenges us to think big, make a plan, and stick to the plan or abort it.

He does not judge the grand mistakes I make but instead comforts me when I'm crying about it. He has learned when to offer advice and when to just listen. He calms me down when I'm freaking out. He grounds me when I'm pissed. And Robert loves to change our environment, all the time, so we don't get too comfortable anywhere, with anything.

We know that, together, we will live a far better life than we ever could imagine as individuals. We don't have it all figured out but every day we move toward an extraordinary future. Some days we take leaps, some days we take baby steps, but what matters is that the desire is there and we're doing something about it.

Robert, you amaze me! You've poured your heart and soul into this project, not just to help our marriage thrive, but also to help other couples build a powerful marriage and successful careers. Every couple that this book helps will have a positive compound effect on their kids and the generations to come.

For your commitment to us, for your love of others, and for many more reasons, I love you.

Love,
Zaira

VOL. I

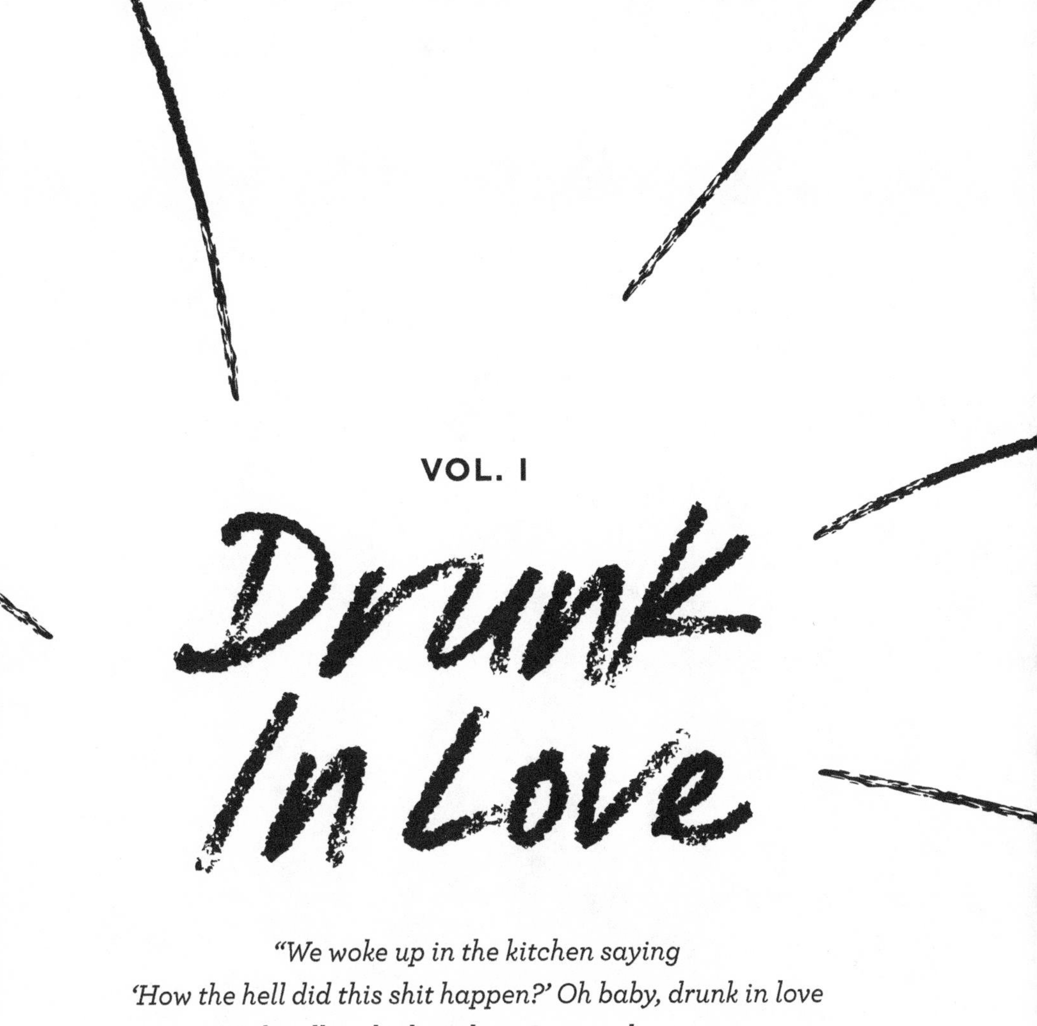

Drunk In Love

"We woke up in the kitchen saying
'How the hell did this shit happen?' Oh baby, drunk in love
We be all night, last thing I remember is our
Beautiful bodies grinding up in that club, drunk in love"

—Beyoncé

CHAPTER ONE

SCARED OF LONELY

"I try to be patient, but I'm hurting deep inside." –Beyoncé

When I departed Kyrgyzstan in December 2012, I knew that my marriage was on the rocks. I had just finished a yearlong overseas assignment in Central Asia. It had been twelve months since I was last home in Hawaii, and I was eager to leave the arid mountains and freezing temperatures in exchange for the warm, sunny beaches of Oahu. I was also anxious to see my wife again.

The trip back took over forty-eight hours as I transitioned between airports in Asia, Siberia, and Seattle, before finally arriving in Honolulu. I was immediately greeted by 85-degree weather and sunburned tourists wearing floral-print aloha shirts and fresh orchid lei necklaces. My wife at the time picked me up from the airport and drove us home. As we drove to the North Shore, we chatted about the dogs, our families, and work as if we were friends who had not seen each other in months.

After we left the city, the country road home took us through the Dole plantation, where endless rows of lush green pineapple bushes cut through the bright orange dirt. As we crested a large hill, I could suddenly see seven miles of beautiful aquamarine ocean and beaches.

As we drove over that crest and I scanned the waves at my favorite surf spots, I began to tear up. After a year of arduous workdays, I was finally home, back to paradise.

My overseas assignment was difficult. I was the chief operations officer for aviation maintenance operations. The pay was great, and the job was rewarding, but the work was nonstop. I usually worked at least twelve hours a day, six or seven days a week.

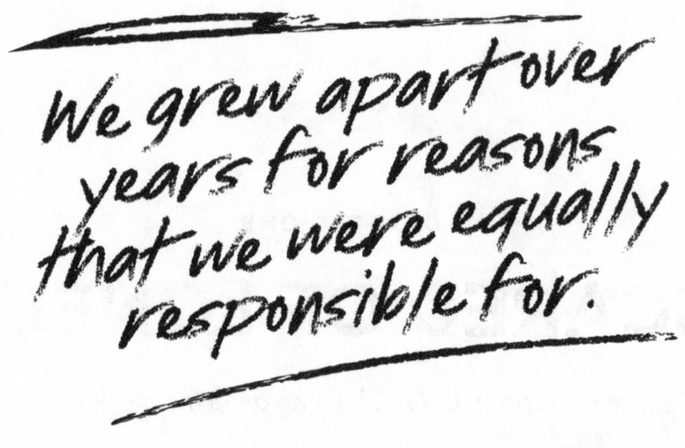
We grew apart over
years for reasons
that we were equally
responsible for.

In exchange for a rewarding overseas assignment, I would receive two years of paid sabbatical to complete my graduate degree at Georgia Tech. It was an offer that I could not pass up. I only had one month at home before having to pack up and leave for my graduate program.

While I was overseas, my wife stayed in Hawaii. We were married for four years and lived in Hawaii for most of that time. This was my first time back to Hawaii since I left a year earlier. In our case, distance did not make our hearts grow fonder. The overseas assignment strained our marriage and, upon my return, I knew that we were in trouble.

Four weeks later, my ex-wife and I filed for separation. The following day, I moved to Atlanta by myself.

My month in Hawaii was made up of mixed feelings. I was excited to be back home in Hawaii but heartbroken that my marriage was clearly ending. I don't blame my ex-wife for the way our relationship ended. We grew apart over years for reasons that we were equally responsible for. Even though we split up on very cordial terms, the divorce still broke me. For years afterward, I felt like I was unworthy of love, and recovering from that experience was no quick process. Although I don't wish divorce on anyone, it did teach me an important lesson: a happy and successful marriage requires constant investment. I learned that the moment you begin to take your partner for granted is the moment that you begin to grow apart. I began to take my ex-wife for granted years before we got divorced, and by the time that we separated, there was no way to bring our relationship back together.

No matter how much you think you love each other, marriage is a fragile agreement. When I married my ex-wife, we thought that we would be together forever, "until death do us part." But despite a great wedding and a few great years together, that didn't happen. After I left Hawaii and moved to Atlanta, I never saw my ex-wife again.

After a couple weeks in Atlanta, I bought a luxury high-rise condo. I remember signing the mortgage paperwork and getting the keys from the real estate agent. After working nonstop for a year, I finally had some time to relax and enjoy life. It was a gorgeous condo with a sprawling view of downtown Atlanta. I was excited to move into my new home and bought a bottle of Moët & Chandon to celebrate. Regrettably, I didn't have anyone to share the experience with.

My experience working like a maniac for a year and then arriving home and getting divorced is analogous to the series of events that many couples experience. People meet and fall in love as young professionals, then they spend the next ten or twenty years suffering evenings and weekends in order to climb up the corporate ladder. They work themselves unhealthy as they advance their businesses and careers and spend more and more time apart. They do all this because they expect some type of paradise awaiting them at the end. For some couples, paradise is living off a pension or 401(k) and never needing to work again. For others, it's a beautiful home in Hawaii. Whatever their intentions, when many people finally do have the time and resources to relax and enjoy life, they also find themselves divorced and alone.

As my marriage ended, and then for quite a while after, I would often wonder, *Are my relationships doomed? Will I ever find love again?*

And then I met Zaira.

LET'S RECAP

- **The first lesson, and probably the most important in this entire book, is that a happy and successful marriage requires constant investment. The moment you begin to take your partner for granted is the moment that you begin to grow apart.**

CHAPTER TWO

BROWN SKIN GIRL

"Pretty like Lupita when the cameras close in." –Beyoncé

I found Zaira late one night in 2012. I was browsing through profiles on Match.com and ZCurl2014's photo caught my eye. I wish I could say that I took one look at her profile and immediately knew that she would be the one, but that wasn't the case. Her profile read like a job posting:

Applicants must...

- be intelligent, easygoing, extroverted, hardworking, have a good sense of humor, and be family oriented.
- be taller than 6'0"
- have gotten a teeth cleaning within the last six months.

She seemed like a no-nonsense type of woman. Actually, I thought, *A teeth cleaning, really? This girl sounds stuck-up.*

Normally I would have passed on a girl like her, but damn she was beautiful! The text of her profile may have been cold and abrasive, but her photos painted a different picture. She had long, curly hair, golden bronze skin, a drop-dead body, warm eyes, and a lovely smile. I suspected that she was some type of hard-working professional, maybe a doctor, which would make sense since Emory University was a top-tier medical school nearby. One of her profile photos was actually a LinkedIn-style headshot. She probably spent her early twenties working her ass off, first in school, and then through residency. She probably didn't have a lot of time to have fun and was tired of fuckboys or players who just wanted to party and hook up. She probably wanted a serious relationship. I also suspected that her life was a sprint, and she wanted someone who could keep up.

It was late at night when I messaged her. I was tipsy after a few too many glasses of wine.

To: ZCurl2014
Subject: It looks like you go H.A.M.
Hey Zaira,
It's clear that you know exactly what you want in life and I respect that. I think it is awesome that you are a professional woman who also knows how to relax and have fun. Like you, I love traveling, great company, and great food—my favorite restaurant in town is Empire State South. What is your favorite spot?
Well, I think we would be a great fit and I hope to hear back from you soon.
Robert

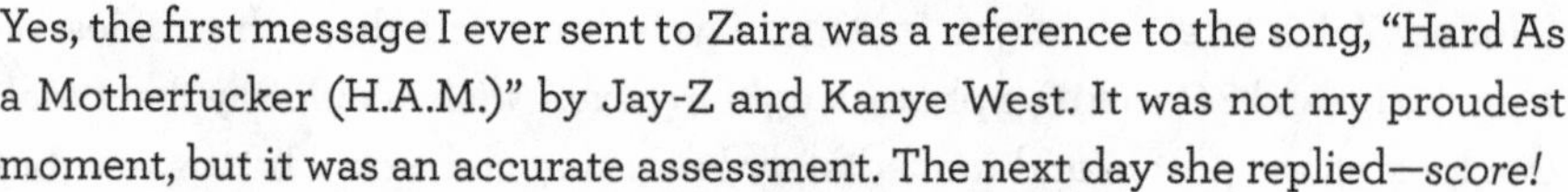

Yes, the first message I ever sent to Zaira was a reference to the song, "Hard As a Motherfucker (H.A.M.)" by Jay-Z and Kanye West. It was not my proudest moment, but it was an accurate assessment. The next day she replied—*score!*

We began emailing and texting each other. We seemed to have a connection and made plans to meet in person at Marlow's Tavern, a local bar and grill. It was a Wednesday and I met her outside at twelve o'clock sharp. She wore heels, a pencil skirt, a blouse, and blazer.

She was more gorgeous in person than in the photos and I was trying really hard not to mess it up. I asked a lot of questions, and spent more time listening than talking.

I intentionally avoided talking about work. Instead I asked her questions about her favorite international trips and where she went salsa dancing in Atlanta, and we talked about our families. Neither of us had mentioned what we did for a living, but I could tell that she was not a doctor. Doctors in residency would never wear heels and a pencil skirt to a workday lunch, nor would they be driving a brand-new Infinity Q35. *She is probably a lawyer,* I thought—*a very hot lawyer.*

After an hour-long lunch, we gave each other a hug and said our goodbyes. It felt like more of a power lunch than a first date.

Our second date was phenomenal. Over the course of five hours, we ate sushi, got dessert at a nearby café, took my dog for a walk, and drank wine while listening to Daft Punk vinyl on my balcony. We didn't have sex, but we kissed each other a lot. Not only was my assessment correct—she was a lawyer—but she owned the whole firm.

I had been on a handful of dates without a lot of luck. I admit that, after being with my ex-wife for over seven years, I was horrible at dating. Zaira was incredibly beautiful, smart, ambitious, and kind. Over and over, I told myself, *I can't believe that this amazing woman likes me. Don't screw this up, Robert.*

On our third date, she finally told me about her career. Years later, she recapped it like this:

> I worked several jobs while I was in law school. I was a bartender, I worked at several different law firms, and I worked at a steakhouse as a server and a bartender. I graduated law school in May of 2011 with the intentions of passing the bar exam and then starting a law firm.
>
> After graduation, I spent the summer preparing for the bar. Every single morning, I drove over to the Emory campus for exam prep classes, then spent the next ten to twelve hours studying. I did this every day. I studied the whole summer. Probably up until being an entrepreneur, it was the most difficult thing I had ever done. My hair was falling out, my body was going through changes; it was horrible. I hated every minute. If I didn't pass, I really thought my world was going to end. I was like, "This is what it's like to be on death row."
>
> I told my boss, "Hey, if I pass the bar, by the way, I am going to start a law firm."
>
> He was like, "Um, sure."
>
> A few weeks later, I passed the bar exam and quit. He was surprised, like he hadn't taken me seriously.
>
> With only a cell phone, computer, and $100, I immediately started my firm. I basically should've had a bed in my office because that's where I spent the majority of the entire day. I woke up for my firm, I spent all day at my firm, I met with clients for my firm, and I changed people's lives with my firm. That's all I did into the early hours of the morning.

She was more gorgeous in person than in the photos and I was trying really hard not to mess it up.

After hearing her story, I began falling in love and our relationship grew from there. On our third date, I cooked dinner for her; on our fourth date, we had sex; on our eighth date, we took a trip to Napa Valley; on the thirteenth date, I told her I loved her; and somewhere between our 89th and 144th dates, I asked her to marry me. She said yes.

In less than six years, Zaira had grown her business from that initial $100 to over $1 million in annual revenue. She started with an office in Atlanta, then eventually expanded to Alabama, Florida, Washington, D.C., and Mexico. She employs over twenty people and has a large team of virtual contractors who support different aspects of the business. She has helped well over 1,000 immigrants to live and work legally in the US—Zaira definitely goes H.A.M.

Women entered the workforce en masse beginning with the Feminist Movement of the 1960s to 1980s. During this time, the percentage of women in the workforce increased dramatically from about 33% of the workforce in 1960 up to 46% by 1994. Inversely, the percentage of men in the workforce has decreased to about 53% during that same time period. Over the past twenty-five years, the percentage of women in the workforce has remained steady, at about 46%.[1]

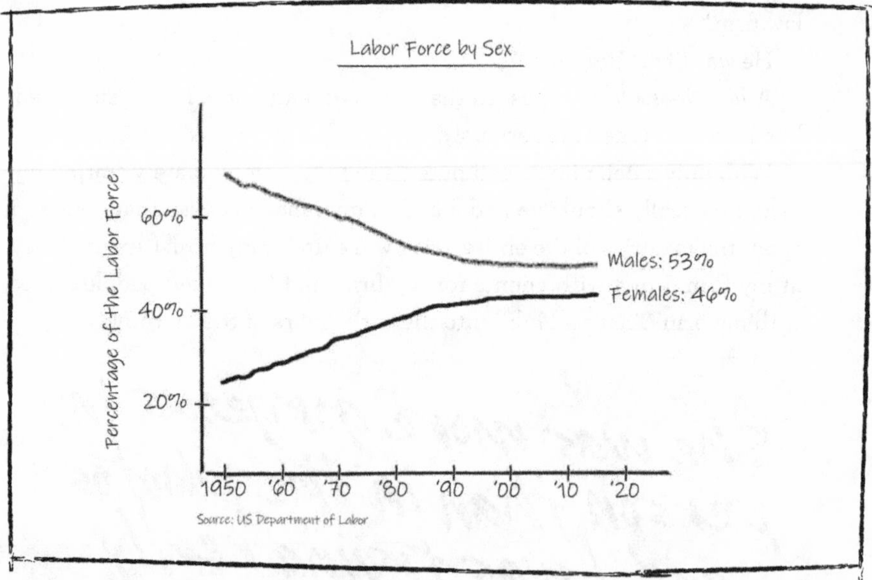

Figure 1. The percentage of men and women in the workforce between 1950 and 2020.

1 "Civilian labor force by sex" (2020), US Department of Labor.

Although the percentage of women in the workforce has plateaued for the past couple decades, the nature of their work has changed. Instead of mostly filling clerical or lower-level positions—like in the 1960s—women are now often in leadership positions. For example, from 1995 to 2017 the number of females on Fortune 500 executive boards doubled, from 9.6% to 22.2%.[2]

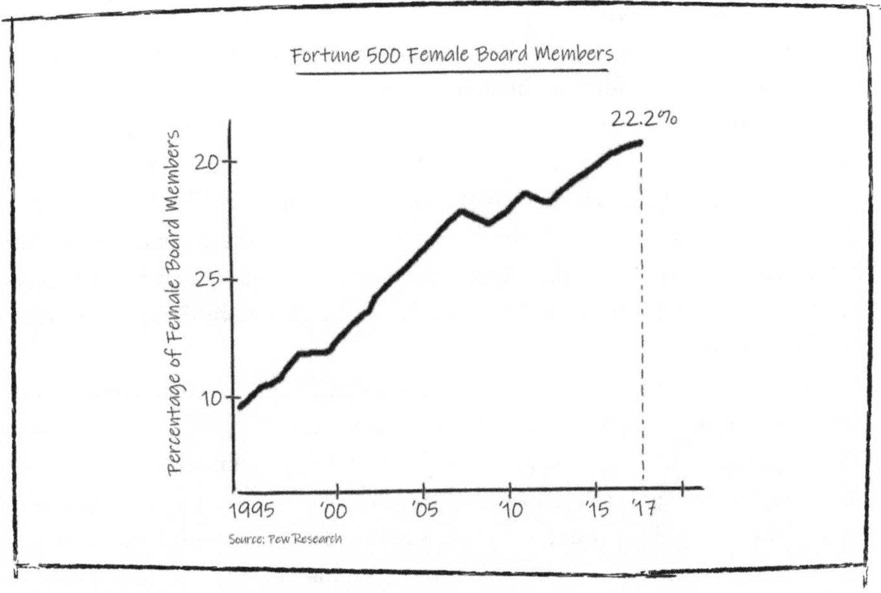

Figure 2. More women are assuming leadership roles at all corporate levels.

Like Zaira, more women are also becoming entrepreneurs. From 1997 to 2017, the number of women-owned small businesses grew by 114%. In 2017, women owned 39% of all US businesses. In the same year, women-owned businesses employed almost nine million people and were responsible for $1.7 trillion in sales.[3]

Of course, women still face many challenges in the workplace. They still tend to make less money than their male peers, are more likely to be victims of sexual harassment or discrimination, and have greater challenges when it comes to balancing their professional careers with pregnancy and family planning. Despite these challenges, women are breaking through the glass ceiling one C-Suite at a time.

The rise of female professionals presents many challenges to society's

2 "The Data on Women Leaders" (2018), Pew Research Center.

3 "The 2017 State of Women-Owned Businesses Report" (2017), Commissioned by American Express.

traditional family structure. Let's face it, in America and most of the world, we have a patriarchal family model. Traditionally, the man of the house had a professional job and made most of the family's income while the woman was the primary homemaker and child caretaker. Even when a woman had a professional career, her job usually took second place to her husband's. This model represented the overwhelming majority of American families for most of our nation's history.

As the American family model shifts, women are no longer as likely to put their careers on hold for their husband's. This is causing trouble for marriages.

In addition to the challenges of a dual career marriage, researchers have shown that marriages that include a professional woman are much more likely to result in divorce than if the woman is supported by the man. In a *Forbes* magazine article, Michael Noer summarized the research like this: "Professional women are more likely to get divorced, more likely to cheat, less likely to have children, and, if they do have kids, they are more likely to be unhappy about it."[4]

Researchers have a difficult time explaining the causal factors behind these statistics. Some speculate that professional women have more opportunities to find happiness outside of the household and marriage, while others argue that male spouses are part to blame since they can be challenged by a woman who is professionally their equal or better. Regardless of the causes, the statistics show that marriages with a professional female partner are less likely to succeed. This is especially true for high-performance females.

A few years ago, a group of Swedish researchers followed women who got promoted to high-level jobs. In particular, they looked at women who became mayors, got elected to national political positions, or became CEOs of companies with over 100 employees. They found that after three years, these high-performing females were twice as likely to get divorced than their non-CEO counterparts. The same trend was not true for high-performance men.[5]

Same sex couples make up less than one half of 1% of all married couples. With so few same-sex couples, it is difficult to say if these same trends apply to LGBTQ partners, but they surely face many of the same challenges as heterosexual couples, and many more.

Surely, a marriage takes two people, and both partners almost always share some responsibility for the success or failure of a marriage. With that said,

---

4 Michael Noer (2006). "Don't Marry Career Women," *Forbes.*

5 Olle Folke & Johanna Rickne (2020). "All the Single Ladies: Job Promotions and Durability of Marriage," *American Economic Journal: Applied Economics, 12.*

these statistics should serve as a warning for any dual professional couple: If you are ambitious and career driven, and marry someone else with those similar values, your marriage may be much more likely to end in unhappiness and divorce.

This was a huge concern for me! Zaira was the definition of high-performance CEO. I was afraid that our relationship would be doomed before it even started.

At first, I thought it was cool to be married to a business owner, but after a while I began to have some concerns. First of all, she seemed to work all the time. Working at the office from 8 a.m. to 8 p.m. was normal for her, she went into the office for a few hours almost every Saturday, and she regularly worked on her laptop or cell phone in bed at night as we watched Netflix.

Of course, I was not much more present. I was in graduate school getting a degree in aerospace engineering, and also worked on several projects and side hustles. I was always writing computer code for helicopter designs, interviewing people for a potential business, or incubating my next idea.

Both Zaira and I operate in a high gear. Most people were walking through life—trying to get from Monday to Friday using as little energy as possible. Meanwhile, Zaira and I were sprinting. People along the way told us that we should slow down, but I don't think that either of us knew how.

I always imagined that me and my future wife would buy a house in the suburbs, have children, and start a family. I pictured both of us working a solid day—her at her business and me at mine, and then we would come home in the early evening, cook dinner together, and help little Robertico with his math homework. In other words, I imagined the same suburban lifestyle and work-life balance that is normal for most middle-class American households.

As our relationship grew, Zaira and I were clearly not on our way to becoming a normal middle-class family. We lived in a high-rise in the heart of Atlanta, not the suburbs. Our work-life balance was completely absent; we worked all the time.

After enjoying life together in Atlanta for almost two years, I was not sure if I even wanted the suburban lifestyle anymore. I enjoyed our relationship just the way it was; however, I began to fear that this lifestyle and dual professional careers was unsustainable, especially if we wanted to eventually get married and start a family.

LET'S RECAP

- Although the percentage of women in the workforce has remained steady since the 1990s, the jobs they are doing are different. Today, women are more likely than ever to be managers, politicians, or CEOs.
- The rise of female professionals presents many challenges to society's traditional patriarchal family structure. Many women are no longer satisfied to put their careers on hold for their spouse's. This is causing trouble for marriages.
- High-performance women who rise to become CEOs or other high-profile positions are more likely to get divorced than their male or non-CEO female counterparts.

CHAPTER THREE

WELCOME TO THE JUNGLE

"I asked her where she wanna be when she 25." —Jay-Z

Part of me still imagined that my relationship would reflect a modern version of the 1950s sitcom *Leave It to Beaver.* Ward Cleaver went to work every day while his wife, Judy, stayed at home, raised the children, and cleaned the house. Every weekday, Ward came home in time for dinner and taught his kids a few valuable life lessons. The Cleavers were the *quintessential* American family.

I admit that I had a lot of anxiety when we started dating because Zaira's entrepreneurial lifestyle was incredibly different from a nine to five job. I knew that our relationship was going to be unlike that of my parents or my peers.

Although I wanted my wife to work, and planned to share house chores with her, I still imagined that she would be the primary homemaker while I pursued my career. I pictured coming home from work each night, cooking dinner together with Zaira, chatting about our day, then watching Netflix and chilling before bed.

As our relationship progressed, I realized that my fantasy of a quintessential marriage was just that, a fantasy. There was no way that we could have a *Leave It to Beaver* lifestyle while both pursuing executive-level positions. Between our dual professions, frequent travel, and other community activities, we had a very nontraditional lifestyle.

If you are in a traditional, patriarchal relationship, and are both happy, that is great. However, I knew that to be happy and stay together, Zaira and I would need to adopt a different way of life. I also knew that Zaira was against the traditional patriarchal family structure. Here's her experience:

> I grew up in Dominican culture. As far as I could tell, all men were cheaters. It didn't matter how beautiful, successful, sweet, or good of a wife or mom

you were: your husband was going to cheat on you. That's just the behavior I saw from a lot of the men in my family and that really sucked.

Also, men in Dominican culture don't have any domestic responsibility in the household. The man was the provider of money and housing; the women took care of the house and family. That's what I grew up knowing and I really didn't know any different until I was an adult. I remember we would eat dinner and the men would get up and leave without helping clear the table. Growing up, the boys never had chores, only the girls had chores. Saturday mornings, the girls had to clean while the boys went out to play or did whatever. Eventually, I was like, "What the fuck? What's up with this?"

Eventually, I was exposed to different types of relationships that I respected more. For example, I had a friend in junior high school whose dad would help her with school projects, pick us up from school, and cook meals for us. That was the first time I saw a father do stuff I had otherwise only seen moms do. It was really surprising.

Then, after college, I saw the marriage between my best friend and her husband. It was the first partnership I can think of where there was true equality, and real partnership to work through things together. And there was love; real, genuine love. They had honesty and integrity. They were both intelligent and independently career driven. I thought that kind of relationship was really cool; something I definitely wanted for myself whenever I met the right man.

As our relationship progressed, I realized that my fantasy of a quintessential marriage was just that, a fantasy.

One day, as I was thinking about how unique my relationship with Zaira was, I walked into a store and saw an oversized painting of two horses. One horse was charging forward in a sprint and the other was by its side in a dashing stance.

Their bodies were almost touching, their muscles were flexed, and their faces were tense but calm. Clops of dirt and clouds of dust swept up behind them as their hooves beat the ground. They appeared to be playing, sprinting back and forth, juking and jiving with each other, enjoying an innocent and free life.

I couldn't help but think of Zaira and me—two strong and powerful creatures sprinting together through the world, side-by-side. The horses, like us, enjoyed the intense feeling of physical and mental exertion. They looked fully present and clearly didn't care about their businesses, their emails, their clients, their next meal, their opponents, or anything else. They were two horses, fully engaged with each other, blissfully living in the moment.

I thought to myself, *How can I channel that kind of energy into my marriage?*

Out of pure curiosity, I began researching horse and animal behavior. For decades, I was told that animal packs—wolves, horses, and lions—were led by an alpha male. This narrative says that males become leaders of their packs by asserting their physical dominance, engaging in aggressive competition, and having sex with multiple partners. I discovered, however, that this old story is demonstrably false.

The original concept of the alpha male became popular after the researcher L. David Mech popularized the term in 1970 with his book *The Wolf: Ecology and Behavior of an Endangered Species*. In it, Mech gave a comprehensive review of wolf ecology and behavior. He provided insight into how they hunt, communicate, mate, and much more. One particular area that he highlighted was social hierarchy and how wolves competed for dominance within packs. The alpha male and alpha female, being the dominant members of the pack, had certain liberties when it came to authority, mating, and eating.[6]

In our society, we regularly view wolves as powerful, intelligent, and mysterious creatures, which is why many authors and self-help gurus began applying the alpha male concept to humans.

This was especially true in dating guides that promised young men that they could become chick magnets by acting like alphas. These pickup artist guides recommended deceptive practices like undermining your date's self-esteem in order to increase your position of dominance. The unfortunate product of this trend is a generation of fuckboys that were disrespectful toward women.

Simultaneously, many leaders and managers also applied faulty alpha male concepts to business and politics. Such alpha tactics included bullying,

---

6 L. David Mech (1970). *The Wolf: The Ecology and Behavior of an Endangered Species.*

browbeating, and showboating. *The Wolf of Wall Street* is a great example of how stereotypical alpha male behavior can result in rampant bullying, disgusting misogyny, and toxic leadership.

The concept of an alpha male has even migrated into our daily lives. For example, Cesar Millan, also known as the Dog Whisperer, says that humans should eat before their dogs and make their dogs earn their food because anything less is a sign of submission. His rationale is:

> The pack leaders always eat first, and any less dominant dog that would try to approach before they are allowed would be severely corrected. The pack leaders lead the pack to the prey and the pack kills it, but the leaders dine first, and then leave what's left for the others.[7]

For a pet owner who is struggling to show their dog who's the boss, Cesar's strategy sounds promising. The problem is that packs of wolves and dogs don't actually behave like that.

Whether it is in dating, business, politics, or dog training, society has been grossly misinformed about the nature of an alpha. It is no wonder that the term alpha, and especially alpha male, has an extremely negative connotation.

I hope that this book can begin to correct many of the misconceptions about alphas and pack leadership.

Since his 1970 publication, David Mech has spent fifty years studying wolves in the wild and has learned that, contrary to his initial research, alphas do not become pack leaders through dominance and competition. Instead, pack leaders are usually caring parents. In wolf packs, the alpha male and alpha female often form lifelong monogamous relationships. Most of their pack members are their children and they care, protect, and nurture their children the same way that humans would do for their families. They become leaders by being caring and loving parents rather than through competition and fighting.[8]

Furthermore, the alpha wolf does not eat first or take claim to whatever they desire. Instead, the first wolf to eat is the first to make the kill, which may or may not be the alpha. Usually two or more wolves make a kill together and then any wolf can immediately join in on the feast as long as there is enough room

---

7 Cesar Millan (2015). "Will Work for Food," cesarway.com

8 Since the publication of his original book in 1970, Mech prefers to call the alpha male and female the *breeding pair,* especially when discussing wolves in the wild; however, he acknowledges that the terms alpha male and alpha female are still appropriate when discussing artificial packs or packs in captivity of nonrelated wolves. *See* L. David Mech, "Alpha Wolf" (2008), YouTube.com. https://www.youtube.com/watch?v=tNtFgdwTsbU

for them to sink their teeth into the elk, bison, or deer. In his later publications, Mech also highlighted the leadership role of the dominant male *and* female in the pack.

If you're like most people, you probably think that the alpha male was the dominant animal in the pack and that he mated with whomever he wanted, protected the pack, led the hunt, and always ate first, while the females swooned for his attention and spent most of their days nursing pups. Once again, this narrative is dead wrong.

Both the male and female pack leaders share roles in controlling the behavior of the pack. Their roles overlap significantly when it comes to hunting as well as caring for the pack.

Mech personally observed a male and female leader jointly defending their pack and killing an intruding wolf. In other instances, Mech observed that the breeding females nurse puppies when they are young, but as the puppies get older, the male leaders also assume responsibility for feeding them. Similarly, the female leaders are more protective of the pack than males, and they will frequently lead a hunt, with or without their male counterparts.[9] [10]

Alpha pairs in wild horse herds also share leadership responsibilities. In the wild, horses form herds over 100 horses strong. Within each herd, they usually form harems, which are smaller groups of three to twenty horses that consist of other mares, fillies, and colts. The harem is generally a family unit led by a lead mare, the alpha female, and a stallion—the alpha male. The alpha female usually leads the harem, sets the pace, steers the harem to water or food, and will lead a retreat if faced with a threat. When traveling, the alpha female leads from the front of the pack while the alpha male, the stallion, leads from the rear of the pack and protects the harem against threats or competitors.

It's clear that throughout the animal kingdom—in wolf packs, horse herds, and many other animal species—the male and female leader share responsibilities. They work together as an Alpha Couple, to keep the pack or herd safe, healthy, and thriving.

I should also note that humans are not the only species in the animal kingdom with LGBTQ relationships. In the primate community it is very common for chimpanzees and bonobos to show bisexual and homosexual behaviors. Furthermore, every major animal group, especially social species,

---

9 L. David Mech (2000). "Leadership in Wolf, *Canis lupus*, Packs," *USGS Northern Prairie Wildlife Research Center.*

10 L. David Mech (1999). "Alpha Status, Dominance, and Division of Labor in Wolf Packs," *Canadian Journal of Zoology*, 77.

demonstrates some form of same-sex parenting, bonding, courtship, or sexual activity. In nature, an Alpha Couple can occasionally be the same sex.

Although Zaira and I do not have children yet, there are a lot of similarities between being a leader for your family and being a leader for your community and business. Similar to parents who want to help their children grow, learn, and succeed, we both want to help our staff develop into better leaders, improve our community, and shape a world where everyone can thrive.

When comparing humans to animals, it is quite absurd that our society's traditional model of marriage stipulates that one partner (usually the female) should stay home and raise the children, while the other partner (usually the male) pursues a successful career. Other than the few weeks following childbirth, there is very little precedence for this model in the animal kingdom.

After uncovering the myth of alpha males, I began to ask myself several questions that I hope to address in the pages of this book: *How can my wife and I both be leaders? How can we channel our animal spirits? How can we be an Alpha Couple?*

LET'S RECAP

- The traditional, chauvinistic, and competition-focused narrative of alphas is grossly wrong.
- In packs of wolves, horses, and other animals, the alpha male and the alpha female share responsibilities in hunting, caring for family, and protecting the pack.
- The Alpha Couple are first and foremost leaders. They become alphas by taking initiative, making decisions, showing empathy, and by loving and nurturing each other and their pack.

Both the male and female pack leaders share roles in controlling the behavior of the pack. Their roles overlap significantly when it comes to hunting as well as caring for the pack.

CHAPTER FOUR

HISTORY

"We could make love and make history." —Jay-Z

Modern humans, *Homo sapiens*, have been walking the earth for about 200,000 years. Although we don't have any written history from our early ancestors, we do know that they lived in groups of couples, families, tribes, and villages.

Anthropologists believe that for most of human history, men and women were generally equal. These researchers examined grave sites in ancient villages from the Neolithic period, the late Stone Age, and discovered that men and woman had similar bone densities, skeletal heights, and diets. At grave sites, males and females had a relatively equal distribution of artifacts such as jewelry, beads, and pottery. This evidence shows that in ancient societies, men and women generally had equal status. [11]

Although we do not have any recorded history from our ancient ancestors, some notable indigenous societies are still around. These include the Ju/'hoansi of Southern Africa, the Aetas in the Philippines, and the Hadza of Tanzania. Many of these tribes still live hunter-gather lifestyles similar to our ancestors 50,000 years ago. These societies offer a glimpse back in time, to how humans have lived for tens of thousands of years prior to the modern era. Interestingly, many of these isolated pockets of indigenous hunter-gatherers share common behaviors and norms.

In the Hadza tribes of Tanzania, hunting is exclusively a male activity and foraging is predominantly female. Foraging is a full-day activity with groups of women and children leaving camp shortly after sunrise, hiking for thirty to sixty minutes, then spending most of the day collecting honey, picking berries, or digging for tubers—a relative of potatoes. Sometimes, women will dig down as much as three feet to collect edible roots. In the evening, after a long day of

---

11 Y. Dong, C. Morgan, Y. Chinenov, L. Zhou, W. Fan, X. Ma, & K. Pechenkina (2017). "Shifting Diets and the Rise of Male-Biased Inequality on the Central Plains of China During Eastern Zhou," *Proceedings of the National Academy of Sciences*, 114.

work, the women hike back to camp, carrying kilograms of tubers for the tribe. In other words, foraging is hard work.[12]

The Hazda men, on the other hand, usually hunt big game solo. Unfortunately, they are rarely successful and "as many as half of the adult men may fail to kill even one large animal a year." On any given day, their chance of success in hunting is only 3.4%. Although big game hunting is an important source of food for the Hadza, it is the women who bring home food routinely.[13]

On the other side of Africa, in Namibia and Botswana, the Ju/'hoansi males generally do the hunting while the females do the gathering. Similar to the Hazda, the female Ju/'hoansi gatherers provide about 70% of the tribe's diet. Unlike the Hazda though, the Ju/'hoansi may occasionally go on gathering missions as far as 10 miles from camp. Although Ju/'hoansi men are the hunters—using poison-tipped arrows to kill animals as large as giraffes—both men and women are expert trackers. Sometimes, women will track an animal while foraging and report their findings to their male counterparts so that a hunting party can pursue the prey. Additionally, a wife may join a husband on a hunt and aid him with tracking.[14] [15]

On the other side of the globe in the Philippines, the Aeta (also called Agta Negrito) is an indigenous tribe of Luzon Island. They share hunting and gathering between males and females. Women regularly participate in hunting game such as pigs and deer and frequently hunt alone, with other females, or in mixed gender groups. Occasionally they will even bring their young or infant children with them on hunts. Although men and women frequently hunt together, the men prefer to use bows and stalking techniques while the women prefer to hunt with dogs and knives.[16]

There are a few other indigenous tribes around the world. Regrettably, their populations are decreasing as modern society encroaches upon them. In some indigenous societies, men hunt and women forage, while in others, men and women both hunt and forage. There really is no universal agreement when it comes to gender division of labor. Even within certain indigenous cultures, gender roles can vary from tribe to tribe.

---

12 H. Hawkes, J. O'Connell, & N. Blurton Jones (1989). "Hadza Hardworking Grandmothers," In Standen & Foley (eds.), *Comparative Socioecology: The Behavioral Ecology of Humans and Other Mammals.*

13 H. Hawkes, J. O'Connell, & N. Blurton Jones (2014). "More Lessons from the Hadza about Men's Work," *Human Nature*, 25.

14 Richard B. Lee (1984/2013). *The Dobe Ju/'hoansi*,

15 Megan Biesele & Steve Barclay (2001). "Ju/'hoan Women's tracking knowledge and its contribution to their husband's hunting success," *African Study Monographs*, 26.

16 M. Goodman, P. B. Griffin, A. Estioko-Griffin, & J. Grovel (1985). "The Compatibility of Hunting and Mothering among the Agta Hunter-Gatherers of the Philippines," *Sex Roles*, 12.

Despite differences in gender roles, there are two common trends that spread across most indigenous societies. The first is that men and women both contribute to the caloric intake of the tribe—with women usually bringing more food home than men. The second trend is that almost all indigenous populations are egalitarian with men and women being respected and treated as equals in the tribe. This is largely due to the fact that men and women both clearly play vital roles in the day-to-day survival of the community. The role of women is not simply to give birth, care for children, and do chores; if they don't work, the tribe doesn't eat. An indigenous woman does not have an option to be a stay-at-home wife.

Although these societies are isolated into small groups of a few hundred people today, archeologists and anthropologists believe that they provide many clues into early *Homo sapiens* society, and that they represent how hunter-gatherers lived for tens of thousands of years up until the Bronze Age.

Beginning about 10,000 years ago, humans invented farming methods. Simultaneously, they invented new metallurgy techniques that propelled humans from the Stone Age to the Bronze Age. During this Agricultural Revolution, humans discovered that they could produce more food through farming and animal domestication. The amount of resources that they could produce increased exponentially and tribes shifted away from hunter-gatherer societies and coalesced in farm villages instead. Subsequently, the human population exploded.

As agriculture ramped up, the roles of men and women began to diverge. The same anthropologists who studied burial sites in the Stone Age also studied burial sites in early Bronze Age societies. They found that after the Agricultural Revolution, the size and bone density of women started to become less than their male counterparts. It appears that women began doing less labor-intensive tasks, like hunting and foraging, and they were also malnourished. Furthermore, they found that women began getting buried with less fanfare then men. It is difficult to say why this trend began, but the evidence is clear that the Agricultural Revolution was a turning point for women. After the Agricultural Revolution, humans clearly began to shift toward a patriarchal society.

As humans began producing excess resources, they began trading goods and services, which led to the rise of artisans, merchant, and laborer classes. No longer did small societies work together for the equal benefit of each of its members, Instead, families became self-interested and worked together to accumulate wealth, resources, and property. As populations continued to increase and certain resources became scarce, families needed a way to protect their resources and consolidate them. Hence, marriage was created as a social contract between families so that families could consolidate and preserve resources. It is no wonder why the first public record of a marriage dates back to ancient Mesopotamia in about 2350 B.C., which was relatively shortly after the Agricultural Revolution began.

Then, beginning about 2000 B.C., civilizations began codifying laws. For example, in 1770 B.C., the Code of Hammurabi, one of the oldest surviving stone-carved set of laws, outlined rules such as "an eye for an eye, a tooth for a tooth." In these laws, the Babylonians also codified marriage and gender inequality. The Code of Hammurabi prohibited women from doing commercial activity and made women the property of men.[17]

There really is no universal agreement when it comes to gender division of labor. Even within certain indigenous cultures, gender roles can vary from tribe to tribe.

Ancient laws like the Code of Hammurabi were the precursor to Judaism, Christianity, and Islam, which in turn informed modern political and legal systems. For thousands of years, the codified gender inequality has persisted throughout most of the world.

Although the trend of gender discrimination began nearly 10,000 years ago, it was not universal. In many civilizations, men and women still had equal status. For example, in Persia, either gender could rule, farm, or serve in the military. In Mayan civilization, women were also treated with great respect and

17 Dr. Amanda Foreman (2016). *The Ascent of Woman.* A documentary.

could participate in politics, farm, and play important roles in religious rituals. In some civilizations such as the Yanshao in China, women actually held higher social status then men, mostly acting as the political and military leaders.

In many societies, women were even rulers. From 51 B.C. to 30 B.C., Cleopatra was the ruler of Egypt. She was a stateswoman and played a key role in foreign affairs. She led her nation through wars, traveled the world, survived the assassination of her lover, Julius Caesar, was exiled, and also ordered the assassination of her own brother.

Cleopatra was a badass but she wasn't the only exception. Throughout the Middle Ages and through the Enlightenment, female leaders helped shape history and society: Joan of Arc led armies; Isabel of Casteel united Catholic Spain under an iron fist; and Catherine the Great ruled Russia. In many cases, the monarchy system that was popular in Europe and other parts of the world actually benefited gender equality. Many of the most powerful women in the Middle Ages were queens, princesses, and regents.

When it comes to women's roles, some societies were better than others. I recognize that despite occasional female regents and leaders, women still faced many challenges throughout the Middle Ages and Early Modern periods. Even when women were rulers, societies frequently experienced male backlash during and after their female reigns. Despite this, women still had occasional leadership opportunities up until about 300 years ago when two really great, but also very chauvinistic, events occurred.

The first major event that significantly changed the role of women in society was the spread of democracy. In America, the Founding Fathers created a nation under the Puritan ideal that all men were created equal—all White men—not Blacks, Native Americans, Asians, or women. Despite monarchy's shortcomings, it did allow women to hold leadership positions and political authority in the absence of their husbands. The early American democracy erased those rights and ensured that women had minimal freedoms.

Even today, the United States Constitution does not recognize the equal rights of women. For a little bit of constitutional background, when the Founding Fathers wrote the Constitution, they intended to protect the rights of White men. The Fourteenth Amendment, adopted in 1868, extended those rights to minorities, but was clear that those rights were for "males."

In 1923, the Suffrage Movement pioneer Alice Paul introduced the Equal Rights Amendment, which said, "Men and women shall have equal rights throughout the United States." Although this sounds like a simple common-sense amendment, it has been stalled in Congress. In 1972, the House of

Representatives ratified the amendment, but to this day, in 2020, the Senate has not ratified the amendment and the United States Constitution still does not affirm equal rights for men and women.[18]

The second major event that hurt gender equality was the Industrial Revolution. From the 1700s to the 1800s, new technologies, factories, and steam power ushered in a new era of productivity. Before the Industrial Revolution, families worked together as a unit. For example, in a family of basket weavers, the husband, wife, and children all worked together in the family business—this is how families got last names like Weaver, Cook, Smith, and Carter. Once the Industrial Revolution began, these artisanal family businesses could not compete with the cheaper products and higher production rates of new factories. So—based on the presumption that men were stronger, and the fact that they couldn't bear children—men became factory workers as women stayed at home to raise children. Over time, women's basket-weaving skills deteriorated as their husbands gained new skills as managers, lawyers, and doctors. Today, we still live in the shadow of the Industrial Revolution, which continues to affect many of our gender bias and societal prejudices.

Fortunately, the Digital Revolution that we live in today is slowly reversing the gender gap. Today, anyone can learn a new skill, get a college degree, or start a new business. Virtual offices and telework are making the traditional nine to five work hours obsolete and businesses are becoming more results driven and less "good ole boy networks." More and more women are rising up the corporate, entrepreneurial, and political ladders.

As a society, we have created better anti-discrimination laws and many companies actively promote equal opportunities for the genders. Some companies even give fathers and mothers equal parental leave. New same-sex marriage laws and many corporate policies also extend equal opportunities to LGBTQ couples. Today, a young parent with an infant doesn't need to leave the workforce for three years. New parents can now continue their professional careers, complete college degrees, or operate their businesses from home while also raising an infant child. Thanks to greater work flexibility, men and women can share more of the childcare burden, or the traditional childcare roles can even be reversed. These changes are ushering in a new era of gender equality.

---

18 Linda Napikoski (2019). "Equal Rights Amendment," *ThoughtCo.*

LET'S RECAP

- In many indigenous hunter-gatherer tribes, the women collect a majority of the food that feeds the tribe. In some tribes, women are just as skilled as the men in tracking prey and hunting live game. Men and women shared work responsibilities for their tribe's survival.
- For nearly 200,000 years, up until the Agricultural Revolution, men and women were equals. The gender inequality that has been prevalent in our society is relatively new in human history and very unnatural.
- The Agricultural Revolution and the Industrial Revolution contributed to the gender inequality between the sexes. Fortunately, the Digital Revolution and modern equal opportunity movement are slowly reversing the gender gap.

CHAPTER FIVE

PUT IT IN A LOVE SONG

"All I'm saying is love is what I'm looking for." —Beyoncé

For most of us living in the twenty-first century, love and marriage go hand in hand. We think that love is one of the most powerful forces in the universe, right up there with gravity. It turns out that love is a relatively new idea. The concept of love as we know it today is less than 1,000 years old.

During the Middle Ages, poets and storytellers known as troubadours traveled throughout Western Europe and shared stories of chivalry and romance. At the time, the idea of marrying for love was revolutionary. It subverted the traditional models of arranged marriages and still influences—and challenges—our ideas about marriage to this day. The troubadours paved the way for future love stories like *Romeo and Juliet*, which was written about 200 years after their movement.[19]

Now, if you are like me and have ever been to a Christian wedding, you may believe that love and marriage is as old as the book of Genesis. After all, love is mentioned multiple times in the Bible, especially the Old Testament, which is more than 2,000 years old.

In total, the word "love" is mentioned 310 times in the Bible. In almost every passage that references love, it is used to describe the relationship between God and his followers and not, as most people mistakenly believe, the relationship between spouses. For example, when the book of Corinthians says, "Love is patient, love is kind," Paul the Apostle is talking about benevolence toward your neighbors and not about love between spouses.

The Bible occasionally talks about the relationship between partners, but in almost all cases it explains that the benefit of a spouse is to have children together or to provide each other security. For example, the Bible says God

19 Michael Bryson & Arpi Movsesian (2017). *Love and Its Critics: From the Song of Songs to Shakespeare and Milton's Eden.*

created man and woman to "be fruitful and multiply," and later says, "Two are better than one, because they have a good return for their labor. If either of them falls down, one can help the other up."[20]

The Bible never says that you should marry someone you love. In fact, there is only one passage that explicitly discusses love between husbands and wives. It says, "Husbands, love your wives, just as Christ loved the church and gave himself up for her to make her holy." So according to the Bible, husbands should love their wives because women are sinful and need men's redemption.[21]

In reverse, the Bible never says that wives need to love their husbands. Instead, it says that wives need to respect their husbands, just like children should obey their parents and slaves should obey their masters. That's it, our entire Christian concept about love and marriage barely mentioned in the entire Bible!

Some conservative evangelist may say amen to the idea that men are superior to women, but I think that is absurd. Love in the context of marriage was simply not an idea that civilizations believed when the Bible was written.

After doing some research, it became clear to me that marriage used to be a logistical and financial ordeal until the troubadours planted the seed for it to grow into something more spiritual. And then, in 1967, John Lennon wrote "All You Need Is Love."

Like many things in our society, the modern stance on love in marriage can be traced back to the Industrial Revolution. With the invention of factories, modern banking, pension plans, and daycare, many families no longer needed to marry off their young in order to protect their farms or consolidate resources. Parents, men, and women began to be financially independent. Since couples didn't need to get married for business reasons anymore, they now needed a new reason to get married. They took the radical step of getting married for love instead. Coincidently, as this trend became more popular, divorce rates began to rise.

I had already gone through one divorce and I didn't want to be another statistic. Over the course of 2014, Zaira and I continued to date more seriously and fell in love. My time at Georgia Tech was temporary and I knew that after graduation I would need to move again to take over a management position in New Mexico.

As my graduation approached, we needed to decide what our future would look like. On this particular night, we went out to dinner at a local restaurant.

---

20 Ecclesiastes 4:9
21 Ephesians 5:25

Afterward we walked home and I tried to talk with Zaira about life after Atlanta: "What is going to happen to us when I move in six months?"

She answered the same way that she answered a dozen times before: "We'll make it work."

When I pressed her to provide more details, she tried to change the subject.

"I'm going to New Mexico. Your business and all of your family are here in Georgia. How do you plan to make this work?"

"I don't know," she replied, "but we'll make it work."

I felt like she was not listening to me, so I continued to raise my voice, hoping that increasing the volume would help her to understand my frustration: "How are *you* going to make it work?"

"I don't know, Robert," she said.

"That's not a good answer, Zaira," I replied, frustrated, as passersby on the sidewalk probably wondered, *"What is that guy's problem?"*

Falling in love with Zaira was easy, but after dating for eighteen months, it sort of felt like our relationship was doomed. I didn't have a good feeling about the upcoming move.

My time in graduate school was a convenient time to fall in love. I was newly single, and I had an easy school schedule that allowed me to relax and recuperate after an intense yearlong assignment. For almost two years, Zaira and I had a great, freewheeling time together. Sure, we had busy lives, but we still made time to walk the dogs in Piedmont Park, attend music festivals, visit her family, and occasionally go to church on Sundays.

Life was good for us. If she was working late, I would bring dinner to her in her office. Likewise, if I was at home typing away on final projects, she would make dinner for us. Her business was going well, my school was going well, and we were really happy, but my assignment in New Mexico was bad news. Our relationship was clearly headed toward marriage, but now we would need to be long distance. Part of my agreement with my company paying for graduate school was that I would take a three-year follow-on assignment to New Mexico. Reneging on that contract was not an option; I needed to move there after graduate school.

Meanwhile, Zaira was the CEO and senior attorney at her law firm. She needed to be in Atlanta for the firm to be successful. Although I loved Zaira tremendously, I did not want to start our marriage as a long-distance relationship between New Mexico and Atlanta. I spent a year away from my ex-wife while I was working overseas and was still scarred from that experience. Although we were not married or engaged yet, we were headed in that direction. Based on my experience, I felt like starting a marriage long distance was a recipe for disaster.

In one form or another, I asked her the same question at least two dozen more times: "What are we going to do when I move?" Her response was always the same: "We'll figure it out."

We were faced with a challenge that many other professional couples are faced with. I had seen it hundreds of times throughout my career: a junior manager falls in love with a young lady with a professional career such as a teacher, pharmacist, realtor, financial adviser, or interior decorator. After dating for two years, the manager applies and gets selected for a more senior position in a different city. The couple is then forced to make a decision. Do they break up and go their separate ways to pursue their careers? Or does the girlfriend leave her promising job, follow the junior manager to their next city, and get married?

When it comes time to move, many couples split up and go their separate ways rather than risk either person's career. My friend Sabrina says the reason she is single is because "timing was never right. I was active duty Air Force and just when I would establish a steady relationship, either he would move, or I would move."

Sabrina is now a doctor, but, like many professionals, she saw marriage as a huge challenge to her professional goals.

Sometimes, one partner (usually female) will sacrifice their career for their partner. Usually the girlfriend tells the boyfriend, "If I'm going to move with you and give up my job, you need to put a ring on it." Thanks, Beyoncé!

If the girlfriend does move, it is almost always bad for her career. She usually leaves a promising job and when she arrives in the new city, she spends six to twelve months looking for a similar opportunity. When she does find a job, it's usually an entry-level position below her experience level and skill set. She performs well, and begins to get ready for a promotion, until she needs to move again a few years later. The process repeats indefinitely and never gives the wife an opportunity to grow and develop in her career field.

Zaira and I had a similar dilemma. If we wanted to stay together, either me or Zaira would need to make sacrifices to our careers. I loved Zaira tremendously, but it felt wrong to leave a job that I also loved. Likewise, I would never ask Zaira to walk away from the company that she founded and built.

Two professional careers, a happy marriage, and a family seemed impossible. John Lennon may have said that "all you need is love," but it didn't feel like it was that simple.

For a relationship to be successful and to really thrive, I believe we need more than love. Partners need to have similar goals, habits, and intelligence—emotional and academic. Additionally, the relationship should support their individual goals as best as possible.

Many relationships have ended in divorce because partners disagreed on wanting children, lived vastly different lifestyles, or had different financial goals. I definitely think that love is important, but as our love for one another ebbs and flows (which it will), we need something else to fall back on. Relationships need to benefit both partners beyond the satisfaction derived from merely giving and receiving love. Love alone is not enough.

Now, less than two years after my divorce, I feared that I was going to repeat history. Zaira and I loved each other and had a lot in common. She was intelligent, lived a healthy life, had great work ethic, wanted to raise a family, and was a great partner. We loved each other tremendously, but as I prepared to move to New Mexico, it appeared that our goals were incompatible. We both wanted to continue to live together, eventually start a family, and have our careers, but it seemed impossible to do all three. To stay together, we needed more than love; we needed a miracle.

If we wanted to stay together, either me or Zaira would need to make sacrifices to our careers.

LET'S RECAP

- The idea of marrying for love is a relatively new concept in human history. Our current concept of love and marriage was invented by poets during the Middle Ages. Before then couples married because they recognized that two is more powerful than one.
- You need more than love to have a successful marriage. To build a powerful marriage, you and your spouse need to have similar interests, habits, and intelligence.
- Relationships need to benefit both partners beyond the satisfaction derived from merely giving and receiving love. A relationship should help each partner live a more rewarding, fulfilling, and happy life. Love is definitely a very important part of marriage, but love alone is not enough.

CHAPTER SIX

1+1

"And it's me and you, that's all we'll have when the world is through." —Beyoncé

Getting married is an investment, but it is an investment that many young professionals don't have much confidence in, considering the millions of divorced Baby Boomers. I was no different, especially given my first marriage.

Zaira told me that she would consider moving with me if we got engaged, but I was still jaded by my divorce and had a different view. I wanted to spend my life with Zaira, but at the same time, I did not want to rush to get married. I knew that putting a ring on it did not automatically result in an unbreakable commitment. If she loved me as much as she said she did, I believed that she should move with me regardless if we were married or not. I wanted to avoid getting forced into marriage for the purpose of getting her to move. I understood her concerns, though. She was afraid to take a risk and uproot herself without the commitment that an engagement ring symbolized.

Since the 1960s, marriage rates have steadily declined and couples that do get married are getting married later in life. In 1960, 72% of the US population was married. Today, that number has decreased to 50%. At the same time, the average age that couples get married has increased from twenty-one years old to twenty-eight years old.[22]

More young professionals are doubting the functionality of marriage. Here's a sample of some comments from my single, never-married, professional friends:

---

22 Cohn, Passel, Wang, & Livingston (2011). "Barely Half of U.S. Adults are Married—a Record Low," Pew Research Center.

My friend Kim, a law firm CEO, says:

> I was raised by a stay-at-home mom so, to me, a mom needs to be at home. I simply don't want to be a mom. I want to be a professional, successful, and powerful woman.

My high school buddy Pete, a teacher, says:

> Marriage is a hard thing to sell to a person like me who grew up in a house with two parents who couldn't have a conversation without arguing about some stupid nonsense. Right now, and for the foreseeable future, I'm perfectly happy being the captain of my own ship.

My friend Amy, a fitness instructor says:

> What's the benefit of marriage that I cannot gain by cohabitating? I wish marriage was more like a renewable contract. At the beginning, you and your spouse get to decide how often you want to re-evaluate. Maybe every five to ten years. Once the term is up, you either renew or walk away with the terms you agreed to when you were in love.

More than a few of my single professional friends proposed the idea of short-term, renewable relationship contracts. Other comments usually highlight the desire for independence, relative ease of cohabitation, and the financial impact of divorce.

Unfortunately, many professionals fail to realize that marriage is more likely to lead to greater happiness, wealth, career success, and life satisfactions. Today, we may not need to marry for basic survival like our ancient ancestors, but marriage can still help us thrive.

Between 1996 and 2001, a group of researchers conducted an ambitious Million Women Study. A staggering 719,671 women participated in this study. The researchers found that women living with a partner were about 57% more likely to report being happy than single women; another group of researchers in Germany found that, on average, married couples who stayed married for two or more years were 17% happier; and similarly, a group of researchers in Taiwan found that the average married couple was over 30% happier than singles. Other studies have found that happiness in a relationship also increases over time, with couples married more than twenty years being happier than newlyweds.[23][24][25]

The Million Women Study found a positive correlation between marriage and happiness, *and* a positive correlation between happily married women and health. On average, happy women were 29% more likely to also be healthy. These happy women were more likely to avoid smoking, maintain a healthy body weight, and sleep eight hours a night—all activities that directly improve health. Happy women also had less detrimental health problems. They had lower risks of cancer, heart disease, stroke, high blood pressure, diabetes, asthma, arthritis, and especially depression or anxiety. And finally, happy, healthy, married women lived longer than their peers.

Numerous studies show similar results for men. One coronary heart disease study found that, after adjusting for age and other health factors, married men were 46% less likely to die from heart disease than single men. Studies in Britain, Switzerland, and the Netherlands reported similar results. Similarly, *Harvard Health Watch* reported that married men live longer, had higher cancer survival rates, and had reduced risk of Alzheimer's disease. Although it is impossible to definitively pinpoint why married men are healthier, the correlation is very clear—married men are healthier than singles.[26][27]

As far as investments go, it seems like marriage may be a good deal if it results in more happiness and better health.

If greater happiness and health were not already a good reason to tie the knot, married couples also make more money. In 2018, the Federal Reserve Bank published a report about the wages of married and single people at various ages. At thirty-five years old, the average single made about $44,000 a year. You would therefore expect that a married couple's income should be about $88,000 (twice that of a single person). In actuality, the married couple made an average of $119,000 a year—over 20% more than their single peers of the same age.[28]

---

23 Liu, Floud, Pirie, Green, Peto, & Beral (2016). "Does happiness itself directly affect mortality? The prospective UK Million Women Study," *Lancet*, 387.

24 Anke Zimmermann & Richard Easterlin (2006). "Happily Ever after? Cohabitation, Marriage, Divorce, and Happiness in Germany," *Population and Development Review*, 32.

25 Hung-Lin Tao (2018). "Marriage and Happiness: Evidence from Taiwan," *Journal of Happiness Studies*, 20.

26 E. Eaker, L. Sullivan, M. Kelly-Hayes, R. D'Agostino, & E. Benjamin (2007). "Marital Status, Marital Strain, and Risk of Coronary Heart Disease or Total Mortality: The Framingham Offspring Study," *Psychomatic Medicine*, 69.

27 "Marriage and Men's Health" (2010), *Harvard Men's Health Watch,* Harvard Medical School.

28 Guillaume Vandenbroucke (2018), "Married Men Sit Atop the Wage Ladder," *Economic Synopses*, 24.

Average Annual Salaries, Age 35		
Single Women	$41,338	Combined Averages Singles: $88,649
Single Men	$47,311	
Married Women	$48,834	Married: $119,208
Married Men	$70,374	

I know that this table also shows a huge disparity in the different salaries between men and women. That topic deserves attention as well. I recommend reading *The Moment of Lift: How Empowering Women Changes the World* by Melinda Gates. In her book, Melinda shares her journey, combined with startling data and inspirational stories that show why women empowerment is more important today than ever before.

Let's face it, our traditional patriarch marriages and nine to five corporate jobs are generally unsuitable for modern dual professional couples, but if couples could crack the code and break through the shortcomings of traditional marriage and careers, there is tremendous potential for couples to be exceptionally happy and successful.

Today, we may not need to marry for basic survival like our ancient ancestors, but marriage can still help us thrive.

When I eventually proposed to Zaira, I definitely was not thinking about how getting married would help me be healthier or more professionally successful. I was actually reluctant to rush into marriage, but I knew that Zaira needed a sign of commitment before she would even consider moving away from Atlanta. Regardless of my hesitation to get married again, I loved Zaira and wanted to spend the rest of my life with her. Before I proposed, we discussed getting engaged and we promised each other that just because we got engaged did not mean that we would rush into a wedding. That was a compromise that I could accept.

Three years into our relationship, we took a trip to wine country in Mendoza, Argentina. In the Andes foothills, we ate a delicious fire-roasted dinner at the restaurant of famous Argentinian chef Francis Mallmann. After dinner, we drank a second bottle of wine in the courtyard, warmed ourselves by the ambers of a wood-burning stove, and then slow danced underneath the Patagonian starlit sky.[29]

Zaira thought that I took her on a romantic dinner because we were celebrating our birthdays. Her birthday was a few weeks earlier and my birthday was the next day. As we danced in the courtyard with our bodies embracing, I asked her, "Are you enjoying your birthday trip?"

"Yes, of course. It is great. Thank you," she replied.

"Zaira, I love you. I look forward to traveling around the world with you for many more years to come." Then, I got on my knee in the grass and asked her to marry me. She shook her head up and down but actually did not say "yes," because she was too choked up with tears streaming down her face.

After I put the ring on her finger, and she eventually stopped crying, we sat in the courtyard and enjoyed the moment under the stars. A few minutes later, I asked her, "You never actually said anything. So, is that a yes?"

"Yes," she said as she still wiped her tears.

We danced another song to the crackle of the fire pit. We talked about our love and shared a glass of Malbec as embers from the burning wood sparked in the background. That was one of the happiest moments of my life.

LET'S RECAP

- Since the 1960s, marriage rates have steadily declined and couples that do get married are getting married later in life.
- Many young professionals doubt the functionality of marriage. They do not see the benefit of being married and many would rather continue with periodic short-term serious relationships. Contrary to their beliefs, data shows many positive correlations to being married.
- Although it is difficult to pinpoint the exact reason, there is a strong positive correlation between marriage and health, happiness, wealth, and professional success.

---

29 *1884 Restaurant,* Mendoza, Argentina.

Let's face it, our traditional patriarch marriages and nine to five corporate jobs are generally unsuitable for modern dual professional couples, but if couples could crack the code and break through the shortcomings of traditional marriage and careers, there is tremendous potential for couples to be exceptionally happy and successful.

CHAPTER SEVEN

S. CARTER

"Let me spell it out for ya." —Jay-Z

About a year and a half into our engagement, I asked Zaira skeptically, "Would you take my name?"

She didn't even put up a fight. "Of course."

My last name was Crapanzano—that's how much she loved me. I inherited it from my adopted parents. It was a good, strong Italian name that meant "the generous family," but unfortunately it wasn't as dignified in English.

"Really?" I doubted Zaira's sincerity, "You would change your name to Crapanzano?"

"Yeah," she nonchalantly replied.

I knew she loved me, but I was afraid that she was delusional. "What about your business?"

"I would still keep it as Solano Law Firm."

Ah, now I saw the cracks in her façade.

"So, would you still be *Abogada Solano*?"—the name that her Latino clients affectionately called her.

"Yeah, probably," she replied, as if she had not thought through this completely.

I helped her consider the dilemma, "So at work you would have one last name, and at home you would have a different last name."

In the legal field, it is very common to name a law firm after the senior partners. For example, Bader and Scott Injury Lawyers, Moore Family Law Group, or Morgan & Morgan. So naturally, when Zaira launched her law firm in 2011, well before she met me, she named the company after herself—Solano Law. In some states, like Georgia, the state bar association even *requires* that law firms include the attorney's name in the business name.

Now, after falling in love with a handsome and charming stud like myself,

Zaira needed to make a decision: Would she take my last name, would she keep her name, or would she hyphenate her name: Solano-Crapanzano?

Most females take their husband's last name. This is the way that the name Crapanzano got passed down from Sicily and how Solano got passed down from Spain, where the two names originated between 500 to 1500 years ago. For most couples, taking the husband's name is the default answer.

But in Zaira's position, her business was tied to her last name, and realistically, changing the name to The Crapanzano Law Firm was a crappy idea.

Our close friend Jen was another law firm owner. Like almost all of our female friends who were entrepreneurs before they got married, she chose the hyphenation option. We considered this option.

"Crapanzano-Solano? That's like twenty letters long. It wouldn't even fit on your driver's license."

She replied, "Okay. Then I won't change my name."

"I don't like that idea either," I said. "A husband and wife should have the same last name. People should know that we are married based on our names. Imagine going to a parent-teacher conference and always needing to explain to our daughter's teachers that we are married but have different names. I would need a permission slip just to pick up our kid from school because I had a different name."

I wasn't actually sure if that was true, but it sounded like a good argument.

Although I consider myself pretty open-minded in many aspects of my life, I guess that I was still traditional in the sense that I thought a husband and wife should have the same last name. In my preconditioned mind, I believed that a couple join their lives together when they marry, and that sharing the same name was an important step in beginning to share their lives. Like most parts of my journey toward understanding Alpha Couples, I needed to do some research.

Sometime between 5,000 to 10,000 years ago, during the first Agricultural Revolution, people began to travel around the world more frequently. When humans began to travel back and forth between cities for trade, they needed a way to distinguish different people that they talked about or traded with.

People got in the habit of describing people by where they were from. For example, Dimitri from Mykonos, Angus of Luxembourg, or Jesus of Nazareth. Solano is a name that describes the hot summer winds in central Spain, therefore, it is probable that the name originated to describe Zaira's family ancestors from that region, long before they migrated to the Dominican Republic.

Sometimes, instead of describing people by where they were from, people described each other by their profession instead. For example, John Smith

(John the blacksmith), George Miller (George the grain miller), or Sean Carter (long before the name was synonymous with Jay-Z, the Carters were the family that carted goods between towns); or they used a name that described a family characteristic, such as the Crapanzanos, the crappy—I mean generous—family.

Then, about 2,000 years ago, the Roman Empire built complex road networks. Trade, populations, and cities grew rapidly. The Romans needed a way to keep accounts of their citizens so they implemented a census—this is why Mary and Joseph traveled to Bethlehem on Christmas Eve.

As cities and populations continued to grow, and people could change cities or change professions more easily, it became difficult to distinguish people by simply describing where they were from or their profession. So, the Romans created the modern surname. Everyone had a surname, it could not be changed, and wives would take the names of their husbands, and children would take the names of their fathers (the patriarchy strikes again). The surname became a way to maintain accountability and, most importantly, to tax the population. Other civilizations around the world implemented similar surname policies, but the Roman tradition is the one that can be most directly traced from Rome, to Europe, and then to America.

?? When people find out that I took my wife's name, they have many different reactions. !!

Up until 500, or even 100 years ago, surnames were still a brilliant invention for civil control. You could, in theory, use a surname to trace your family lineage back to the dawn of Christ. But this is 2020. Today, we have Social Security cards, passports, DNA, the IRS, and two-factor authentication. We have much better ways to verify someone's identity than by tracing the origin of someone's surname. The fact that we continue to treat it normal that a wife takes a husband's last name is rather absurd.

One evening during dinner, we began the discussion again and I offered the solution. "I'll take your name. I'll change my name to Solano."

"What?" she replied, perplexed.

"I'll take your name. Problem solved."

"What about Crapanzano?" She asked, "What will your dad think?"

"Which one?" I jokingly asked.

She chuckled and immediately understood what I was saying. Since I was adopted and knew my biological parents, I had two different fathers with two different last names. I was adopted at four years old. When I was born, my name was Roberto Antonio Caraballo, but when my adoption was finalized, my adopted parents changed my name to Robert Anthony Crapanzano. My adopted parents will forever be my mom and dad, but over the years I also met my biological father, and then my biological mother (who was separated from my dad). Over the years, I built relationships with them and their families. I have two fathers, two mothers, and three different families—even more if I add my in-laws.

I explained, "I was born a Caraballo. This isn't the first time my name was changed. And what about my moms' names— what about Dailey or Negron? Besides, I don't need to keep a last name to show how much I love my parents. So, I'll just take your name—Solano—because I love you."

"Okay." She said.

"Okay!" I replied.

When people find out that I took my wife's name, they have many different reactions. Women usually respond with wonder, joy, and amazement—"You did what? Oh my gosh! That's so cool! You're so progressive!"

Men, as you can imagine, have a much different reaction. They usually give me an inquisitive response. They say things like, "That's different," but I know that many of them think, "*That's weird.*"

On one occasion, I met an old supervisor a year after I got married. He is a good guy, but very right-wing conservative, and I would generally categorize him as a ballbuster.

When he saw me, he looked at my name badge and exclaimed, "Solano?! That's right. I did hear that you changed your name. Dude, you lost your man card."

I thought his statement interesting because I didn't remember reading the rule that changing your name would disqualify someone's man-card club membership. I also wondered if I had been missing out on any club benefits, but most of all, I thought about how completely absurd this whole name changing thing is. These are the small ways in which the patriarchy is reinforced.

Why does a wife need to take a husband's name? We have been brainwashed to conform to this old archetype that no longer provides the genealogy history that it did 200 years ago.

People will argue that Zaira and I should have kept our own names, but as I already explained, I'm traditional and think that Mr. and Mrs. [Same Name] has a special ring to it.

Some people will argue that changing a name affects their professional reputation, and this is a somewhat valid argument, but the truth is that the most valuable relationships are the ones that we continue to regularly maintain. Most of these people are active in my life had no problem shifting from Robert Crapanzano to Robert Solano. Once I changed my name, most people didn't even bat an eye. Perhaps other people, especially professional women, have had different experiences, but it seems like we spend a lot of time debating a name change that has very little impact on most of our professional careers.

I know through firsthand experience that changing your name sucks. I have a lot of sympathy for the hundreds of millions of women that have done it over the past 200 years. The whole process is a huge ordeal to change your Social Security card, driver's license, passport, bank accounts, credit cards, frequent flyer accounts, Amazon account, mortgage, and Facebook name. I estimate that I've easily spent at least 100 hours of my life trying to change my name. As an attorney, Zaira's hourly wage is $350. I joke that I saved her $35,000 by taking her name instead of the other way around.

There are a lot of reasons that may impact your choice of a surname, but we shouldn't pick a last name just because it's the husband's. Some couples may even find that it makes sense to create a unique surname together, one that allows both partners to start a new legacy, a new tribe, and a new pack.

Zaira and I were hesitant about the plan, initially, because we were preconditioned by decades of past experience and thousands of examples. When we realized that it was better for us as a couple to use her name rather than mine, we made a decision and stuck with it. In retrospect, it was a decision that we both thought a lot about, but that had very little impact on our lives, professional careers, or happiness.

Some women will read this and say, "Yes! That's right. I don't need to change my name. My husband should change his name instead!"

Even after reading this, there will be some chest-thumping chauvinistic men or proud and independent women who refuse to change their last names. For these people, I remind them that surnames were originally a tool created by emperors to control their citizens and take their taxes—fight the power. Couples need to choose what makes the most sense and brings them the most joy, and they shouldn't worry too much about the rest.

LET'S RECAP

- The use of surnames began after the Agricultural Revolution when individuals needed a way to distinguish people who performed different professions or who were from different towns. Later, governments like the Roman Empire relied on surnames to manage populations and collect taxes.
- The tradition of passing the male surname between generations is a tradition that no longer serves a functional purpose.
- Couples should pick a surname, or keep their own names, based upon what makes the most sense for their individual circumstances.
- For young professionals, your future is greater than your past. Whatever name you pick, the most important friends and colleagues in your life will accept it effortlessly.

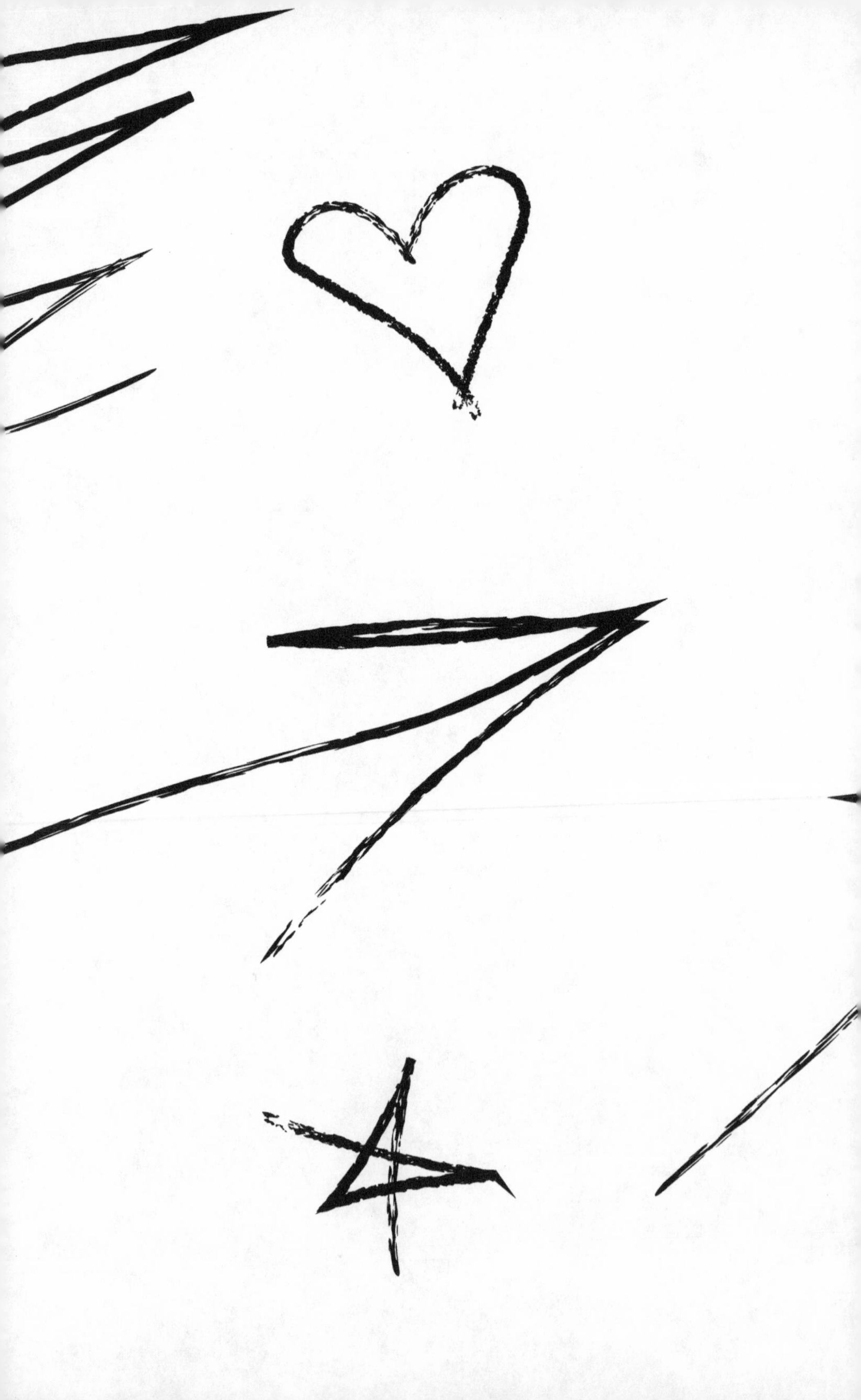

VOL. II

Upgrade U

"Island hopping off the Amalfi coast
Mafios, oh baby, you ever seen Saturn?
No, not the car, but everywhere we are
You're sure to see stars, this is high level not eye level."

—Jay-Z

CHAPTER EIGHT

HARD KNOCK LIFE

"But since when y'all niggaz know me to fail? Fuck naw." —Jay-Z

Before I graduated from Georgia Tech, I called my human resources manager and asked him if I could get an assignment on the East Coast instead of New Mexico. I told him that I met a girl, fell in love, and planned to marry her. Then I explained that a job in New Mexico would make our relationship very difficult. Since I signed a contract in exchange for attending graduate school, I could not refuse an assignment without incurring a significant amount of debt. But there was no harm in asking for a new assignment if it might benefit my relationship.

Two months later, my human resources manager called me back to let me know that an assignment became available in Orlando. It wasn't Atlanta, but it was much closer. Zaira agreed to move with me, and in the summer of 2014, we moved to Florida. Flights between Atlanta and Orlando were cheap and quick, so it was relatively easy for Zaira to get to work. After a few months, Zaira and I developed a routine.

A typical Monday went like this: Zaira woke up before me at about 4:30 and began getting ready for the day. The sound of the shower water running followed by scuffling noises in the bathroom and then closet were usually enough to wake me up. In the closet, I could hear Zaira zip her suitcase as she finished packing her clothes. I looked over and saw that she was already dressed, which meant that she was probably almost ready to go to the airport. I grabbed my iPhone from the nightstand and checked the time—4:46 a.m.

"Almost ready to go, babe?" I asked her, but since she was already dressed, I knew she would be ready in about five minutes.

"Almost, a few minutes. Can you help me zip my dress?" she replied as she walked over to the bed and turned her back toward me so that I could zip her. She wore pumps and a sleeveless red dress that tapered at the bottom. She was sexy, and if she covered her shoulders with a blazer, she was ready to go to the boardroom or courtroom.

I got out of bed, zipped her dress, and then put shorts and a T-shirt on. I brushed my teeth and grabbed my wallet and car keys. Zaira was ready now and walked toward the door with her suitcase.

"I'll take the dogs with us. Do you want to take them for a walk and then I'll pick you up downstairs?"

"Sure," Zaira looked for the dogs who were still sleeping, one on the foot of the bed and the other on the couch. On a normal day, the dogs wake us up in the morning, but 4:50 a.m. was too early for even them. "Let's go Sasha. Sierra, get off the couch!"

We stepped outside and prepared to lock the door behind us. "Got your boarding pass?"

"Oh, thanks for the reminder," she said. She opened up her email, sent her pass to the printer, and then ran back inside to grab it. Spirit Airlines was always a pain in the ass if you didn't have a printed boarding pass when you checked in. Our forgetfulness had cost us $10 on many occasions.

Thirty minutes later we arrived at the Orlando airport, gave each other a farewell hug and kiss, Zaira petted the dogs, and then she checked in for her 6:30 a.m. flight. After dropping her off, I returned home with the dogs, and then got ready for the day and went to work.

If her flight was on time, which was uncommon for Spirit Airlines, she would land in Atlanta by 7:45 a.m. She would take an Uber from the airport to her office and be there ready to start her day before most of her staff began to show up for their 9 a.m. meeting. Her new employees were always surprised when they found out that she commuted from Orlando to Atlanta every Monday morning.

For the next four days, Zaira worked in Atlanta. She kept her apartment in Midtown, which she used as a crash pad when she was there. She didn't spend a lot of time there because without me or the dogs to be a distraction, she could grind out a ton of work. Often, I would text her in the evenings around 9 p.m.: "wyd?"

She would text back, "Still at office. I'll call you on my way home."

While Zaira was in Atlanta busting her ass, I stayed busy in Orlando. After completing my graduate degree, I decided to continue my education and pursue a Ph.D. Most of my classes were distance learning. So, in addition to working forty to fifty hours a week, I also worked about twenty hours a week on school.

I would get home at about 5:30 p.m., and then, at about 6, I would open up a bottle of wine, sit in front of my computer, and work on research, essays, and discussion boards. I worked on my classes and drank until about 11 p.m., which was usually the time that Zaira was getting finished up with her work too. I would make a quick late-night dinner as I talked to her for a few minutes and then we went to bed in our separate homes. That was the way that Monday, Tuesday, and Wednesday nights went.

On Thursday, Zaira would catch the 5:30 p.m. flight from Atlanta to Orlando. I would pick her up from the airport and we would be home in time for a late dinner. Zaira spent Monday to Thursday in Atlanta and Friday through Sunday in Orlando. With the exception of a few research papers and occasional emergency client phone calls, our weekends were relatively normal. Zaira was just like any other executive who commuted on an airplane to the office. We lived like this for almost two years.

I felt bad that Zaira did most of the commuting and I would try to go to Atlanta about once a month to reduce her travel burden. Unfortunately, my work schedule was more structured than Zaira's. I had to be in the office Monday through Friday and worked normal business hours. Our office did not allow telework, so If I wanted to go to Atlanta for three or four days, I needed to take paid time off.

As a CEO, Zaira had more flexibility in her schedule. She could leave the office early afternoon on Thursday to catch a flight and could telework from home on Fridays. Her travel was also a tax-deductible business expense, which helped reduce the financial burden of flying back and forth.

During this time, Zaira and I also attended a lot of business conferences together, and in our initial icebreaker conversations, other professionals always asked us, "Where are you guys from?"

We used to respond, "Uh, well. We live in Florida, but our offices are in Atlanta and Birmingham," and then I watched their mind struggle to process the information. In many instances, they physically shook their head side-to-side as if their subconscious was saying, "*No. That's not possible.*"

"Wait. What?" they would say, "You live in Florida but work in Atlanta and Birmingham? How do you do that?"

They would usually shake their head *no* at least one more time before they began to understand our living arrangement. After explaining a few more details, they would say something like, "Wow. That's amazing that you can make that work."

In the world of small business, meeting an executive that flies as much as Zaira is like seeing a unicorn. The same would be true for many professions, with the exception of maybe a consultant. As a society, we think that a normal professional career and family means that you live in the suburbs, drive to work each morning, and then drive home each night. Although this will probably continue to be the norm for the next ten to twenty years, I expect that more and more couples will have intercity relationships like Zaira and me. This trend will continue because:

- Cheaper flights, faster screening through TSA precheck, and more connections at regional airports have made flying more convenient.
- More companies are offering flexible schedules like the compressed week, which lets employees work nine hours a day and then take off every other Friday. Three-day weekends every other week make travel easier for long-distance relationships.
- More companies are offering telework, where employees can work part or all of the week from their home office or anywhere else that they can get Wi-Fi. The recent coronavirus pandemic accelerated this trend as it forced many companies to implement telework policies.
- Corporate managers are changing jobs and locations every two to four years to get promoted and gain experience, often leaving friends, family, and high-school-aged children behind.

Zaira and I are proof that you can have a successful intercity relationship. We still travel a lot, but not as much as we did between 2015–2017. Although we were apart for four days of the week and worked our asses off during our time away from each other, we still spent almost every weekend together.

When Zaira had told me, "We'll make it work," I doubted her, and when Zaira first proposed that she would commute back and forth between Florida and Atlanta, I thought she was crazy. With the exception of a few airline pilots, I never knew anyone who traveled that much for work. At first, I called our relationship long-distance, but as time passed and we continued to see each other almost every week, our relationship no longer needed a special name. It was just our relationship.

Zaira and I are proof that you can have a successful intercity relationship.

Many people argue that in a dual professional relationship, one partner usually needs to make a sacrifice in their career for the benefit of the other person's career. Sometimes our friends will say, "Zaira made a sacrifice for you by moving to Florida." But it wasn't a career sacrifice. Thanks to cheaper travel, telework, digital work, and other changes in the workspace, professional couples have more career options today than any time in history.

The term sacrifice implies that you give up something that you value for the sake of something else that you value more. Zaira did not give up her career for the sake of our relationship. Zaira definitely had to work hard to maintain our intercity relationship and career. If anything, she sacrificed her sleep and comfort on many occasions as she flew back and forth on budget airlines. Commuting back and forth was a hard life, but Zaira never had to sacrifice her career. Quite the contrary. Moving to Florida forced Zaira to explore new business strategies and management practices. For the first two years, she commuted back and forth, but over time, she made policy and staff changes that allowed her to spend less time in Atlanta and more time in Florida. These changes propelled her business's growth and resulted in her tripling her revenue from $400,000 per year to over $1.2 million. Additionally, she learned how to create virtual work teams. This means that when the coronavirus pandemic struck the world in the spring of 2020, Zaira and her team were well prepared to telework from home because of the changes that she began implementing in 2016.

Instead of sacrificing her career, Zaira decided that she would temporarily sacrifice some of her happiness in exchange for a successful business and relationship. She made that decision before she had any clue how she would actually do it. I am extremely grateful for her commitment to our relationship and her career and I tried the best I could to reciprocate and meet her halfway when able. Her decision forced us to find opportunities. The first opportunity we found was in getting reassigned from New Mexico to Orlando. The next opportunity was low-cost flights so that we could commute back and forth from Orlando to Atlanta. The next opportunity was new virtual teamwork software like Zoom and Slack that allowed Zaira to spend more time working remotely. The reason that we are able to have two successful careers and a powerful marriage is actually because Zaira *refused* to sacrifice.

In life, we often hope that opportunities will find us—I hoped that I would find a beautiful, smart, and intelligent woman who would have a professional career and could also move with me every two years—rarely does life happen that easily. Instead, we must find the opportunities ourselves. We need to decide what we want and what we are *not* willing to sacrifice. As Zaira showed me, we usually need to make those decisions before we actually have a clear path on how we will proceed. However, once we make those decisions, then we can begin to see opportunities open up for a better life.

LET'S RECAP

- **Two individual careers are challenging for most couples. When faced with this challenge, to avoid making a career sacrifice, you need to find opportunities to continue your career.**
- **Cheaper flights, flexible work schedules, and telework are a few recent trends that have given dual-career couples greater opportunities to each be successful.**
- **Sometimes, you will still need to temporarily sacrifice your comfort and happiness for your career if you want it bad enough.**

CHAPTER NINE

LIFTOFF

"We gon' take it to the moon, take it to the stars." —Jay-Z

We made long distance work, but it sucked! While we were in a happy relationship, it was truly a miserable lifestyle. Mondays can be hard enough and waking up at 4:30 a.m. made it even harder. I hated waking up early on Monday and hated driving to the airport even more.

Although flights were cheap, when you add up at least eight flights per month, the Ubers, and the Atlanta apartment, commuting cost us about $3,500 per month. To top it off, we were also separated from each other at least four days a week. We always wanted to make the best use of our short weekends together, so usually Zaira worked until 8 or 9 p.m. each night while she was in Atlanta. As a result, when I did pick her up from the airport on Thursdays, she was usually physically and emotionally burnt out. It took her at least a full day in Orlando to recover from the stress of her Atlanta work, and she always dreaded Sunday nights on the eve of another long workweek.

Eventually, I got fed up with our situation. One day, I broke. "I can't take you to the airport anymore," I told her matter-of-factly one particular day that I was in a bad mood. "I really don't like waking up early, so you need to start taking an Uber.'"

I expected Zaira to resist the idea. Of the five love languages, Zaira's language is Acts of Service.[30]

I thought that taking her to the airport and picking her up was a way for me to show her that I loved her, and likewise, I thought that she expected me to pick her up as a sign of my love. I expected her to be disappointed, but instead she said, "Okay. That makes sense."

"Same goes for picking you up," I added after my first victory. "Instead of me sitting in rush hour and then waiting in the cell phone lot, you should just Uber."

---

30 Gary Chapman (2015). *The 5 Love Languages: The Secret to Love that Lasts.*

"Okay. That's fine." She said as I tried to discern if she was really okay with it, or if she was just saying that to avoid a fight. At the time, I thought, *That was much easier than I expected.*

A few years later, I asked Zaira about that conversation and she shared what she initially thought. "I was like, 'This fool gonna leave me. He don't want to be with me anymore. Look at that, he won't even take me to the airport.' "

After that conversation, Zaira began to Uber herself to the airport. With this small change, I was able to sleep in until my usual wake-up time of 7 a.m. and start my Monday mornings well rested. When Zaira returned to Orlando on Thursdays, I was able to cook and have a stress-free dinner ready and waiting for us. She could vent to me over dinner about her long week, and I listened sympathetically because I was not already stressed out by an hour-long rush hour drive to and from the airport. A simple Uber of $20 each way led to a much more relaxing morning or evening. This was a small sacrifice, but one that we could tolerate in exchange for the benefits.

We decided that we wanted and deserved higher standards for our lives. As soon as we elevated our standards, we became receptive to new opportunities.

At the same time, Zaira decided to start flying Delta instead of Spirit. It was more expensive but allowed her more comfort and schedule flexibility. Since I didn't need to take her to the airport before work, she switched to the 10 a.m. flight instead of the 6:30 one. Now, with this small financial sacrifice, Zaira woke up refreshed, she was able to work in the Uber on her way to the airport, at the airport she could get a quick breakfast at the Delta lounge, and then she could work on her flight. The extra cost probably saved our relationship.

Like many people, Zaira and I initially tolerated unhappiness because of money, and I get it—a $59 Spirit Airlines flight is a great deal compared to a $220 Delta flight—but life is too short to be unhappy. In our case, investing in our happiness cost us a net of $0.

Let me explain. Taking an Uber to the airport cost $20, but it allowed Zaira to work another thirty minutes and saved me two hours of sleep. These small changes doubled our happiness and thirty more minutes of productivity resulted in more revenue than $20. Similarly, Zaira was able to work in the Delta lounge and Delta flight, which more than made up for the extra $150 to buy a Delta ticket (which was also a business tax deduction). If she could use that time to get just one additional client, she could make over $500 in profit.

For a long time, I approached life with the belief that transportation was a means to an end. I never saw the value in having a nice car or flying first-class—everyone arrives at their destination at the same time. As a result, I always looked for the cheapest deals and tolerated discomfort and unhappiness as a result. Upgrading to Uber and Delta helped me realize that the way we travel is just as important as why we travel or where we travel to. Now I completely understand why CEOs of large corporations fly first-class or on private jets.

This experience—figuring out the logistics of our long-distance relationship—really taught me to be intolerant of unhappiness. We decided that we wanted and deserved higher standards for our lives. As soon as we elevated our standards, we became receptive to new opportunities. We became happier, but also increased our productivity and became a stronger couple.

We all have things in our lives that make us unhappy. It is natural and healthy to desire more in life whether it is more money, better health, more travel, stronger relationships, nicer homes, or more productivity. Most of us tolerate our own unhappiness because we think that the thing that will make us happy will cost too much or will require too much work, that we don't deserve it or we think it is impossible to achieve. Other times, we tolerate unhappiness because we are afraid what other people may think. Here are some examples of things that I am still tolerating:

- My dog occasionally pisses on our stairway landing. It happens about once a month. We clean it the best we can, but there are many days where I still catch a faint hint of urine afterward. I tolerate it because I think that it would be impossible to eliminate. I think that if we replaced the carpet with hardwood, she would just find some other area of the house to urinate in.
- I really want a beach house near a surfing destination, but the idea of owning a beach house seems financially impossible.

- We have an employee who consistently performs below standard. He has a good personality, so we continue to tolerate his poor performance.
- High-traffic areas in our yard always have dead grass. I love drinking coffee in our garden, the flowers are beautiful, but every time I look at the dead grass, I get frustrated.

I know that I should just replace the carpet, buy a beach house, fire our underperforming employee, and hire a landscaper, but I tell myself toleration stories. We will always have subpar areas of our life that we tolerate. Even the wealthiest people in the world have parts of their life, business, or relationships that they want to improve. Usually, the reasons that hold wealthy people back from being happy are the same reasons that hold us back. Instead of stressing about buying a $250,000 home, they stress over buying a $5 million home. Similarly, wealthy people may also take undesirable jobs just because they pay more. For example, an actor may turn down a role in a fun independent film that pays crap in exchange for a supporting role in a shitty major film. The indie would bring the actor happiness, but he makes financial excuses to justify his unhappiness. The scale may be different, but the human feelings remain the same. Building a fulfilling and rewarding life is a process that never stops.

We will need to occasionally do things that make us unhappy—we will need to kiss a client's ass to make a sale, work on part of a case that we don't enjoy because we are the only one who can do it, or we will need to live in a subpar house until we can increase our income. But, if we are serious about living a rewarding life, we need to decide that we will not tolerate unhappiness. If something is negatively affecting your happiness, set your sights on finding a way to improve it.

Improving your life has a compound effect because it opens new avenues to improve your life even further. If you let old pains stop dragging you down, you can seek out pleasure more easily. For Zaira and me, we decided that we would try to make our relationship work, and only then did an Orlando job became available. We decided that we would not wake up early on Mondays and only then did we learn that we were more productive and happier taking Uber. We decided that we would not tolerate flying on "The Worst Airline in America" and then realized that flying Delta improved our productivity and covered the cost of better flights—many sections of this book where written while sitting in a Delta lounge or while on a Delta flight. We are still on the journey, but today, we live a much higher quality of life than we did five years ago. This journey began in earnest when we decided that we would not tolerate unhappiness anymore.

LET'S RECAP

- Small upgrades to your environment and how you spend your time can have exponential changes to your business and happiness.
- Most people tolerate discomfort and unhappiness in order to save money. In many instances, and this is especially true for entrepreneurs and executives, investing in life upgrades can lead to greater productivity, more clients, and greater income.
- If you want to live a rewarding life, decide that you will not tolerate unhappiness. Once you make that decision, opportunities will follow.

CHAPTER TEN

FLAWLESS

"Mama taught me good home training.
My Daddy taught me how to love my haters." —Beyoncé

When Zaira and I first got married, our life was hectic. I had a full-time job as a program manager, and I worked another 20 hours each week on my Ph.D. Meanwhile, Zaira was flying back and forth to Atlanta and trying to figure out how she could live in Orlando while still managing her businesses in Atlanta and Birmingham. Simultaneously, we launched our nonprofit organization. And all of this while trying to build our new marriage. Time was a precious asset.

For three years, I was always working, studying, or traveling. I was tired. During this time, I ate like crap, drank way too much alcohol, and neglected my physical and mental health. I started to have issues with my eyesight, regular headaches, and a difficult time concentrating or staying awake at work.

Eventually, I realized my Ph.D. studies caused a lot of my unhappiness. I dreaded the start of each semester. Although I enjoyed working with a great group of peers, I hated the frivolous writing and soul-crushing dissertation process. I also had very little time for my own health and well-being while I was in school.

I really wanted to be called "Doctor," so I continued with my studies despite my unhappiness. Eventually, I was three years into the program. In addition to about $50,000 of employer-sponsored financial aid, I had also spent about $25,000 of my own money on tuition. To earn a doctorate, all I needed to do was complete my final dissertation. I knew I could complete the disertation in two years, but I dreaded the thought of suffering for six more depressing semesters. I couldn't quit because I was well over halfway done, and I felt like I had an obligation to my professors, my parents, and siblings who were so supportive of me during the process.

One day, I was struggling with this thought and I asked myself, *If you were going to die next week, would you be happy spending your last week on Earth continuing your Ph.D. research?*

Of course not! I replied to myself, *If I was going to die, I would spend my last week enjoying it with my friends, family, and Zaira!*

Okay, I asked myself again, *If you die in fifty years—that would make you eighty-five years old—when you look back on your life, is this Ph.D. going to be the crowning achievement that defines your life's success?*

No, I replied once again, *I want to be defined by the friendships I built, the business that I will build, the people that I helped, and the legacy I leave behind with my family.*

Do you need a Ph.D. to do any of that? I asked.

"No, not really." I said aloud.

In that moment, I realized that I was wasting my time and energy toward doing something that did not help me achieve my most important life goals. I started my Ph.D. for the wrong reasons. After I realized that I hated it, I continued it because I felt like that is what society expected of me. Despite the sunk cost and concerns of others, I knew what I needed to do.

After months of nervous deliberation and self-doubt, I submitted my resignation letter. The following day, I felt a huge wave of relief as I shed thousands of pounds of stress. I immediately started spending more time in the gym, spent more stress-free time with Zaira, and began reading and writing for leisure, which eventually led to this book.

In that moment, I realized that I was wasting my time and energy toward doing something that did not help me achieve my most important life goals.

Shortly after I quit my Ph.D. studies, I came across a quote by Gary Vaynerchuck: "Stop doing shit you hate." I loved this mantra and made it part of my personal philosophy.

As I learned by quitting my Ph.D., when we stop doing things we hate, we can use our energy to do more things that we love. For me, this meant living a healthy lifestyle, building a powerful marriage, and sharing my stories to help other professional couples. This mantra has completely changed my life and marriage.

We all have things that we hate, dislike, enjoy, and love. In a simplified model of our lives, we can put these activities on scale with things we hate at one end and things we love at the other end. For me, my Ph.D. studies were at the far end of the hate scale. Moving up the scale are things I dislike such as sitting in traffic, cleaning toilets, and flying Spirit Airlines. On the other side of the scale are things that I enjoy, such as helping clients, international travel, and surfing. Finally, further up the scale are things that I love, such as spending meaningful quality time with family. I call this the Happiness Scale.

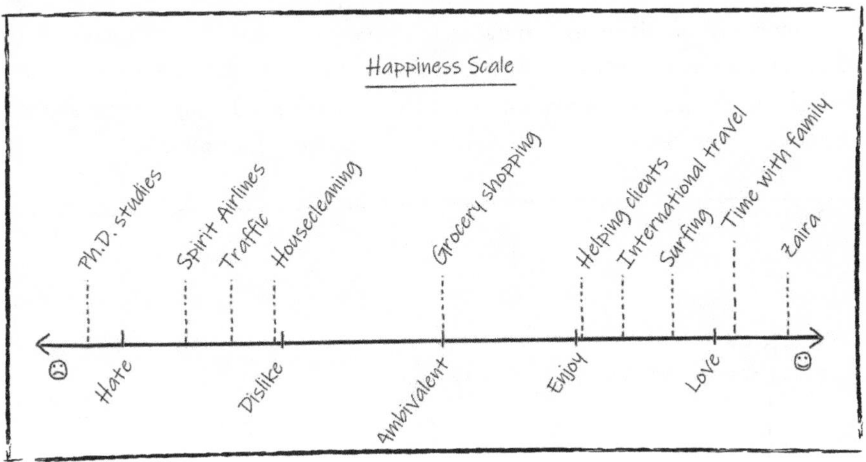

What I observe is that if I tolerate something in my life that I really dislike, then there is usually something else that I am tolerating that I equally dislike. For example, when I was tolerating unhappiness from my schoolwork, I was also tolerating being out of shape, worsening health issues, and being disengaged at work. This was during the same time that Zaira and I were also tolerating early morning trips to the airport and weekly flights on Spirit Airlines. When I stopped tolerating being miserable in my schoolwork, I also stopped tolerating sitting in traffic, flying Spirit, or being out of shape.

It is as if we accept a level of unhappiness that we will tolerate in our lives.

If we tolerate one area of our life that brings us unhappiness, we are much more likely to tolerate other areas that bring us similar unhappiness. For example, if you tolerate a job that brings you unhappiness, then you would also tolerate an unhappy marriage. Each of has an internal standard for how much unhappiness we are willing to tolerate and this standard cuts across many different aspects of our lives to include our work, homes, cars, health, friends, clients, staff, children, and relationships.

On the surface, tolerating one thing that makes us unhappy may not seem like a big deal, but if we tolerate unhappiness in one aspect of our lives, there are almost always other areas of our lives where we have equally low standards. For this reason, we made it a goal to continuously increase our standards.

By definition, the things that we hate are the lowest on the list of things that make us happy. They should be the first things that we eliminate from our lives. Once we eliminate the things we hate, we can begin to avoid other activities that we dislike, which means that we can spend more time doing the activities that we love.

For me, when I raised my standards, I created more time and energy to devote to surfing, enjoyable travel, new entrepreneur activities, and my marriage. My overall happiness and enjoyment in life increase tremendously. I increased my standards from “Ph.D. studies” to just below “grocery shopping.”

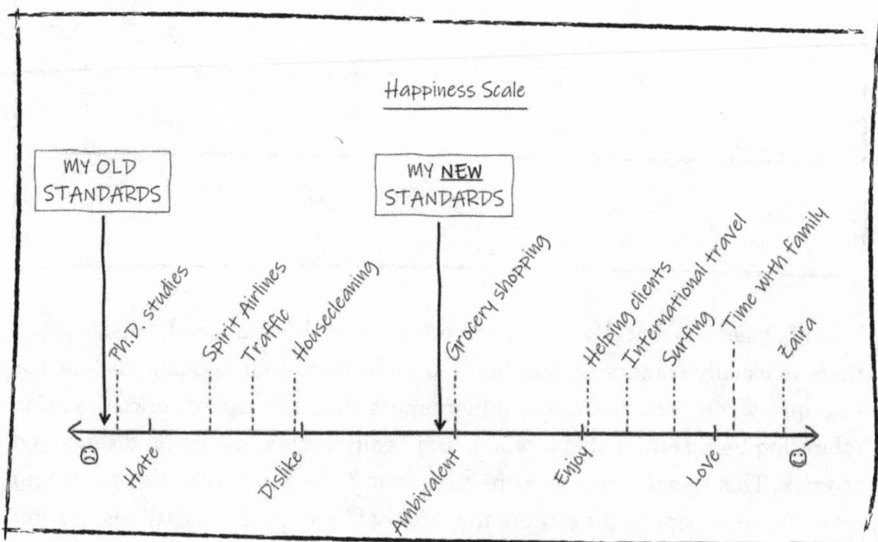

It is as if we accept a level of unhappiness that we will tolerate in our lives. If we tolerate one area of our life that brings us unhappiness, we are much more likely to tolerate other areas that bring us similar unhappiness.

When I tell people, "Stop doing shit you hate," occasionally someone will reply, "We always need to do some things that we hate."

"No," I reply forcefully, "you don't."

If you think that you need to do things you dislike, you are deciding that you will tolerate those things. I guarantee you that it is possible to live a life where you never need to do things that you dislike.

It is understandable why some people think like this. After all, most of us have lived our entire lives doing things we dislike. Our parents ingrained this into us when they told us to eat our vegetables, school reinforced this by burdening us with classwork and standardized tests, and now most professional careers continue to persuade us to do things we dislike by enticing us with lucrative wages. But we do not need to listen to our parents anymore, we are finished with school, and if you are unhappy in your current job, there are hundreds of others out there that you would enjoy. The only reason that we do things that we dislike is not because we need to, it is because of our standards.

To raise your standards, the first step is to decide what actually needs to get done. In my example, I learned that I really did not need to complete my PhD. Similarly, I attended tons of meetings at my office because I imagined that my boss would be impressed with my eagerness to participate. I realized that I was doing this to make someone else happy and not myself, so I stopped going. As a result, I began to get more work done and enjoy my time at the office more. Interestingly, no one has ever commented about my reduced meeting attendance and my boss is rather happy with my increase in performance and new projects.

Sometimes, instead of avoiding necessary tasks, a better option is to make those tasks more enjoyable. For example, Zaira and I fly back and forth to Atlanta frequently. We disliked the task of flying because we were flying Spirit Airlines and sitting in traffic back and forth from the airport. We were able to make that task more enjoyable by flying Delta Comfort class, visiting the Delta lounge before our flights, and by hiring Uber Black cars to take us to and from the airport. Now, flying frequently is a low-stress activity and on many days, I actually look forward to the ability to work or read on the flight without office distractions.

Of course, I understand the objections. There are always undesirable things that need to get done. For example, we need to file our annual taxes, we need to wash our laundry, and we need to commute to work. But just because these things need to get done does not mean that *we* need to be the ones who do them. This is why a good way to raise your standards is to hire help.

As a young professional or entrepreneur, many of us begin our early twenties doing everything ourselves. We clean our own apartments, do our own grocery shopping, drive ourselves to the airport, mow our own grass, and file our taxes. New entrepreneurs also do everything for their businesses: they write their own copyright, serve as the receptionist, complete sales, run marketing, manage bookkeeping, and lead human resources. We do everything because when we are young, and have very little money, we need to be everything and everyone. Unfortunately, most of us never break that habit, even after we are older, wealthier, and have more productive ways to use our time than spending a Saturday cleaning our houses. It is a struggle to transition from doing everything ourselves to doing only the things that we enjoy.

One of the techniques that helped me make this transition was to decide how much I valued my free time—which is different than my hourly salary. I started by thinking about something that I really dislike. For me, that thing was sitting in traffic. Then I asked myself, *How much would I pay to avoid sitting in 60 minutes of rush hour traffic?*

Today, I would pay $100 to avoid an hour of traffic. This dollar amount is my *toleration budget*. This budget helps simplify decisions to clear monetary evaluation. If sitting in traffic will earn me $100 or more, then I will sit in traffic—for example, to meet a new client. However, if I could avoid an hour of traffic by paying someone else $100 or less, then I will pay $100—for example, paying for an assistant to deliver an urgent package during rush hour. This toleration budget is the same for everything that I dislike—sitting in traffic, scrubbing toilets, filing taxes, editing videos, or mailing Christmas cards. I will pay someone or some service to do those tasks for me if it cost $100 or less per hour, otherwise I will do them myself.

It is important to think of our toleration budget as the *value of our time*, and not how much a task should cost.

Zaira really hates folding laundry. When I asked her, "How much would you pay to avoid folding laundry for an hour?"

Her response was, "I would pay someone $15 an hour."

"No," I replied and repeated the question. "How much would you pay to avoid folding laundry *yourself?* Your time is worth more than $15 per hour."

After a moment of thinking she replied, "Well, my hourly fee is $350. So, let's say $350 an hour."

"Okay," I challenged her. "So you would pay $350 to avoid folding laundry for an hour?"

"Of course not!" she exclaimed, like I had insulted her.

"Your toleration budget is not the same as your hourly wages," I explained. "Let me help you. Would you pay $50 to avoid folding laundry for an hour?"

"Yes," she replied.

"How about $100?"

"Yes," she said without hesitating.

"How about $150?"

"Yes," she said after a short pause.

"How about $200?"

"Maybe," she said after a longer pause.

"How about $300?"

"Ew," she winced. "That's hard. You are triggering my money story. I wish I had *fuck you* money like that." Zaira continued, "Okay, I think $200 is my limit."

Our toleration budgets are different than our hourly wages or consultation fees—we're not talking about real money here. We are gauging how much we dislike something. Zaira, for instance, really hates laundry. Other people may find laundry enjoyable, in which case they should imagine some other task that they hate. Our wages and fees definitely influence our toleration budget, but other factors also influence it, such as our disposable income, the amount of free time we have, our current standards, and whether we are on a fixed or flexible income.

Toleration budgets not only help us raise our standards, but they also simplify decisions. Anytime we have a task that we dislike, we simply need to ask ourselves, *Can I hire someone to do this for less than my toleration budget?*

If the answer is yes, then, without hesitation, you should pay someone else to do it.

Now, I should warn that this strategy can lead to financial ruin if you set a toleration budget that exceeds your financial means. You should not set a budget so high that it sends you into debt and poverty.

Here are some examples of how I use my toleration budget to elevate my standards. As a reminder, my toleration budget is $100 an hour.

> **Scenario:** Our friend visited for the weekend and her flight landed during rush hour. It would take me at least 45 minutes to drive to the airport to pick her up, and then another 45 minutes back. ($150 budget)
>
> **Decision:** When she landed, I called her an Uber Black Car which cost me $36. As an added bonus, she felt like a world-class celebrity when I told her that a black Escalade was waiting for her outside baggage claim.
>
> **Scenario:** I have an old dog. I love her, but if I leave her home all day, she

will urinate and crap on the living room floor, which requires about ten minutes to clean up. ($16 daily budget)

Decision: I hired a dog walker for $10 per day. Now I come home to a flawless house and I'm greeted by a happy dog instead of piss and shit.

Scenario: After a long day, I wanted to get home, exercise, and then work on my book, but I realized that I had no food at the house for dinner. Going to the grocery store would have cost me about an hour of my evening. ($100 budget, not including cost of groceries)

Decision: During my lunch break, I ordered groceries through Amazon. When I arrived home, the groceries were sitting on my doorstep. The groceries were about $15 more expensive than going to the local grocery story. I had a great workout, plenty of time to work on my book, and a great dinner.

Sometimes, outsourcing a task exceeds our toleration budget. Here are some examples where I needed to do undesirable tasks because outsourcing them would have cost too much.

Scenario: I need to file an LLC and EIN for my new business. To hire a local business lawyer would cost about $1,000. Alternatively, a less reliable online service would cost about $350, plus registration fees. Both of these would still require at least an hour of my time.

Decision: I spent two hours on a Saturday and registered my business myself ($200 budget).

Scenario: My boss told me that I needed to attend a three-hour mind-numbing meeting. My expertise was relevant for only about fifteen minutes of the meeting. If I skipped it, I probably would have received a negative report, which could eventually result in me missing a promotion and losing my job.

Decision: I attended the meeting ($300 budget), but to reduce my dislike, I sat in the back row with my notebook and a few reports that I needed to read. Although it probably looked like I was taking diligent meeting notes, I was actually preparing a technical evaluation of an unrelated project.

The most important aspect of building the lives that we desire is to continue to grow and raise our standards. Setting a toleration budget and paying that amount, despite mental reservations, is an important step in elevating our standards. Most of us have wealth stories that make this kind of growth uncomfortable. Work to retell yourself the stories you need to be happier.

Here is another scenario that was particularly hard for me and that challenged my wealth story: A while ago, I saw a pair of cargo pants that I liked. I was in a rush, so I bought the pants without trying them on. When I got home and finally did try them on, the waist fit well, but the legs were too big. They fit like parachute pants; not a style that I liked.

My plan was to return the pants and get my money back. The problem was that going to the sporting goods store would add at least thirty minutes to my commute. It would take me thirty minutes of my time, valued at \$50, to return a pair of \$40 pants.

What did I do?

Nothing. I did not return them. Commuting an undesirable thirty minutes to get a \$40 refund was less than my toleration budget. So, I kept the pants on my shelf for ninety days, saying to myself that I would return them if I ever happened to drive over to the area of town where the store was.

Zaira lamented, "You need to return those pants and get your money back."

"I will," I consoled her, "next time I am in the area."

Breaking through our subconscious money barriers is very difficult.

Months passed, and I never needed to go to the store. Eventually the ninety-day refund period expired, and the pants continued to sit on my shelf, cluttering my life and bringing me some uneasiness. Finally, after I got tired of looking at them every day, I donated them with our spring cleanings. Some happy soul will receive a \$40 brand-new pair of cargo pants for \$5 at Goodwill.

My subconscious scolded me: I can't believe you threw away \$40 because you didn't want to drive thirty minutes!

I claimed the pants as a donation tax deduction, but I still felt like I basically wasted money. I imagined what my parents would have thought if they knew that I bought a brand-new pair of pants and then basically threw them away because I thought my time was too important to drive thirty minutes. The unfortunate truth is that most of society views these behaviors as wasteful. This is especially true if you grew up in a middle-class family like me. These are the types of subconscious obstacles that we need to break through if we want to elevate our standards.

Of course, donating a pair of pants is not wasteful. I paid $40 to the store, which employed the staff that sold them to me, the warehouse workers that packaged them, and the manufacturers that made them. I also donated them so that someone else will hopefully be able to enjoy the pants. Nothing about donating my $40 pants was wasteful. Instead, I had to retell my story to realize it would have been wasteful if I sat in traffic for over thirty minutes when I had more productive uses of my time.

Breaking through our subconscious money barriers is very difficult. I admit that I had a hard time writing that Zaira would pay $200 for someone to do laundry. I told myself, *People are going to think that we are so bougie. They are going to say, 'That is so wasteful—$200 for laundry, seriously? Who the hell do these people think they are?!'*

I have had similar thoughts the first time we hired our housekeeper at $150 per week, or when we spent $800 on our first first-class tickets, or when we spent $30,000 on a professional development retreat. All of these experiences were great, and I found them incredibly enjoyable and rewarding, but my personal wealth story screamed, shouted, and clawed through my subconsciousness the entire time.

Over time, I have learned to welcome these thoughts. More often than not, they are an indication that I am on the right track. I recognize that as long as Zaira and I are continuously developing personally and professionally, and at the same time maintaining a positive income-to-expenses ratio, it really does not matter how much we pay for laundry, Ubers, housecleaners, dog walkers, hotels, assistants, or private jets. Our concerns about wastefulness and what other people think are inevitable as we push our standards higher and higher. Over time, our higher standards become commonplace, and our subconscious learns to accept our higher standards of living. But at first, this growth is very uncomfortable. Establishing a toleration budget, and sticking to this standard no matter what, is a very invaluable technique to elevate our standards and attain more happiness.

LET'S RECAP

- We all have things that we hate, dislike, enjoy, and love. If you tolerate one area of your life that brings you unhappiness, you are much more likely to tolerate other areas that bring you similar unhappiness. This is why you should aspire to raise your standards in all areas of your life.
- Determine your own toleration budget—how much you would pay to avoid doing something you hate. If you can hire someone else to do that task for you for less than your budget, you should.
- Breaking through your subconscious money barriers is difficult. You will inevitably have very uncomfortable internal arguments as you raise your standards. Learn to welcome these arguments as an opportunity for self-development and growth.

CHAPTER ELEVEN

99 PROBLEMS

*"You some type of lawyer or something?
Somebody important or something?" —Jay-Z*

Making the bed, washing the dishes, and folding laundry may seem like minor tasks, but when added together, properly cleaning an average three-bedroom house can easily take ten to twenty hours per week. As busy professionals, that is a tremendous amount of time that you should spend doing more important things. This is why most dual-career couples need a housecleaner. As an added benefit, a housecleaner can help you and your spouse avoid a lot of arguments about household chores.

If a housecleaner is the first position that most professional couples should outsource, then the second position they should outsource is an assistant.

I used to think that assistants were only for rich people or Fortune 500 CEOs, but that isn't true anymore. Most entrepreneurs and busy professionals, even those who run small businesses, probably need an assistant. Zaira and I have had assistants for three years now and today, I could not imagine a life without one or two of them. Assistants are, believe it or not, very practical.

Generally, there are two types of assistants: *personal assistants* and *executive assistants*. Which one you hire first will depend on your own personal needs and how much you can afford. If you are just beginning your career, you may combine these roles into one position, but eventually you should try to separate them for reasons that I will describe soon.

Before we hired our first assistant, we were still flying back and forth to Atlanta regularly. Additionally, Zaira and I attended business conferences about once a month, and I traveled separately for work about once a month also. Between five to ten days of the month, we were both traveling away from home at the same time.

The problem was that we had two dogs that we needed to take care of. At $50 per night, our average boarding bill was $250–$500 per month. I estimated that for less than $500 a month, we could hire an assistant who could watch our dogs while we were out of town, help Zaira with scheduling client phone calls, film social media clips for the law firm, run minor errands for us, and also supervise handymen and contractors when they worked on the house—at the time, we were getting new carpets, paint, and appliances.

We posted a short advertisement on Facebook and, the following day, we interviewed a candidate in our living room. Although both Zaira and I had interviewed hundreds of job applicants before, this was the first time we interviewed someone in our living room. It made Zaira feel awkward. We got lucky and the first person we interviewed was a rock star—we hired her on the spot.

If a housecleaner is the first position that most professional couples should outsource, then the second position they should outsource is an assistant.

Before we knew it, our assistant became a vital part of our lives. She took the dogs to the vet, picked up laundry, took Amazon return packages to the post office, helped decorate the house for Christmas, designed and mailed our personal and law firm Christmas cards, bought us each other's birthday and anniversary gifts, created new client handouts, filmed YouTube tutorials, created our wedding photo album, took the cars to get washed, did the grocery shopping, scheduled spin classes, brought us lunch, sent birthday gifts, booked flights, organized our closet, made hotel reservations, packed our suitcases, drove us to the airport, planned our vacation itineraries, hired handymen, scheduled massages, shopped for us, wrote our monthly newsletters, scheduled date night, and did at least ninety-nine other tasks that I have a difficult time remembering.

As you can imagine, these tasks would have taken countless hours for Zaira and me to do. In actuality, for most of our lives, we did these errands ourselves and never thought twice about them. It wasn't until we had an assistant that we realized just how much time we wasted on these unimportant tasks. Most of them were necessary but did little to help us move closer to our personal and professional goals. For example, there is nothing particularly rewarding about making hotel reservations, taking the car to get an oil change, or, the quintessential assistant task: picking up dry cleaning. With the help of our assistant, we were able to focus our energies on our marriage, happiness, and growth instead of routine errands.

One evening, I walked into the bedroom, flipped the light switch on, and *pop*—a light bulb in our ceiling fan blew out. One of the light bulbs was already blown, so now only two of the four bulbs turned on. I hated our ceiling fan light fixtures. They were straight out of the 1980s with shiny gold brass, dull white blades, and two pull chains—one to change the fan speed and the other to turn the lights on and off.

We had four of these outdated light fixtures throughout the house. When we bought the house two years earlier, we planned to change the lights, but we never got around to it. We always seemed to have higher priorities and the energy required to change them always seemed not worth it. If I wanted to change the lights myself, I would have needed to drag Zaira to Home Depot for her to pick out a light fixture, and she hates Home Depot just as much as I hate Bath & Body Works. I could have found an electrician to do it, but I would have had to search for one on the internet, read their reviews, and then call a few of them until I found someone trustworthy for the job. It was already nighttime, so I would have needed to wait until the following day to call them.

The entire task of replacing our ceiling fans would take several hours, therefore, I continued to tolerate my geriatric light fixtures because replacing them required too much energy.

This day was different though because Zaira and I had an assistant now. I cursed the light fixture and then I pulled out my phone and created a to-do task in Asana (the app that we currently use to manage our assistant's tasks). The task read, "Replace ceiling fans."

At our next weekly meeting, our assistant asked, "I saw that you added 'Replace ceiling fans.' What would you like me to do for that?"

"We hate our ceiling fans," I replied. "Please search Home Depot or Lowe's for a few different replacement options. Next week, show us what you found, and we'll pick the one we like. After we give you the go-ahead, please order them and then hire an electrician to replace them. Sound good?"

Our assistant has a key to our house, she has a credit card, has the login information for our Lowe's and Home Depot accounts, and is around us enough that she has a good understanding of our tastes and style. With a little guidance, she was able to accomplish the entire task and a few weeks later we had four brand-new modern ceiling fans. With an assistant, the entire task of replacing our light fixtures required only a few minutes of my time, versus hours of work, spread out over multiple days, if I did it myself. Leveraging an assistant for the task required much less activation energy on my part.

In another instance, Zaira and I wanted to host a Thanksgiving Turkey Giveaway, where we intended to give away turkeys and entire Thanksgiving meal kits to underserved Latino communities. We talked about it for years, but never did it because we expected it to take hours and hours of our time. We expected that we would need to find a venue, advertise the giveaway, shop for the groceries, package the food, organize the event, and give away the turkeys. Each of these tasks could easily consume hours of our time. As busy professionals, the idea of a Turkey Giveaway, which felt good but did not result in direct revenue, seemed like a daunting task on top of our already busy schedules.

After a few years of talking about it, we finally decided to execute the Turkey Giveaway; we gave the task to our assistant. To get started, we sent her a text, "Please schedule a thirty-minute meeting with Zaira and me to plan our Turkey Giveaway." (Notice when we have an idea, we tell our assistant to schedule a meeting for us. Even a small task like scheduling a meeting requires mental energy and time.)

We met with her for about thirty minutes and gave her initial guidance and then two weeks later she back briefed us on her plan. She was a member of a local church and planned to use her connections with the church and community to give away the turkeys after Sunday service the weekend before Thanksgiving. We liked the plan and gave her some more detailed marketing and execution guidance. She led the advertising campaign with the help of her pastor. She shopped for the food, picked it up, and organized the event.

In all, we had about four planning sessions leading up to the event. Planning the event took about four hours of mine and Zaira's time; meanwhile, our assistant spent nearly thirty hours on the task. That is thirty hours that Zaira and I did not have to spare.

The Sunday before Thanksgiving, we arrived at the church and the pastor spoke for twenty full minutes about the generosity of people like Abogado Solano. (Interestingly, he talked in the Spanish masculine tense and pointed to me the entire time. Clearly our assistant failed to explain that *Abogada* Solano was a female.) After the sermon, we gave away Thanksgiving meals to about fifteen families and spent nearly two hours providing free immigration legal advice. It was a tremendously rewarding experience and one that we only accomplished because we had the help of our assistant.

As a busy entrepreneur or professional without enough time in the day, hiring an assistant is an absolute must. Even if only for a few hours each week, assistants can give you more time to do the things that you enjoy.

LET'S RECAP

- If you are a dual-career couple, you need a housecleaner. As busy professionals, your time is better spent doing more important things than washing clothes, mopping floors, or cleaning toilets.
- Busy professionals also need an assistant, even if just for a few hours per week. Hiring a part-time assistant is very practical and can help you offload dozens of time-consuming errands.
- We tolerate many things in our life because the time and mental energy required to change is a barrier to higher standards. An assistant can reduce this barrier and make change easier.

CHAPTER TWELVE

DIVA

"Na-na-na diva is a female version of a hustla." —Beyoncé

For two years, we had one employee as both our personal *and* executive assistant. We eventually split the roles because we needed someone with more office and corporate experience for certain tasks. For example, we needed someone who could effectively manage our schedules, prioritize emails, and engage with our professional staff on behalf of the CEO. If Zaira received an email from our CPA requesting a copy of our W-2s, we needed an assistant who could understand the problem and contact our firm administrator and bookkeeper to get a copy of the forms, preferably before we were even made aware of the problem. Most entry-level assistants barely have any experience filing their taxes, let alone are they able to understand the corporate functions of a CPA or bookkeeper. If you keep running into issues like this with your assistant, it might be time to find an executive assistant.

The skillset required to operate in an office environment are much different than the skill set required to take the dogs to the vet, meet the electrician at the house, or drop off laundry. And likewise, the wages of experienced office personnel are higher than the wages of someone who runs errands. While a personal assistant wage is $10–$15, a great executive assistant will cost $15–$20 at the low end and $30–$40 per hour for the more experienced "professional" executive assistants. It would be foolish to pay someone $30 an hour to pick up the laundry when you could pay someone $12 an hour, which is why we now have separate personal and executive assistants.

But hiring an assistant, whether personal or executive, can be very hard for people. Let's face it: booking a flight, making dinner reservations, or writing a weekly email seem like very minor tasks that most of us could complete in ten minutes. It may feel weird to pay someone $15 an hour to do such a minor task that we could otherwise do ourselves. Initially, having an assistant may make you feel uncomfortably entitled, but you are not immediately a diva if you have an assistant pick up your Starbucks iced caramel macchiato; you are an effective executive.

Independently, picking up coffee, returning Amazon packages, and checking mail may seem small and inconsequential, but collectively all these tasks add up to a tremendous amount of time and energy; energy that of most of us would be better served doing more productive and rewarding work. Of course, the assumption in this last statement is that we use our extra time and energy to do more productive and rewarding work. I admit that sometimes I spend too much of my free time watching Netflix or scrolling through Facebook instead of being productive—a constant struggle.

Another reason why hiring an assistant is very hard for people is because most executives love feeling in control. They want to set their own schedule, select the flights and seat options that they like, make dinner reservations at the restaurant that they choose, and handle minor problems in the office the way that they want to handle them. Hiring an assistant and giving him or her tasks to complete requires that we give up control of those tasks.

If we want to attend a conference, we should ideally be able to tell our assistant, "I want to go to the South by Southwest Conference in March. Please register me and book my travel to depart on Thursday and return on Monday."

With that simple guidance (low activation energy on our part), our assistant should research the conference, check our calendar for any conflicts, and register us for the conference (assuming they have an expense account, which they should). They should already know that we prefer flying Delta first class, a window seat, and not the first row. They should also know that we prefer to stay at the nicest Marriott hotel in the area but would make an exception if the conference was collocated at a different hotel chain. They should also know to arrange for a dog sitter, e.g. check availability with our personal assistant. After all the details are finalized, they should know how we like the event to appear in our Outlook calendar. They also know to send us a confirmation email and itinerary. They also should know to make dinner reservations at least twice during our stay and spa reservations on Sunday if there are no other scheduled conference activities during that time. They know all of this through experience, and also because these policies and procedures and our preferences are outlined in our *Executive Assistant Manual*, an ever-growing reference document so our assistant, and any future assistant, knows how to be most effective.

It is often a hurdle to give someone this full level of control over our personal lives. Our assistants literally decide when we travel, where we stay, what we eat, and what we do. But the true power of executive assistants is not in their ability to book travel, it is in their ability to control your time. It may be hard to get to this level until you have a full-time executive assistant, but once you do, you should be able to tell your assistants your priorities. Your assistants should have complete control of your calendar and schedule your time to support your objectives.

The true power of executive assistants is not in their ability to book travel, it is in their ability to control your time.

For example, at the beginning of the quarter, I tell my assistant, "These are the recurring meetings that I need on my calendar—the daily stand-up, weekly marketing and sales reviews, and quarterly employee performance reviews. I want an hour each day during lunch for open-door time with anyone from staff. At the end of each day, I want fifteen minutes blocked off to respond to text messages from my clients and followers. Other than that, I need at least four hours each week to focus on our upcoming launch in Latin America and two hours each week to audit the sales funnel. Oh, and make sure I leave the office by 5 p.m. on Wednesdays so that I'm home in time for date night."

In this way, you can put your schedule on autopilot. When you use less energy managing your own schedule, you can use more energy to focus on the more important priorities. Whether personal or executive, our assistants have the clear responsibility to anticipate our needs and alleviate us from routine tasks so that we can focus our energies on our priorities that really matter. Best of all, Zaira and I have more free time to have a fun relationship and work on meaningful projects rather than worrying about domestic logistics.

LET'S RECAP

- While your personal assistant primarily runs errands and personal tasks, your executive assistant should be more focused on businesses. Although you can combine these roles, you should eventually consider separating them as your business grows.
- For an assistant to be effective, you must give him or her guidance and give them control over your schedule, activities, and other areas of your life. They should also have an expense account. This can be very difficult for professionals who like to be in control.
- You should leverage your assistant to achieve your personal and business objectives. An assistant can free up a lot of time and energy—which you can use to be more productive at work, do more rewarding activities, or spend building your relationships with your spouse, family, or friends.

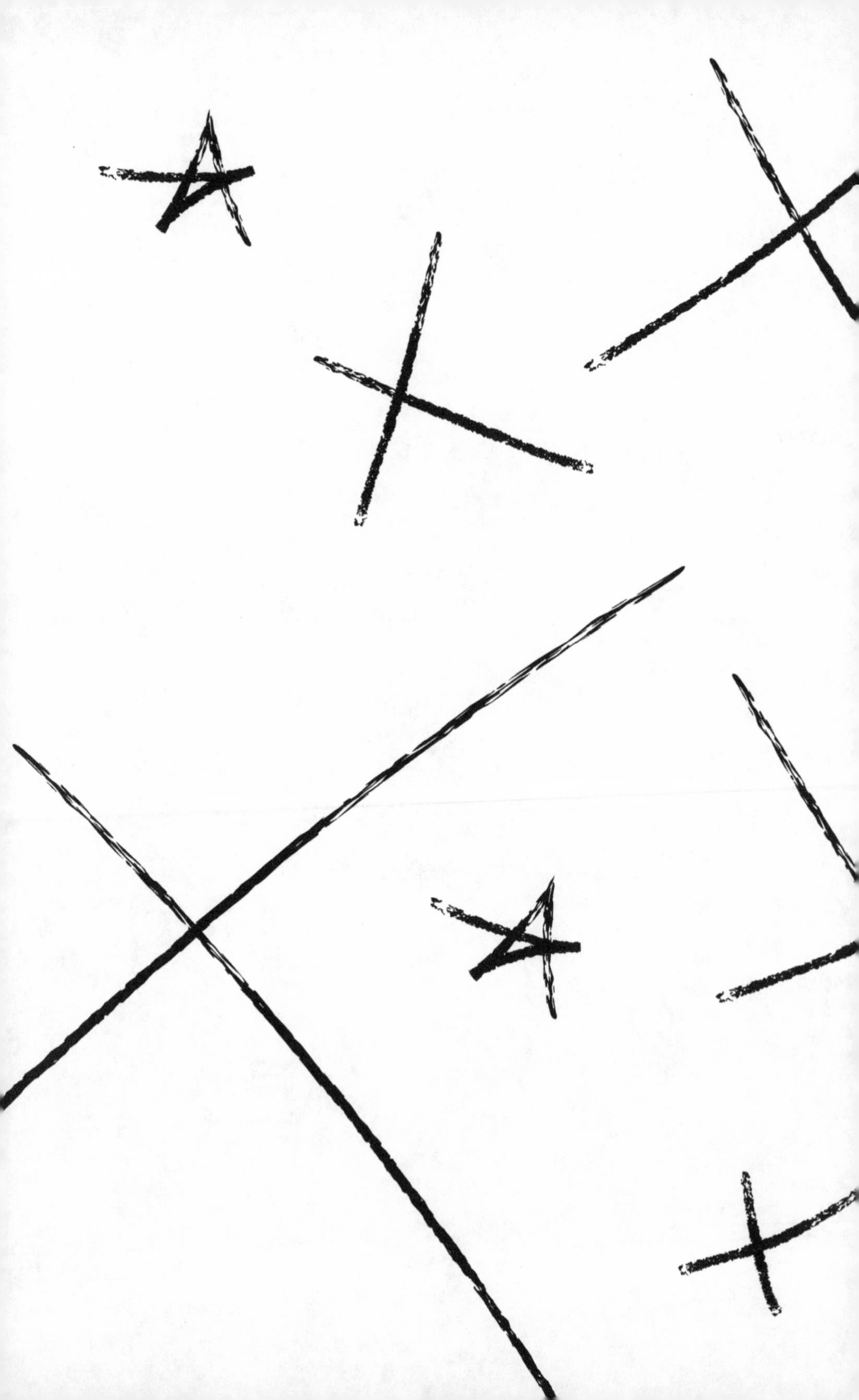

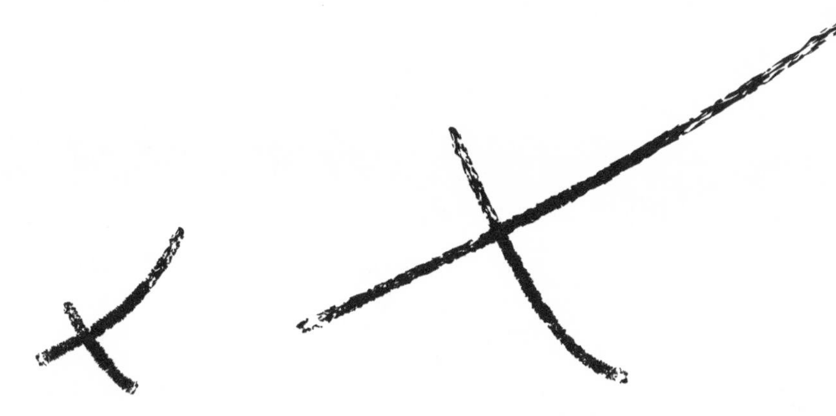

VOL. III

Dead Presidents

"I got a good life, man, pounds and pence
'Nough dollars make sense, while you ride the bench
Catch me swingin' for the fence
Dead presidents, ya know?"

—Jay-Z

CHAPTER THIRTEEN

THE STORY OF OJ

"You ever wonder why Jewish people own all the property in America? This how they did it." —Jay-Z

For most of my life, I have had a relatively fixed income. I got promoted and received pay raises on a predictable schedule, I saved money toward retirement each year, and always paid slightly more than my minimum mortgage payment. I have taken multiple vacations each year and enjoyed good dining. I have usually had a few thousand dollars in credit card debt, but rarely a car loan. For most of my adulthood, I have budgeted my finances down to the penny. I'm not a frugal saver, but I want to know where my money goes. Each month, I have automatic deductions that go to my retirement accounts and mortgages. Then, I live off the rest. At thirty-eight years old, this strategy helped me live an enjoyable life while also saving up a few hundred thousand dollars.

Zaira, on the other hand, saved money because she was too busy to spend it. She began her business right after law school with exactly two months' rent in her bank account with $100 to spare, which she turned into over $1 million in annual revenue in just a few years. The $100 to $1 million story sounds great, but it neglects to emphasize how special she was to even have two months' rent saved up. Most college students live hand to mouth—whatever they make, they spend—but Zaira was able to save about $4,000 while finishing her final year in law school, and while studying for her bar exam. Throughout college and law school, she did not have the help of her parents; instead, she took out student loans to cover the cost of tuition. She covered her living expenses by working as a resident assistant, then a bartender, and then a law clerk. The fact that she was able to save nearly $4,000 by the time she graduated law school is a testament to her hustle.

Even as a new business owner, Zaira saved and saved. When I met her, she was making over $100,000 a year, but still lived like a college student. Her apartment was sparse, and she did not own a dresser, a couch, or a guest bed.

Her apartment was barren and empty. It looked like she just moved in, but in fact she had lived there for over two years. When I visited her, we usually hung out, relaxed, and watched TV in her bed—not because we had a nonstop sex life, but because her bed was the only furniture she owned. I thought it was extremely weird to date this lawyer who drove a new Infiniti Q35 sedan, but who had no apartment furnishings or décor. At first, I thought it was because she was extremely frugal, but the real reason she lived that way is because she worked twelve to fourteen hours a day, six or seven days a week. The only thing she did in the apartment was sleep.

Zaira saved almost all of her income. The only nice thing she owned was her car, which was paid off. Everything else she shoved into savings, retirement accounts, and toward paying off her student loans. Although Zaira and I had slightly different strategies in our early twenties, our investment strategies helped us build a comfortable nest egg that continues to grow, mostly tax-free.

I asked Zaira what prompted her to start saving money so early in her career and her response was:

> I don't want to work forever. I don't want to work forever to have to earn a living. If I do want to work forever, I'll volunteer or I'll do work that I enjoy, but I don't want to have to work. I don't want my lifestyle to depend on the money that I make by working. I want our savings, and pension, and businesses, and IRAs, or whatever to support our lifestyle without needing to work. I don't want to spend my days stressed out forever.

This is called an investment mindset. As Robert Kiyosaki, author of *Rich Dad Poor Dad*, explains, "The philosophy of the rich and the poor is this: The rich invest their money and spend what is left. The poor spend their money and invest what is left."[31]

Both Zaira and I had investor mindsets, which we began practicing before we graduated college.

There are many different ways to invest. You could work for a company that gives stock options, you could buy rental properties, or you could start a business with the hopes that it will one day pay you dividends. For most people, the easiest and safest way to invest is through their 401(k), IRA, Thrift Savings Plan (government employees), or other retirement plans. These investment options usually offer great tax benefits and can give you investment diversity

---

31 Robert Kiyosaki & Sharon Lechter (1997). *Rich Dad Poor Dad.*

if you also invest in businesses, real estate, or stocks.

If you are a professional couple (doctors, lawyers, engineers, dentists, pharmacists, software managers, etc.), you and your spouse can save a million dollars in twenty years or less. To do this, you simply need to save at least 15% of your income into retirement accounts. If a retirement account earns an average annual interest rate of 8% (a.k.a. annualized return on investment or ROI), you can have $1 million by the time you turn 45 years old. This assumes that your starting salaries at age 25 are each about $45,000 per year ($90,000 combined) and that, by the time you are 45 years old, your salaries gradually increase to about $120,000 ($240,000 combined). Here is what the numbers looks like at 25, 30, 35, 40, and 45 years old.

Age	Combined Salary	Annual Savings (15%)	Total Net Savings
25	$90,000	$13,500	$16,200
30	$115,010	$17,251	$133,342
35	$146,970	$22,045	$335,900
40	$187,810	$28,172	$672,423
45	$240,000	$36,000	$1,216,593

Note that increasing your combined salary from $90,000 per year to $240,000 per year requires consistent annual pay raises of about 5% per year. For most jobs, annual pay raises average about 2%-3% per year. In order to continuously increase your salaries by at least 5% per year, you will need to grow your business, get promoted, and continuously take on positions of greater responsibility that also pay more. You're not going to triple your income unless you grow proportionately as a professional and leader.

As you rise up the ladder, many employers will offer 401(k) or a Simple IRA matching up to a certain percentage of your salary. For example, 3% matching would be $1,500 on a $50,000 annual salary. In these companies, if you contribute $1,500, your employer will contribute another $1,500 for a total of $3,000. As a rule of thumb, most young couples should begin saving for retirement by taking advantage of contribution matching if available. This is basically free money, so take advantage of it. Even as the owner of her own small business, Zaira offers herself and her employees Simple IRA matching. Paying part of her retirement savings through the law firm's matching program provides additional tax benefits.

After you max out employer matching, then the next best option is usually to invest in a Roth IRA. A Roth IRA has huge lifetime tax advantages if professionals begin saving as entry-level employees. Whether IRAs or 401(k), I recommend investing in an S&P 500–type index fund.

Here is the detailed chart, which assumes saving 15% per year, 3% employer matching, and an 8% annual ROI.

Age	Combined Salary	15%	Roth IRAs	401(k)/ Simple IRA	Employer Matching	Net Savings
25	$90,000	$13,500	$10,800	$2,700	$2,700	$16,200
26	$94,524	$14,179	$11,343	$2,836	$2,836	$34,510
27	$99,275	$14,891	$11,913	$2,978	$2,978	$55,141
28	$104,265	$15,640	$12,000	$3,640	$3,128	$78,320
29	$109,506	$16,426	$12,000	$4,426	$3,285	$104,296
30	$115,010	$17,251	$12,000	$5,251	$3,450	$133,342
31	$120,791	$18,119	$12,000	$6,119	$3,624	$165,751
32	$126,862	$19,029	$12,000	$7,029	$3,806	$201,846
33	$133,239	$19,986	$12,000	$7,986	$3,997	$241,977
34	$139,936	$20,990	$12,000	$8,990	$4,198	$286,524
35	$146,970	$22,045	$12,000	$10,045	$4,409	$335,900
36	$154,357	$23,154	$12,000	$11,154	$4,631	$390,556
37	$162,115	$24,317	$12,000	$12,317	$4,863	$450,982
38	$170,264	$25,540	$12,000	$13,540	$5,108	$517,708
39	$178,822	$26,823	$12,000	$14,823	$5,365	$591,312
40	$187,810	$28,172	$12,000	$16,172	$5,634	$672,423
41	$197,251	$29,588	$12,000	$17,588	$5,918	$761,722
42	$207,165	$31,075	$12,000	$19,075	$6,215	$859,950
43	$217,578	$32,637	$12,000	$20,637	$6,527	$967,910
44	$228,514	$34,277	$12,000	$22,277	$6,855	$1,086,475
45	$240,000	$36,000	$12,000	$24,000	$7,200	$1,216,593

These are estimates. Your results may vary. You can download your own version of this sheet, and additional info about 401(k)s and IRAS, by visiting robertsolano.com/retirement-calculator

As you become more experienced, you can begin investing in different index funds or stocks, or you can diversify your investments based upon your unique circumstances, careers, and goals, but the key is that you need to start investing as early as possible. I cannot stress this enough!

If you are older than 25 and have not begun saving for retirement yet, I recommend that you start now. You may need to shift the $1 million mark a few years later, or you may want to save more in order to catch up.

Everyone's life goals and circumstances are slightly different, but this is generally the strategy that Zaira and I use, and it has worked out well for us. Of course, couples should do their own research, but investing early has helped many couples become millionaires.

If you are a professional couple, you and your spouse can save a million dollars in twenty years or less.

As an added benefit, disbursements from investments usually fall in different tax categories than regular income. While regular income for an upper-middle class family is taxed at about 32%, investments are usually taxed at a lower rate. The national capital gains tax rate is about 20%, and some investments, like Roth IRAs, have future tax rates of 0%. Generally, our current US tax regulations favor wealthy investors more than high-income earners. A financial adviser or tax accountant can provide more details about investments and tax rules.

You might be asking, "Is it difficult to save 15% of your salary each year?" Of course, it's hard!

Recently, Zaira and I met another couple for dinner. Our friends were accountants and owned an accounting firm. Over dinner, the couple talked about how happy they were to buy a new house that they completely remodeled. Over dinner they passed around their cell phone, which had photos of their new 6,000-square-foot home featuring a pool, waterfall, basketball court, indoor garden, wine cellar, mahogany library, and massive marbled kitchen. The property cost $1.5 million. It was an absolutely gorgeous home and we were incredibly happy for them, but it put our three-bedroom townhouse to shame.

After dinner, I commented to Zaira, "Maybe, together, they have a 30% profit margin, which is very efficient, but that is still a huge mortgage."

Zaira and I shook our heads in disbelief. Their business was nearly identical in revenue to Zaira's, but they had an in-ground pool with a grotto and waterfall. They were living like ballers, meanwhile Zaira and I had a small yard with burnt grass that was barely large enough for our Labrador.

"Do the math," I told Zaira as I drove us home. "What's a mortgage for $1.5 million?" Zaira plugged in some numbers on a mortgage calculator website and reported, "About $7,500 per month."

Our mortgage was $2,100 and our HOA was $400, which meant they paid about $5,000 more than us per month, plus taxes.

The weird reality is that Zaira and I saved a combined $5,000 per month. If we reduced our savings and moved from downtown out to the countryside where they lived, we could also have bought a similar home. A $1.5 million home seemed like stratospheres above our current standard of living, but when we looked at our numbers, it was not unachievable. It was hard to justify saving so much of our income when we had friends that seemed to be earning the same amount of money as us but living such an incredibly better life.

Envy is a dangerous emotion because it leads us to compare our lives to others. Usually we do not know all of the details. Just because we knew their businesses' revenue and their mortgage value does not mean that we knew anything about their saving strategy, disposable income, or their relationship. For all we know, they live in a beautiful house but still live frugally in other areas of their lives. Although Zaira and I lived in a modest home and I drove an older Mazda, we regularly indulged in five-star meals and international trips. That same couple could have left our dinner conversation and said, "I can't believe that Robert and Zaira took three weeks off to go to Italy. They stayed in a castle on the beach—can you believe that! How could they afford that?"

When it comes to finances, it is okay to talk with other people to understand financial management strategies, but ultimately, the only people you should compare yourself to is who you were yesterday, who you are today, and who you want to be in the future. Even in this book, I share a lot of my own personal finances because I think it is important to understand how different people think and make decisions. Some people reading this may have much less wealth than us and others will have much more. Either way, I hope you can learn something from Zaira and me, good or bad, without comparison, judgement, or envy.

This is one of the reasons I hate the word *rich*. A lot of people say, "I want to be rich."

When people say this, usually what they mean is that they want to be like someone who has more money than themselves. We can never be rich because there will always be someone with more money than us. Rich is merely a word for financial envy, which is a horrible and unproductive emotion to have.

Many rich people—the people driving around in Maseratis, popping bottles in the club, and flaunting Louis Vuitton purses—have very little wealth, which is another way of saying they are not saving.

Instead of wanting to be rich, we should want to be wealthy.

The word *rich* also does not differentiate between someone who has money and someone who spends money—these are two extremely different things. Many rich people—the people driving around in Maseratis, popping bottles in the club, and flaunting Louis Vuitton purses—have very little wealth, which is another way of saying they are not saving.

Instead of wanting to be rich, we should want to be wealthy. Investing is the most well-documented and proven way to become wealthy. The investment mindset has helped more people become millionaires than any other strategy in human history. Even someone who makes minimum wage can become a millionaire if they have the right investment mindset.

I admit that I did not always invest 15% of my income into retirement. Some years, I barely invested 5%, but I always invested something. Today, Zaira and I actually invest more than 15%. It's actually closer to 20%. At a minimum, our goal is to max out our Roth IRAs, 401(k)s, and Simple IRAs each year. After that, we diversify our investments by paying additional principal toward our mortgages or investing in our businesses. In the future, we look to expand and purchase additional rental properties and commercial real estate, or to invest in additional businesses. Generally, I think that residential real estate investments are overhyped—real estate is usually a low-risk investment but also has lower returns than other markets or businesses—but as part of a diversified investment portfolio, a few properties can be a good strategy.

If Zaira and I continue our retirement saving strategy, saving a minimum of 15% of our income per year with an average annual return of 8%, we will save over $6 million by the time we are sixty-five years old. This is a strategy that has worked for me even throughout the 2008 recession and through the coronavirus pandemic. Despite periodic dips in the market, continuous diversified investments and dollar cost averaging has helped us maintain steady growth over the long run.

Over $6 million in savings, combined with income from our properties, businesses, royalties, and other investments, will allow us to live our desired standard of living from the ages of 65 to 105, whether we decide to work or not. Yes, we expect that a healthy lifestyle and medical advances between now and 2085 will allow us to live comfortably to 105 years old. We also have some buffer in our plan in case we want to indulge in luxury expenses. Ultimately, it is our investments and not our income that will help us achieve financial independence and live an extraordinary life.

Although Zaira says that she does not want to work, I personally do not believe in the classic definition of retirement; I have no desire to stop working.

I may retire from one career in exchange for another business, but I never want to stop working. My goal in life, every day, is to do work that I find enjoyable. If I am enjoying my work and I'm able-bodied, I plan to work forever. But, like Zaira said, retirement for us is reaching a point where we can work because we want to and not because we have to.

LET'S RECAP

- If you don't want to work forever, you need a well-planned investment strategy. It is hard to save money, but you need to start investing today if you want financial freedom in the future.
- Many highly skilled professionals couples can save $1 million by the time they are forty-five years old if they begin saving 15% of their salaries early in their career.
- High-income earners, the doctors and lawyers with high-paying jobs, usually get taxed more than any other group. In contrast, US tax laws favor investors and business owners.

CHAPTER FOURTEEN

DON'T HURT YOURSELF

"Who the fuck do you think I is?
You ain't married to no average bitch, boy." —Beyoncé

After two years of living and working back and forth between Georgia, Alabama, and Florida, we realized it was untenable. Zaira was the office manager, human resources, marketing director, sales associate, and attorney. She wanted to spend more time in Florida, but we did not see any way that she could escape her duties in Georgia and Alabama.

We knew that there had to be a way for her to spend more time in Florida and began to experiment with different techniques. For a while Zaira installed webcams throughout her offices and put up a 60-inch TV screen that displayed her from our Florida home office. Throughout the day, her face was always on the screen and at any time her staff could walk up to the monitor and talk to her through Skype as if she was sitting there in person. I gave her hell for this and told her that "Big Sister is watching" was very *1984*—not a fan of sci-fi, my joke went over Zaira's head.

The Big Sister approach was a Band-Aid. It helped her spend a few extra days in Florida, but as soon as an attorney quit or sales began decreasing, she would need to rush back to the Atlanta office to get the ship back on course. She implemented the webcams, Skype video calls, timecard software, and a few other tools. Some helped and some did not. She was constantly trying something, failing, and trying something else, hoping that something would let her spend more time in Florida and less time in Georgia and Alabama. Despite her best efforts, she just could not spend more than a few days away from her Atlanta and Birmingham offices.

Around the time that she was struggling to figure it out how to spend more time in Florida, a friend recommended Zaira hire a business coaching firm called How to Manage a Small Law Firm, or just HTM for short. We were desperate for any opportunity that could help our situation and this one seemed promising. Zaira invited me to join her for one of their first live meetings at the Ritz-Carlton in Key Biscayne, Miami.

After driving for three hours from Orlando, we arrived at the Ritz. I circled around the hotel a few times to see if there was any street parking available.

"Just valet," Zaira said as she pointed to the team of porters that waited to take my money.

"Okay, fine," I said reluctantly. "Do you have cash for tip?"

Zaira pulled her wallet from her purse, "Yeah, I have two dollars."

We pulled up and got greeted by a team of valets. One of them on each side of the car opened our doors.

"Do you need help carrying your bags?" they asked with a generous smile.

"No, we can take care of it," I said as I refused their help and pulled our bags from the trunk.

As we walked into the lobby, I looked at the valet ticket in my hand, *$35 per day. Damn that's expensive.*

The Ritz-Carlton was beautiful. There were fresh orchids by the dozens and the furniture was colorful and ornate. The oversized purple chairs would look gaudy in any other setting, but in the marble foyer of the Ritz, they made me feel like I entered an *Alice in Wonderland* tea party.

When we got to the receptionist, three staff members stood behind the counter with equally gracious smiles. "Good evening and welcome to the Ritz-Carlton. Could I have the name for your reservation?"

"Solano," Zaira told the receptionist.

"Ah, yes. I have you right here. Welcome Mr. and Mrs. Solano. While I check you in, could I get you something to drink?"

She must have seen my eyes thinking about her question, *Something to drink? Did she mean a bottle of water?* That's what I normally get at the Hampton Inn.

After she noticed my inquisitive look, she clarified, "We have water, soda, wine, or perhaps a margarita."

Damn, margaritas? I could tell that this was going to be a fancy weekend.

"How about a champagne?" I asked—*I felt fancy.*

"Of course, sir," she turned to Zaira. "And for you ma'am?"

"Yeah," Zaira said as she shook her head with a smirk. "I'll take a champagne too."

One of the other receptionists whisked away and came back sixty seconds later with two flutes of sparkling wine.

As we walked to the elevators, trying to balance our champagne in one hand while carrying our luggage in the other, I asked Zaira, "How much does this workshop cost?"

"I think it's about three thousand dollars," Zaira replied nonchalantly.

My eyes widened, "Three thousand dollars!"

I had never attended a conference that cost that much. Most conferences or workshops I attended usually cost a few hundred dollars, at most. This was an astronomical price. After a few brief moments, I thought about the nice hotel and great customer service, then I changed my tone, "Well, I guess if you include three nights at the hotel plus meals at the conference, it's not that much."

"No," Zaira corrected me, "that doesn't include the room or meals."

I felt lightheaded, and my vision began to blur. "Are you serious? Three thousand dollars, not including the room or food?"

"Robert," Zaira replied calmly, "It's okay. The business is paying for it, and it's tax deductible." *Oh, the benefits of being an entrepreneur.*

Over the next three days, we attended workshops and learned skills on marketing, business plans, and policies and procedures. The workshop was focused on helping small law firm owners like Zaira, but I learned valuable lessons that I could apply to my own work. The instructors were exceptionally interesting, and their lessons made me think about business in a new and exciting light. The workshops were much different than the politically correct and regimented corporate training programs that I was accustomed to.

After that first meeting, Zaira joined the coaching program and began meeting regularly with her team of coaches. Through the program, she hired a fractional CFO and COO. Zaira could not afford to hire these positions full-time, so the fractional hires allowed her to get expert advice and assistance for a few hours a week without the cost of hiring a full C-suite.

Throughout the next year, we attended about eight different workshops and quarterly meetings... Zaira spent over $30,000 the first year.

Spending $30,000 on coaching and consulting made me very uncomfortable. It was more than I paid for my car, and weekends at the Ritz-Carlton felt like an opulent and unnecessary luxury.

I occasionally challenged her, by asking her things like, "Are you sure that this is worth it?" but for the most part, I let her make her own decisions. At the time, we were engaged, not married, so I felt like it was her money and she was free to use it how she wanted.

Over the course of a year, her business coaches and fractional executives encouraged her to restructure the business. Soon, she hired more paralegals, two sales associates, multiple marketing companies, and a law firm administrator. This last hire was a huge mindset shift. Her law firm administrator cost $20,000 to recruit and onboard, and then another $90,000 per year in salary. This salary was more than twice as much as her average employee. In less than a few months, the law firm's monthly operating expenses tripled from about $15,000 per month to over $45,000 per month.

Throughout the next year, we attended about eight different workshops and quarterly meetings. Including the fractional executive services, Zaira spent over $30,000 the first year.

The amount of money that she was investing in the business was huge. If these new hires and new operating procedures did not work, they would break her law firm and drive her to bankruptcy.

As our wedding day approached, I became more concerned about Zaira's spending. Since I had previously been married, I wanted to elope and have a small wedding. We found a resort in Mexico that promised to be a cheap destination wedding for about fifty of our closest friends and family, but the cost soared as Zaira added options for custom flower arrangements, aerial drone video, and a live mariachi band. Since these were options that Zaira wanted, not me, she agreed to pay for all of them.

At the same time, my work moved me from Orlando to Tampa. For years, Zaira had yearned to own property so she decided to buy a house in Tampa. I would have liked to help her pay for the wedding or house, but I was paying for my Ph.D. studies, recently bought a new car, spent thousands of dollars on our honeymoon reservations, and bought her engagement ring. My bank account was tapped out.

I was broke and Zaira was paying for the wedding, a house, and tripling her business overhead all at the same time. Everything indicated that we were headed for financial disaster.

Whenever I expressed my frustration and told her that she was spending too much, Zaira shut me down. She prided herself in being independent and did not like other people telling her how to spend her money. I could understand her position except that her coaches were telling her to spend!

Many of Zaira's business and lifestyle coaches preached an abundance mindset. In essence, they encouraged Zaira and other business owners to spend, spend, spend. They believed that there was plenty of wealth to go around as long as business owners were blindly optimistic about the future. They encouraged entrepreneurs to buy luxury cars, move to nicer houses, and of course, spend more money on coaching and personal development. These business coaches relabeled my investment mindset as a scarcity mindset and discussed it with contempt and disdain. The only time that they discussed investments was when they discussed investing in nicer cars, hiring more staff, or investing in more coaching.

At one workshop, different from the HTM program, a life coach told Zaira that she should always fly first-class—starting immediately. At the time, we were flying about six times per month. First-class flights would have cost us over $4,000 per month. We did enjoy flying Delta Comfort, and could afford the extra cost of that, but first-class flights would have very quickly put us in debt.

Although Zaira didn't immediately begin flying first-class, she did slowly start increasing her spending. She got tailor-made dress suits, bought multiple pairs of Christian Louboutin shoes, ate at fine dining restaurants more often, and was unhappy if we stayed at any hotel that was less than Ritz-Carlton quality. I was further concerned because she continued to spend more and more on coaching. The first year, she spent $30,000 on coaching; the second year it doubled to over $60,000 per year. At one point, she spent $30,000 for a single five-day VIP workshop. In my opinion, her so-called abundance mindset was wasteful and reckless. Zaira's abundance mindset seemed completely at odds with my investment mindset.

At one of the workshops, Zaira confided in me, "Robert, I'm afraid that I'm going to grow and leave you behind."

I was also afraid that we were growing apart, but not in the way that she believed. I countered her argument and told her, "I'm afraid that I am going to grow and leave *you* behind."

Implementing her new strategies required a lot more work on her part. Despite all of the improvements, it seemed like her next goal was always just out of reach. She would make progress in one area of her business, and just when she thought she could relax, a key employee would quit and bring her back into the relentless grind. She was always stressed and complained about work nightly. Meanwhile, I had a healthy balance between work and pleasure, especially after I quit my Ph.D. My work as a program manager was challenging but intrinsically rewarding. Best of all, I was home every day by 6 p.m. and rarely worked on nights or weekends.

Many people struggle their entire life to achieve financial security, but I was already there. I had a stable job making over $100,000 a year, I had rental properties that generated additional income, and I had an achievable plan to save $6 million over the next thirty years.

What frustrated me more was that Zaira's abundance mindset gradually started to cost me a lot of money. Early in our relationship and marriage, we still shared expenses by using our individual accounts; if we went out to dinner, she would pay for it one time and I would pay for it the next time. As Zaira's standards increased, she demanded that we eat at nicer and nicer restaurants. Instead of getting Philly cheesesteaks and PBRs like we used to when we started dating, she wanted to eat at the white tablecloth seafood restaurant. Of course, I wanted her to be happy, so I took her to eat where she wanted and paid when it was my turn for date night. Don't get me wrong, I enjoy a Michelin-star restaurant, but I also enjoy eating a greasy sandwich on a picnic bench. Zaira was becoming much harder to please, and it was costing me.

I was credit card–free before I got engaged to Zaira, but soon, I had over $20,000 in credit card debt as I tried my best to keep up with her abundance mindset. I still saved toward retirement each month, but after that I was essentially broke.

Zaira was correct: We were growing apart. Zaira was taking more financial risk and spending more money on the business and herself. Her goal was to grow rapidly to maximize revenue. Meanwhile, my goal was to maximize my investments. I wanted to live below my means and build assets, but I could not keep up with Zaira's lifestyle. My investment mindset seemed to be incompatible with her abundance mindset.

I complained. I told her that her spending habits were making me spend more, but she didn't seem to listen to me. It was like, in her mind, she was still singing the Destiny's Child song "Independent Women"—"Try to control me, boy, you get dismissed."

I wasn't trying to control her, though. Instead, I was trying to protect us from getting financially damaged. We were about to get married. If she bankrupted herself, she would bankrupt me too. I was always taught to live below my means and that your monthly expenses should be less than your income. From my perspective, Zaira was spending way more money than she was earning. I knew she had some savings that she was dipping into, but I wasn't really sure how much she had saved or how much runway she had before her bank account hit zero. It made me scared, nervous, and uncomfortable.

Luckily, Zaira's investments in employees, marketing, and coaching worked. After that first year, her annual revenue increased from $400,000 per year to $750,000.

Zaira did not like talking about money with me, but eventually she agreed to sit down and list out all of our assets, liabilities, and income. This was the first step in trying to align our goals and mindsets leading into our marriage. Zaira did have some savings, and she shared with me how much she was willing to invest in the business and how much she saved in reserves.

Additionally, I discussed my credit card debt and explained to her where my monthly expenses were going. We readjusted the way we split our household expenses, which helped me pay off my credit card debt faster. I explained to her that I was spending too much money on nice dinners, and we agreed to curb some of our personal spending. We also agreed that our recurring 401(k) and IRA investments were off-limits and that no matter how much we invested in the businesses we would not reduce those investments—that made me very happy.

Furthermore, we began to discuss business financials. She shared with me her annual revenue goals, monthly profit, and overhead figures, and we began meeting with a CPA together. By structuring the conversation around the business plan instead of our emotions, we were able to have a much more productive conversation that helped address my concerns, showed Zaira that I was not trying to control her, and that also helped Zaira refine her business strategy.

This is a practice we continue to this day and even as I was preparing to publish and launch this book, Zaira and I discussed the investment cost of self-publishing, projected sales, and expected revenue and profit.

We always support each other in our goals, but we learned that support is not blind. With any major project, we challenge each other to articulate our personal, business, and financial goals. We don't always achieve our goals, but the simple act of discussing them ensures that we stay synchronized and it resolves a lot of our emotional concerns.

Luckily, Zaira's investments in employees, marketing, and coaching worked. After that first year, her annual revenue increased from $400,000 per year to $750,000. Within three years she was at $1.2 million in revenue, and the business continues to grow.

After we got married, we took a three-week honeymoon to northern Italy. When we were in Italy, Zaira checked in with her team for about an hour each day, but otherwise we had plenty of time to eat the best pizza ever, drink delicious Barolo wine, and make love on our honeymoon. It was the first time since she began Solano Law Firm that she was able to leave the office and relax for more than a week.

Eventually, Zaira was able to work from our home office most of the time. Soon, she was able to go for months in between her visits to her Atlanta and Birmingham offices. Two years after our honeymoon, we were even able to take another three-week vacation to Europe, except that this time she completely unplugged. She didn't check her email, call staff, or meet with clients at all for three whole weeks. Amazingly, the business and great team she built continued to operate just fine without her. It is a lifestyle that I would have never imagined for us a few years ago.

We were living the good life. It seemed like Zaira's abundance mindset had paid off and that we had resolved our financial differences, at least for a while.

LET'S RECAP

- Coaches can help you identify your blind spots and break through the obstacles and limiting beliefs that prevent you from achieving your goals.
- The risk associated with growing a business can be very challenging for many couples. The key to overcoming these challenges is open and honest communication. It usually is best if you can separate your relationship emotions from discussions about business strategy, and discuss each of those separately.
- You and your spouse need to be aligned on whether you will have an abundance mindset, investment mindset, or how you will merge the two. If you are not aligned, you will grow apart.

CHAPTER FIFTEEN

BILLS, BILLS, BILLS

You're slowly making me pay for things your money should be handling." —Beyoncé

"What do you mean you haven't been paying yourself?" I asked Zaira.

"We are in a cash crunch," she told me. "Sales were low before the holidays."

"Okay," I said as I contemplated the impact of this. "Well, when was the last time you paid yourself?"

"Um," she thought for a few seconds. "I can't remember."

I was shocked by her reply. "You can't remember!"

"I don't know. I think I paid myself before Thanksgiving." It was now early February.

"Three months! What have you been doing for money?" I asked, dumbfounded.

"I've been using my savings," she said, which explained a little.

I rolled my eyes and shook my head, then replied, "Okay. Well if you don't get paid in the future, can you let me know?"

I was surprised, not because she did not tell me, but because nothing had changed in our lives. Zaira continued to pay the mortgage each month, she still paid for date night when it was her turn, and we even spent the holidays with family and bought Christmas gifts for all the kids. I knew Zaira had a good amount of money in her savings account, but I didn't know she had been dipping into it in order to keep everything normal.

She didn't intend to be deceitful or hide anything from me, she just had a much different relationship with money than me. She prided herself in being an independent woman, and as long as she was paying her share of household expenses, she thought it was unnecessary to discuss her personal finances. Zaira was fine with withdrawing from her savings because she expected the business to pay her back sometime in the future.

In contrast, if I went three months without getting paid, I would be eating ramen noodles, renting our spare bedroom on Airbnb, and renting out the Mazda on Turo.

Honestly, I was not completely sure how much Zaira normally got paid. Once, when we first got married, we sat down and listed out our individual income and then divided the household expenses between ourselves, but over the years, Zaira's salary had fluctuated as her business grew and I was not sure how much she made now.

We kept separate bank accounts, we alternated who paid for meals, we split household expenses evenly, and when we went on vacation one of us paid for the hotel while the other paid for flights and meals.

At this point, we were married for two years, but still managed our expenses like we did when we were dating. I didn't question it because as long as Zaira was paying her share of expenses, everything was good to go. Eventually though, my growing credit card debt really bothered me and the three months without Zaira getting paid was a huge concern of mine. We were growing apart financially, and I knew that our marriage would not survive if we continued like this. We needed to learn to make financial decisions as a couple, we needed to live a lifestyle that supported both our individual desires and our relationship goals, and we needed to learn how to balance my investment mindset with Zaira's abundance mindset.

At first, we had decided that we needed a joint account, especially for household expenses, vacations, and date nights. We agreed that we would each put a certain amount in the joint account each month. It worked out well for a while, but we had a lot of moments where we got confused or disagreed about things.

For example, the first year that we filed joint taxes, we got a big refund check for $7,000. Zaira wanted to put the money into a savings account, but I was anticipating a refund check so that I could pay off some of my credit card debt. I paid more taxes than her throughout the year. Normally, I filed as a single; my tax refund was about $5,000. I felt like I was owed that money.

In another instance, after Zaira become profitable again, she had a particularly good quarter. She took a $10,000 disbursement. She discussed this in one of our tax planning meetings, but I did not know where the money went. I assumed it went into her savings, but I wasn't really sure.

Zaira had periods where she brought home a lot more money than me, but likewise I had periods where I brought home a lot more money than her (like during her cash crunch). With one of us having flexible income, and the other having fixed income, our strategy of splitting bills or contributing part of our salary to a joint account was failing. It seemed like there was a huge financial disconnect between us.

We kept separate bank accounts, we alternated who paid for meals, we split household expenses evenly, and when we went on vacation one of us paid for the hotel while the other paid for flights and meals.

Zaira did not want to give up control of her money, and in a testament to the strength of her subconscious, she mistakenly misplaced both her joint credit card and joint debit card. Out of necessity, Zaira began using her personal account for joint expenses. Eventually, she stopped contributing to the joint account at all and I became the only person contributing or using the joint accounts.

What I came to realize is that the only way we could resolve these issues was by transitioning to a completely joint account. Instead of splitting bills, or budgeting part of our salaries for joint expenses, we needed to treat all of our income as one. Everything we earned, whether it was our salaries, tax refunds, rental property income, or investment disbursement, would be joint income. This was the only logical way that we could really share our income and expenses fairly. I cautiously delivered this idea to Zaira.

"I think we should have our paychecks deposited into the joint account. What do you think?"

"What's wrong with the way we are doing it now?"

"I feel like we aren't actually splitting expenses evenly"—counseling taught me to frame disagreements in the way that I feel—"and I'm having a really hard time getting ahead on my credit cards."

"Well," she fought the idea. "Why don't we just work through our budget and adjust the numbers?"

"We've been trying to set a budget for three years and it's not working." I tried to deliver it softly: "Let's just give it a try. I'll start putting my pay into the joint account next month and I'll start paying all of our household expenses from the account."

Zaira made excuses and tried to wriggle out of it.

"Look," I told her. "I surveyed a bunch of couples for my book and did a bunch of research. This is how most of the successful couples manage their money."

She ignored my research and confessed, "I'm afraid that you will tell me how to spend my money,"

Zaira was a powerful, independent woman. Her own feeling of independence was strongly correlated to her own personal financial independence; this was part of her relationship with money. Fortunately, I anticipated this.

"I know," I told her. "We will still have our own accounts. Each month we will pay all of our expenses and then take a disbursement for the rest. So, for example, if we have $4,000 left over, I get $2,000 and you get $2,000 to spend on whatever you want."

Zaira was not convinced.

I added, "You can spend your money on whatever you want. I promise that I will not judge your spending at all."

I showed this flow chart to Zaira.

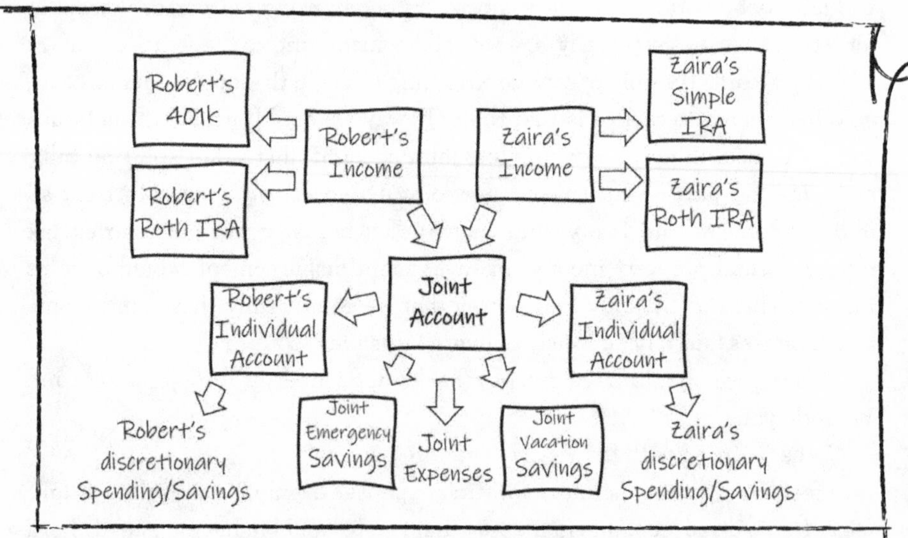

I explained how we would continue to max out our 401(k)s, Roth IRAs, and Simple IRAs, and that everything else would go to our joint account. From there, our joint account would be the central hub that we used to fund our individual accounts, joint savings, and joint expenses. I reiterated once again, "You can use your individual account for anything you want. That is your money to spend on anything. Could we just give this a try, please?"

I am really glad that we moved to our current system and it has resolved a lot of tension in our marriage. Zaira still thinks that we could have gotten by if we each transferred our fair share into the joint account, but this strategy presents problems. One of the biggest problems is that couples that use this strategy constantly need to evaluate what a *fair share* is. As demonstrated by our disagreement about taxes, what one partner considers fair is not always the same as the other partner. It is also challenging to calculate a partner's fair share when they may have a few months that they don't get paid and other months where they take home $10,000 bonus checks.

Any strategy that requires partners to contribute a fair share—and this is true for many aspects of marriage to include household chores or childcare—has shortcomings. For example, if Zaira and I agreed that we would contribute 50% of our income to the joint account, then when we have a big disparity in our income, one partner would have a lot more disposable income than the other. This can lead to resentment if one partner makes a lot more money than the other.

Instead, our financial approach has both Zaira and I giving 100% to the marriage. It's not her money or my money, it is *our* money. Depositing all pay to a joint account and then splitting the disbursements completely evenly eliminates all potential disagreements about fairness. All income is joint income, therefore there is no such thing as a fair share.

Merging our finances in a joint account also forces communication. Every month, we look out our expenses and see how much we are spending as a couple, not as two individuals. This strategy also helps us balance our mindsets. As a couple, we agreed to max out our retirement contributions, which satisfied our investment goals, and we each have plenty of joint and individual discretionary spending, which supports an abundance mindset. During periods of feast or famine, we equally share in each other's success or burdens. We also set a certain amount aside each month for emergency funds and vacation savings.

Finally, we implemented quarterly financial review meetings where we sit down and review our financial goals and progress, and discuss any issues or concerns. When we first started merging our accounts, we met almost every week to discuss our spending and budget, but once we became conformable and reached stasis, we reduced the frequency to once a quarter. During these meetings, we discuss our spending habits and our future goals, for example, buying a larger home in two years. These meetings are in addition to our quarterly calendar meetings and our quarterly tax review meetings with our accountant, where we adjust our income and expenses to minimize our tax burden. I should also highlight that Zaira meets with her bookkeeper and CFO every week to discuss business-specific income and expenses.

Any strategy that requires partners to contribute a fair share—and this is true for many aspects of marriage to include household chores or childcare—has shortcomings.

Other couples have different approaches. I know some husbands who are satisfied letting their wives manage all of their household expenses; I know some single-income families where one spouse gives a monthly stipend to the other; and other couples are perfectly content maintaining completely separate bank accounts and fairly splitting the household bills. There are many ways to manage your finances but merging finances into a joint account is, in my opinion, by far the best. Merged income requires trust between partners, financial responsibility, and active communication—usually couples that struggle with a merged bank account have a hard time because they lack one of these elements. Merged income can actually be a catalyst to confront these issues and improve trust, responsibility, or communication.

Dave Ramsey is the best-selling author of *The Total Money Makeover* and numerous other financial advice books. His advice has helped millions of people get out of debt and build wealth. On his radio show, a listener called in and asked Dave if he thinks that couples should have their income go to a joint account. Dave quickly and definitively responded, "Yes, if you want a quality marriage and if you want a high probability of building wealth."

Although he is not a relationship coach or counselor, he noticed that the couples who merge their income into a joint account and work together toward financial goals have a lower rate of divorce and much healthier relationship. In his show, he continued to explain, "Where you spend your money and how you spend your money is a result of your value systems. Jesus said it this way, 'Your treasure is where your heart is.' When you plan your money out together, you are sharing your fears. You are sharing your dreams. You are sharing your goals."[32]

Merging our income into a joint account helped Zaira and me align our goals. We learned how to balance investments with abundance and create a lifestyle that supports our long-term goals and short-term happiness. I eventually paid off my credit card debt, we have frequent and open financial communication, and we have a much healthier relationship with money. Tackling our finances and confronting our relationship with money helps us continue to grow as a couple.

LET'S RECAP

- You should have financial planning meetings with your spouse every quarter. Depending on your situation, you may need to meet weekly or monthly until you develop steady state operations.
- Although there are a few different ways to manage joint finances, the best approach is for couples to merge all income into a joint account and then divide funds proportionally from there.
- Merging finances encourages financial discussions, improves trust, and helps partners align their financial goals.

32 Dave Ramsey, (2018). "Married? Separate Bank Accounts? That's a Bunch of CRAP!" *The Dave Ramsey Show*, YouTube.com.

CHAPTER SIXTEEN

A MILLION AND ONE QUESTIONS

"Cats around my way was buying brand new whips and shit." —Jay-Z

"We're millionaires," I told Zaira.

She chuckled at me and shook her head as if I were joking.

"No babe, for real," I lifted the paper and showed it to her. "We are millionaires. Look at the numbers. Our net worth is over a million dollars."

Zaira and I were having a financial planning meeting. For months I begged her to sit down with me to review our finances, but finances are a trigger for Zaira, and she will make any excuse she can to avoid discussing them. Generally, she is afraid that a budget is a way for me to control her. On this occasion, she finally agreed to spend an evening talking about finances. In exchange, I promised her that I would order her favorite Indian food for dinner afterward.

This was the first time we reviewed our finances together since our wedding two years earlier. A lot had changed since before we got married—we bought a house together, I was promoted at work, and Zaira's business grew from $600,000 to $1.2 million in revenue. This meeting was long overdue.

I showed Zaira the sheet of paper. On the left side was a heading for *assets* and on the right side *liabilities*. In the asset section, I wrote the names and values of our bank accounts, condos, house, cars, and 401(k)s. In the liability section I listed our outstanding mortgage balances and debt. After I subtracted the liabilities from the assets, I underlined my answer twice and then put my pen down.

She looked over it for a few seconds then said, "No, you can't add our mortgages."

"I didn't," I said as I pointed at the column of addition and subtraction formulas. "Look, I added the property value here under assets, and added mortgage value here under liabilities, and here is where I subtracted liabilities from assets."

Zaira still doubted me. She opened up the calculator on her phone and started adding and subtracting the numbers herself. She went down the list, adding the assets in the left column—$280,000 for the condo in Orlando, $375,000 for the condo in Atlanta, $450,000 for the townhouse in Tampa, $15,000 for our car, our savings accounts, our 401(k)s, and other retirement accounts.

Then she subtracted the liabilities—three mortgage balances and $10,000 in credit card debt.

"One point zero four. I guess you were right," she conceded.

I'm always right.

I sat back in the chair and looked at the numbers again. "Dude, that's kind of a big deal. We're millionaires."

After our meeting, we ate dinner and continued on with our daily life.

Zaira and I didn't come from wealthy families. Zaira is the daughter of immigrants from the Dominican Republic. She was raised in New Jersey by a single mother who barely spoke any English and worked as a seamstress just to make ends meet.

Similarly, my parents were middle-class blue-collar workers. My dad was a construction worker and my mother was a receptionist at the community college. Although they had good middle-class jobs, they frequently needed to make their salaries stretch to support me and my handful of siblings. Our families were rich in love, but humble in financial wealth.

To some people, a million dollars may not seem like a lot of money, but, like lower- and middle-class children, I dreamed of being a millionaire. I watched *Lifestyles of the Rich and Famous* and then *MTV Cribs*. I pointed at the television and said things like, "I'm going to be rich like that when I grow up." To this day, whenever I give someone a tour of our house, I always walk into the bedroom and say the *Cribs* tagline, "This is where the magic happens."

Zaira and I were now millionaires, but it turns out there are a lot of different ways to define *millionaire*. When television shows and magazines talk about millionaires, very rarely do they make a distinction between individuals with a net worth over a million or an annual income over a million. And to muddy the water even more, income could be differentiated between individuals with a pretax income of over a million or an adjusted taxable income over a million. There is also a lot of debate on the net worth of small businesses like the law firm or the future value of pensions, which we did not account for in our calculations. Millionaire is a very ambiguous term when you dig into the details.

Zaira and I were millionaires because our net worth exceeded $1 million, but we definitely did not have stacks of money at our disposal. In fact, when we became millionaires, I still had $10,000 in credit card debt that I struggled to pay off. There are a lot of different opinions on what income and wealth levels make up the different economic classes. I like to use this model, which I adapted from US Census Bureau statistics.

Income Group (% of US Households)	Household Income	Net Worth
Poor or near-poor (20%)	$20,000 or less	Less than $0
Lower middle class (20%)	$20,000–$50,000	About $0
Middle class (40%)	$50,000–$120,000	$0–$500,000
Upper middle class (15%)	$120,000–$260,000	$500,000–$2.5 million
Upper class (4%)	$260,000–$420,000	$2.5 million–$10 million
Top 1%	$420,000 and up	$10 million and up

Adapted from "Income Limits for Each Fifth and Top 5 Percent of All Households," 2018, US Census Bureau.

To put these numbers in context, the average middle-class American earns $55,000 per year, just barely above lower middle class. Today, it is nearly impossible for a couple to live a middle-class life on one salary alone. This is yet another reason why, in the US, dual working marriages are now the norm and not the outlier. A dual working couple, each making an average salary, earning about $110,000 per year combined, is what it takes to be middle class in America.

Zaira and I were fortunate. We worked our asses off in high school, college, and early in our careers. We also had family, friends, and mentors to help use during our professional journey. As a result, we both had good careers where we each earned about $100,000 per year. This put us in a weird place where we were well above the average middle-class couple. We still felt like middle class—we drove a six-year-old Mazda SUV and lived in an average three-bedroom townhouse—but at the same time, we took sailing trips to Greece, went wine tasting in Tuscany, and had a net worth over $1 million, which we knew were very un–middle class. We were on a path to upper class.

As a college student, I knew very little about investments. I had a vague idea that I wanted to buy stocks because that is what people did to get rich, but I did not really understand how to do it or why I should.

When I was a freshman at West Point, I attended a mandatory two-hour-long lecture on personal financing. The instructor taught us about Roth IRAs,

401(k)s, and other topics that I had never heard of before. The instructor told us that compounding interest was PFM (Pure Fucking Magic). I did not fully understand everything yet, but I took away from that class a desire to max out my Roth IRA, and that is exactly what I did. That same year, as a freshman, I began saving money to my Roth. At first it was whatever I could afford, but eventually I began maxing it out. Ever since I had that freshman lecture, I have always saved between 5% and 20% toward retirement.

Zaira, on the other hand, was always a saver. She grew up with the mentality to "save for a rainy day." Her single immigrant mother taught her to save out of necessity because they had so little money growing up, but similar to me, she did not know much about IRAs or retirement accounts.

A year after she started her business, her income grew exponentially to over $100,000 per year, but she had a problem. She was making more money than she ever imagined, but she also had over $200,000 in student debt. She was conflicted on how she should prioritize her savings versus paying off debt. One day, she complained to her best friend about her debt and her friend, a marketing director for a financial adviser, recommended that Zaira meet with her boss.

Zaira met with the financial adviser who developed a strategy for Zaira to pay off her student debt and who also helped her set up automatic contributions to her Roth IRA and Simple IRA. Two years later, Zaira paid off her $200,000 student debt and was also maxing out her retirement contributions.

Both Zaira and I stumbled into retirement saving. As students and young professionals, we were extremely fortunate to have financial mentors and coaches who showed us a path to retirement savings. It is because of mentors and coaches like these that Zaira and I have been so fortunate in life and can call ourselves millionaires. For their advice and guidance, we will be forever grateful. I hope that our experiences in this book can pass on some of those lessons to our readers.

I had a great childhood, but I still want to give my children a better life than I had. I want to have generational wealth so that I can give an amazing life to my children and grandchildren. I don't only want to be in the top 1%, I want to be in the top 1% of the top 1%. I want to have such high standards that I only ever do the activities that I absolutely love. I want to have more money than I could ever spend—what Zaira affectionately calls *"Fuck You" Money* (FYM).

The idea of FYM is that you have so much of it you can say "fuck you" to anyone without any fear of financial repercussions.

Zaira and I both want to have enough money that we can freely and fearlessly express ourselves without worrying about financial impacts or what our bosses, clients, staff, investors, or peers will think. We want enough money so that we can live our desired lifestyle without ever stressing about our income, bills, expenses, or the cost of anything.

I sat back in the chair and looked at the numbers again. "Dude, that's kind of a big deal. We're millionaires..."

You and your partner should define what financial freedom means to you. For some couples, financial freedom may mean having enough money to quit your job, build a dozen churches in Haiti, or buy a beach house in Hawaii. Here are a few real-life examples of how other couples set goals for financial freedom.

Actress Sarah Jessica Parker's financial goal was to build a financially stress-free life for her children. Today, Sarah, who is married to Matthew Broderick, has a net worth of over $100 million, but that was not always the case. She grew up in poverty and remembers standing in welfare lunch lines, the electricity getting shut off, and her family skipping Christmas because they could not afford it. In 2000, as *Sex and the City* released its second season, and before Sarah Jessica Parker was a household name, her financial goal was to build a better life for her children. As an up-and-coming actress, she explained her motivation: "The thing I want most for my children—I would like for them to not be aware of money, which means I have been very aware of my financial situation."[33]

Similarly, Jay-Z and Beyoncé are focused on their family. Jay-Z has already shared his plans to leave his record label to his children and he raps about wealth with lyrics like, "Generational wealth, that's the key. My parents ain't have shit so that shift started with me," and "Financial freedom my only hope. Fuck livin' rich and dyin' broke. I bought some artwork for one million. Few years later, that shit worth eight million. I can't wait to give this shit to my children."[34]

---

33 Geraldine Fabrikant (2000). "Talking Money with: Sarah Jessica Parker; From a Start on Welfare to Riches in the City," *The New York Times.*

34 Jay-Z (2017). "Legacy" and "The Story of O.J.," *4:44.*

In 2011, LeBron James made it his goal to reduce high school dropout rates of at-risk children in his hometown of Akron, Ohio. Seven years later his nonprofit helped open the I Promise School and has pledged $41 million to provide over 1,100 students with full-ride college scholarships. LeBron, who is married to his high school sweetheart Savannah, is one of the best all-time NBA players. Despite his extraordinary success on the court, he says that "to be able to open up a school and give back to my inner city" has been his greatest professional accomplishment.[35 36]

Whatever you call it, I recommend that you set a goal or definition for what financial freedom means specifically to you and your spouse. Having a clear vision and goals can help motivate you to build wealth.

Occasionally when I talk about our desire for wealth, a few people get offended. Their immediate response is usually, "Money can't buy happiness."

I admit that my subconscious also thinks this sometimes—the product of fourteen years of Catholic school. When I recognize my subconscious thinking this, I remind myself that that dogma is bullshit. *"Money can buy happiness!"*

Some of my most memorable experiences with Zaira were sitting on the deck of a sailboat in Greece, listening to Daft Punk on the balcony of our luxury condo in Atlanta, standing front-row at a Jay-Z and Beyoncé concert, watching New Year's Eve fireworks in Hawaii, and riding a hot air balloon over Napa Valley. Those experiences are some of the most enjoyable of our life, my relationship with Zaira is stronger because of them, and they all cost a lot of money.

Of course, money cannot buy happiness directly, it is merely a tool. Huge bank accounts, stacks of Benjamins, and Scrooge McDuck–style pools of gold coins are relatively useless. Instead, money is a tool that we can use to buy things, and those things can make us happy. For example, money bought the airplane tickets, sailing trip, luxury condo, concert tickets, and many other things associated with our memorable and happy experiences. In our day-to-day lives, money buys date night dinners, gym memberships, our beautiful home, health care, professional coaching, marriage counseling, and hundreds of other things that we enjoy. Money also pays for support staff and assistants who help us reclaim time to do more things we love, like gardening, traveling, writing, or spending time with each other. Money also supports our nonprofit organization

---

35 Alyson Shontell & Arielle Berger (2016). "LeBron James created a foundation that has pledged to give more than 1,100 students full rides to college, which could cost ~$41 million," *Business Insider*.

36 Michael Singer (2017). "LeBron James: Opening school is my most important professional accomplishment," *USA Today*.

Zaira and I both want to have enough money that we can freely and fearlessly express ourselves without worrying about financial impacts or what our bosses, clients, staff, investors, or peers will think.

which provides scholarships to underrepresented minority students.[37]

We all spend money on things that make us happy, but many of us still try to convince ourselves that money can't buy it. We tell ourselves of this because society taught us wrong. Throughout our lives, we all develop a relationship with wealth and money. As a child, your parents, teachers, and pastors taught you that greed is sinful, money is the root of all evil, and that you should learn to be happy with what you got. As an adult, the mainstream media tells you that greedy mortgage lenders caused the 2008 recession, protestors say that the wealthy 1% are destroying America, and politicians say that "billionaires should not exist." For most of your life, society has tried to convince you that money is evil—it's all bullshit. Money can buy happiness. If you can accept this, you can be more effective at using money as a tool to build a happier life.

LET'S RECAP

- Today it is nearly impossible for a couple to live a middle-class life on one average middle-class salary.
- You and your partner should define what financial freedom means to you. Having a clear vision and goals can help motivate you to build wealth.
- Money can buy happiness. If you can accept this, you can be more effective at using it as a tool to build a happier life.

37 The Crapanzano-Solano Initiative, a 501(c)3 nonprofit. For more info or to donate please visit robertsolano.com/scholarship. 100% of donations go to scholarships for underrepresented Black and Latino minority students.

CHAPTER SEVENTEEN

CAN'T KNOCK THE HUSTLE

"Bouncing on the highway switching fo' lanes, screaming through the sunroof, money ain't a thang." —Jay-Z

Whether you realize it or not, we all enter our marriage with a relationship with *Money*. It is as real and tangible as our relationship with our spouses. In other words, I have a relationship with Money and I have a relationship with Zaira. Similarly, Zaira has a relationship with me and a relationship with Money.

Now, we could approach our relationships with Money in two ways. Zaira and I could share our relationship with Money and we could have a beautiful open and honest relationship between the three of us, or we could continue to keep our relationship with Money private. Zaira could have her relationship with Money, and I could have mine, and the two could never mix. I could treat Money like a side chick. I could check my bank accounts when Zaira is not around, take Money out on dates to the bank with just the two of us, and never talk to Zaira about her. That kind of relationship with Money is not healthy—it is called an *affair* and can destroy a marriage.

Part of the reason why many of us keep our relationship with money a secret is because that is another bullshit lesson that society teaches us. Society teaches us that we should not talk about our salaries and that we should keep our account balances a secret. As a result, most of us are embarrassed by our wealth and income. This is especially true if we make a lot more money than our parents, family, or peers.

I'm not immune either. I try to build a healthy relationship with money, but even as I write this, I am afraid of what my parents, sisters, cousins, and coworkers will think as I admit being a millionaire. If I was single, I would probably be more comfortable telling my parents that I was dating a stripper than telling them that I was a millionaire.

Another reason why many of us are embarrassed by money is because we all have a benchmark for how much something should cost. We are afraid to spend money on things that exceed our unconscious cost threshold. If we were to think about buying a $100,000 Porsche Cayenne Turbo, or subconscious screams, "No one needs a car that cost that much!" (also bullshit; I need that car).

Society teaches us that we should not talk about our salaries and that we should keep our account balances a secret. As a result, most of us are embarrassed by our wealth and income.

Most often, we benchmark our idea of value against the average of the people that we spend the most time with (past and present). For example, growing up, I frequently visited my grandmother and she always took us to restaurant that had a $2.99 children's' buffet. We loved going there as a family because it was such a great deal. If you asked my parents if they would ever pay $1,000 for a dinner for two, their answer would be an astounding "Are you nuts! Fuhgeddaboudit!"—it would be a bad value for them.

As an adult, my wealth story is invariably swayed by my parents. I've eaten $1,000 meals before and without fail, I think, "*What would my parents say if they knew how much I spent on this twenty-one-day dry-aged Wagyu tenderloin?*" For people who came from humble families, it is hard to enjoy luxury items without feeling guilty.

All of these factors affect our relationship with money. It is hard to get over these feelings of guilt and shame—Zaira and I still struggle—but one lesson that has helped us build a better relationship with money is an understanding of the Law of Exchange.

The Law of Exchange dictates that in a free-market exchange of goods or services, money is a tool used to exchange items of value between two people or organizations and the amount of money we receive for delivering a good or service is proportional to the amount of value that we deliver. With the exceptions of lying, cheating, or stealing, the only way that you can earn money is by delivering a proportional amount of value.

For example, one of my side businesses is a Hawaiian shave ice cart. We sell a product that is similar to a snow cone. It costs me $1.20 to make a snow cone, which is mostly ice, ice cream, and syrup. If I disregarded the value of my product, I would sell the cones at cost for $1.25. Instead, I charge $5 for a Big Kahuna snow cone.

When I started the company, I felt guilty selling these for $5—it was mostly frozen tap water. Then I learned to accept that the only reason that I could sell it at that price is if I delivered more than $5 in value. I was not just delivering a snow cone. I was quenching someone's taste buds at a hot baseball game, I was delivering them an authentic Hawaiian experience in Florida, I was giving them an Instagram-worthy delicacy, and I was sharing plenty of Aloha spirit and cheer. My customers who paid $5 for my shave ice value the experience of the shave ice much more than the mere cost of sugary syrup. When I accepted this, I got rid of any shame or guilty I had.

As another example, a typical Solano Law Firm client works an hourly wage job. A client may work an entire month for $2,000. Without the Law of Exchange, Zaira would feel guilty charging him $2,000 for only five hours of her time. Zaira may feel like she is ripping him off or diminishing the value of his hard-earned work. However, the Law of Exchange dictates that Zaira can only earn $2,000 if she delivers a service that is worth more than a month's worth of that man's time. For example, the client may be in jail and need Zaira's help getting out on bond. In exchange for $2,000, Zaira delivers the client the possibility that he may get out of jail. The high possibility of getting out of jail is worth more than the client's $2,000 because it will allow him to continue to work and provide for his family.

As a salaried employee, I get paid based upon the value that I deliver to my stakeholders. Although I do not have a direct relationship with customers, I still deliver value to my supervisors, customers, contractors, and community. If I continue to deliver more and more value, I will continue to get promoted and receive pay raises.

You do not need to have shame or guilt about money. It is an important tool for business and our personal happiness. The more value that you deliver, the greater wealth you can earn. This is the only honest way that you can ever earn money or wealth. You should be proud of your wealth because it is a sign of the amount of value that you have delivered to the world.

While writing this book, I asked Zaira, "Remember the day we were at the kitchen table and I told you we were millionaires. How did that make you feel?"

She replied:

> Hungry. I was like, *"Really, this is what it means to be a millionaire?"* This is not what I expected. We have assets, but I want to have a million in cash. To me that's a millionaire—not having assets. And so, it just inspired me to hustle more and grow financially. I didn't feel any different than I did the day before. We still owe money on our homes, and we're not going to pull out that money from our retirement accounts anytime soon. So, to me, it just really didn't make a difference. There is so much more that I want to achieve with my business. I have so many more goals. And there is so much more I need to learn about wealth. I still don't consider myself a millionaire, but one day, I will.

LET'S RECAP

- **A healthy and open relationship with money is required to have a healthy marriage. Keeping money secrets is akin to having an affair—it can destroy a marriage.**
- **You should not be ashamed of honest-earned wealth because of The Law of Exchange. The amount of wealth that you accumulate is proportional to the amount of value you deliver to the world, and you should never be ashamed of delivering value to your customers, stakeholders, or community.**
- **If you want to earn more money, you need to first understand the value of your products and services, and then increase the amount of value that you deliver to your customers, clients, and stakeholders.**

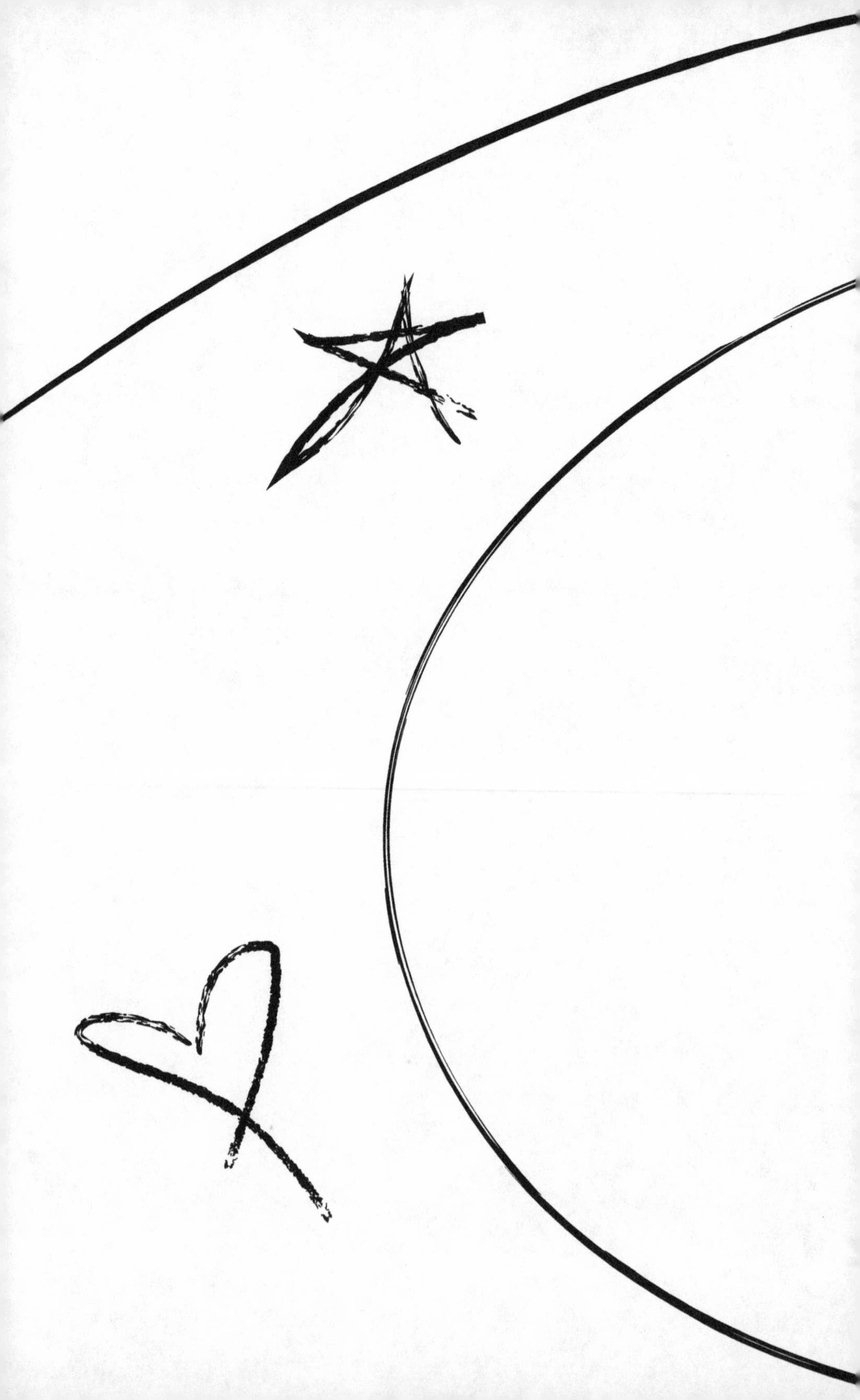

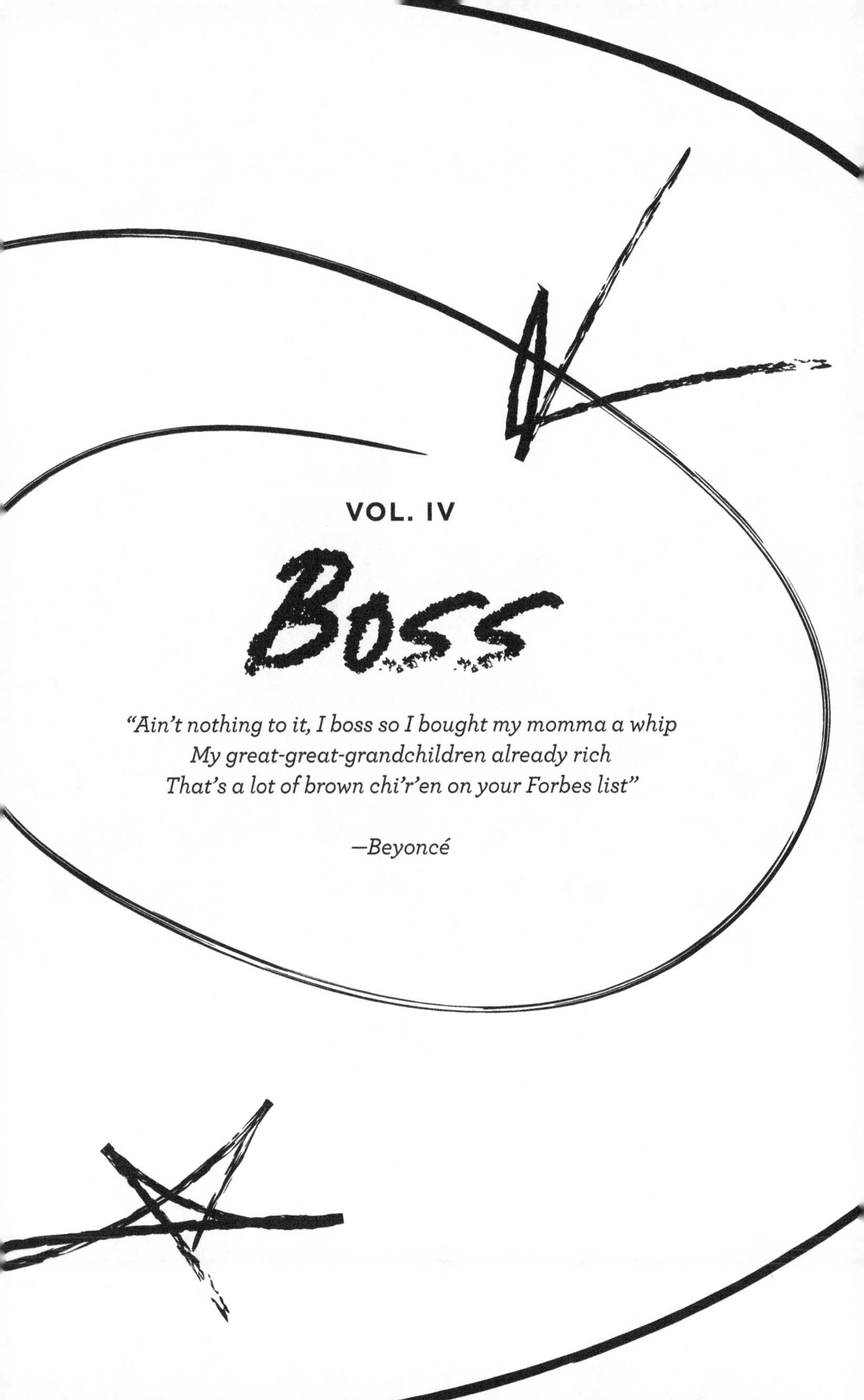

VOL. IV

Boss

"Ain't nothing to it, I boss so I bought my momma a whip
My great-great-grandchildren already rich
That's a lot of brown chi'r'en on your Forbes list"

—Beyoncé

CHAPTER EIGHTEEN

RENEGADE

"No lie, just know I chose my own fate. I drove by the fork in the road and went straight." —The Carters

Zaira's business is a fundamental part of her and, therefore, a fundamental part of our relationship. More so than my corporate job, Zaira's business has shaped our relationship and our life, for better or worse. Our entrepreneurial relationship has been a growing process, and I want to share with you some of the lessons that we've learned along the way, but first, I have a confession.

I hate the word entrepreneur. I use the word frequently in this book because it is easier than saying business owner, cofounder, or partner, but the term really irritates me.

The first reason I don't like the word is that it is hard to spell. The second reason I dislike it is because too many people glamorize the entrepreneur lifestyle. On the one hand, people think that as an entrepreneur they can be their own boss, set their own schedules, and not need to answer to anyone. Zaira eloquently captured this sentiment like this:

> I'm a Renegade. I just want to do whatever the fuck I want; whenever the fuck I want, all the fucking time I want. That's my problem. That's been my problem since I was a child. I never want to do bad stuff; I just want to do what I want to do. That's why I always wanted to own my own law firm. I hate boundaries, and I don't like rules. I wanted to be my own fucking boss.

While entrepreneurship does provide some freedom, it also carries a tremendous burden. As the CEO of a seven-figure law firm, responsible for over a dozen full-time employees, Zaira may be able to set her schedule, but she can never stop working. Responsibility follows every day, and it doesn't make a difference if it is 9 p.m. at night or 3 p.m. on a Sunday, if there is urgent work to do, she needs to do it. Sure, she has a lot of freedom as a small business owner, but in many ways, she is a slave to her business. CEOs have a tremendous amount of responsibility.

The entrepreneur lifestyle may seem fashionable, but anyone who has run a seven-figure business, or had more than a handful of full-time employees, can tell you that the entrepreneurial lifestyle is not glamorous. It is more often a constant struggle of never-ending stress.

While entrepreneurship does provide some freedom, it also carries a tremendous burden.

When we first started dating, I had a hard time understanding Zaira's struggle. As a corporate employee, I always believed in work-life balance. I worked hard while I was in the office, but completely shut down the work side of my brain when I came home. Rarely would I check my work email or even discuss work when I was home. Zaira, on the other hand, talked and thought about work every second of the day. Almost every night, she worked from home, usually on her laptop until a few minutes before going to bed at night. I had a really hard time understanding why Zaira had no work-life balance.

Ultimately, the way that I began to understand Zaira better was by helping her with her business. Although I did not work in the business full time, I tried to help her when I could. I built websites for her, managed marketing campaigns, interviewed potential employees, ran her social media pages, and designed her office (cubicles, conference rooms, break areas, etc.). Working with her part-time gave me a greater appreciation for her struggle as an entrepreneur.

Today, when it comes to the law firm and our other businesses, we are always "on." We cannot have a conversation without talking about business in some fashion. Business is definitely not the only focus in our lives, but it manages to weave into every aspect of our existence. Most of our vacations are business trips, most of our friends are business colleagues, most of our readings are business books, networking events double as date nights, and many of our friends raise their children in their businesses. Including my nine-to-five corporate job, we each regularly work eighty hours a week and spend much more time beyond that talking and thinking about our businesses.

Working eighty hours a week may sound absurd, but for entrepreneurs, there is no such thing as work-life balance. There is only life, and life includes the business, our relationship, our family, and friends. They all support each other. Instead of work-life balance, we have work-life integration.

We schedule date nights and reading time at the beach the same way we schedule conference calls, performance reviews, and quarterly calendar meetings. We regularly talk about business at home at all hours of the day, night, and weekends. The business is an extension of our relationship. We love each other. We love the world. We want to develop a deep and meaningful relationship, and we want to have a meaningful impact on the world—the business is an extension of this love.

This does introduce numerous challenges to our relationship. We do have a limited amount of energy available every day. Although we leverage assistants and helpers to reclaim more time and energy, our natural tendency is to channel that energy into our work. As you can imagine, this does not leave a lot of extra time for our hobbies, fitness, or sex. For these reasons, we've learned that it is very important for us to block off time for these activities. This is why we are religious about Wednesdays and Fridays being work-free and TV-free evenings. Wednesday night is the one day that we always cook dinner together and then spend the rest of the evening going for an evening walk, playing board games, or just sitting on the couch talking. On Fridays we usually go out to dinner and a date. This strategy helps maintain our mental and physical intimacy.

While the interweaving of our relationship and business may seem beautiful, another often overlooked aspect of entrepreneurship is the risk associated with owning a small business. Too many entrepreneurs think that their brilliant idea or company will make them a fortune. They devour the rags-to-riches stories and think that they could be the next Gary Vaynerchuck, Sara Blakely, or Grant Cardone. While a small minority of entrepreneurs will make it big, most will be lucky to just get by.

The glamorization of entrepreneurship has led many great people to shun corporate jobs to pursue the dream of being an entrepreneur. This is an unfortunate trend. Most new entrepreneurs soon find out that being a small business owner usually requires at least twice as much work as a corporate job for half the pay. For example, if Zaira was a lawyer in a large law firm, I know that she would already be a senior partner making over twice as much as she regularly makes now.

According to Google, an entrepreneur is "a person who organizes and operates a business, taking on greater than normal financial risk in order to do so."

Personally, I prefer to operate a business with *low* financial risk. Or, better still, I prefer to make money *without* organizing and operating a business at all. Developing a new product or service, hiring staff, and managing operations are difficult tasks that I would prefer to avoid if needed. Entrepreneurship does have the potential to be very rewarding, but it can also be very risky and disproportionately challenging. This is one of the reasons why I continue to work my corporate job while also pursuing side hustles in my spare time.

Compared to most small businesses, larger corporations usually provide higher pay, better benefits, retirement plans, corporate mentorship, and training opportunities. Sure, my corporate job has some drawbacks, but it also has many benefits. For example, I lead the development of advanced technologies, I execute billion-dollar budgets, I work with hundreds of amazing and highly talented people, I receive regular mentorship and education, and I gain invaluable experience in contracting, negotiations, and financial management. In addition to all those benefits, I also have a great salary, health care, and a retirement plan. What I sacrifice in freedom and flexibility, I make up for with greater benefits and stability.

Another truth that few people talk about is that small business growth is cyclic. Small businesses have hard times and good times. Some months Zaira will make more money than she ever dreamed possible, and other months she questions her life choices as she cries herself to sleep.

Zaira has succeeded in growing the business 33% to 125% annually, but this growth requires a lot of hard work and investment. In 2017, Zaira hired her office administrator. This was an expensive hire. It cost over $10,000 just to find and recruit her and another $10,000 to train her. These costs and her entire salary came out of Zaira's pay. For four months, Zaira did not pay herself anything to cover the initial investment. For four months, the work didn't stop, but the pay sure did. Imagine working eighty-plus hours a week as an attorney and CEO for free!

Zaira reinvests a lot into the firm too. Company retreats, family days, coaching, and marketing are all investments that are required for growth, and growth allows Zaira to help as many clients as possible. But these investments cost a lot of money, which usually comes out of Zaira's pay.

For Zaira and me, my corporate job and her small business provide diversity between risk and rewards. My corporate job provides our family with financial stability, while Zaira's business provides us with less secure but higher-potential financial opportunities. Our different careers also provide us with a diversity of thought. While Zaira thinks like a small business owner, I think like a corporate manager. We can share ideas that help improve our management strategies. Zaira summarizes it like this:

> I have pretty much total control of my success and failure. I have the ability and the freedom to choose what I want to work on and what I don't. I have the ability to impact our lives in different ways than Robert can. I have the ability to generate income for our family in addition to what's routine and expected. If we need or want more money, I could work harder, go on speaking tours, or hop on sales calls to get a quick jump in profit for our family. I also take on a lot of risk. Just like I can add a lot more income to our family, I can lose it all much quicker than Robert could. The business could dry up due to factors outside of my control; for example, coronavirus. If this lockdown gets worse, we will need to come up with some new ideas to keep the business going.
>
> Our different jobs are a lot like our relationship. Robert is the type of personality that likes a lot of structure while I thrive in chaos. I probably need about half the structure that he does, and it's challenging. I appreciate Robert. I appreciate him for keeping our life, our finances, our vacations, our schedules all in order. But, I'm just like this fish in the sea that's just going all the time. Having to slow down or stopping to smell the roses or having a plan and structure is a challenge for me. But I appreciate that about Robert—he grounds us when it comes to that.

My wife is the entrepreneur in our relationship, not me. Sure, I'm launching Alpha Couples and have a few small side hustles, but as of now, entrepreneurship is my hobby and not my full-time career. For Zaira, being the CEO of Solano Law Firm has been her full-time hustle for almost a decade. I truly appreciate her hard work and dedication to building Solano Law Firm, and I'm glad that I have been able to join her for the ride.

Although Zaira and I are not parents yet, many entrepreneur mothers will even tell you that being a small business owner is more difficult than raising a child. I am sure that Zaira will agree that being an entrepreneur is the most difficult thing she has ever done in her life, but also the most rewarding—it's cliché because it's the truth.

LET'S RECAP

- Both entrepreneurship and corporate employment have their respective benefits and drawbacks. Owning a business and being a CEO is a tremendous burden. It can be extremely rewarding at times but also carries heavy responsibilities and tremendous financial risk. Corporate jobs, on the other hand, usually offer higher pay, better benefits, and greater mentorship opportunities than small businesses.
- If you want to be an entrepreneur, forget the idea of a work-life balance. Instead, find happiness in the interweaving of your personal and professional life.
- As an entrepreneur, your natural tendency is to channel all of your spare energy into your business. Be deliberate in scheduling time for your fitness, health, and intimacy—otherwise, these areas of your life will get neglected.

CHAPTER NINETEEN

BIGGER

"Look up, don't look down, then watch the answers unfold." —Beyoncé

So, by this point in the book, you have a housecleaner, a personal assistant, you're flying first-class once in a while, taking Uber Black cars, and have a nanny to help with the kids. Congratulations, you are taking big steps to increase your quality of life and happiness. As you invest more and more in raising your standards and improving your life, two questions that you need to ask yourself are:

1) What am I going to do with the extra free time that I have?
2) How am I going to afford these changes?

Let's start by talking about free time. When you invest in raising your standards—for example, hiring an assistant—you will inevitably reclaim your free time and generate more energy. If you are an Alpha personality, your natural tendency will be to use your newfound energy and time to work more. You will spend more time checking email, reviewing résumés, or talking with employees. We never have enough time to do these tasks, so if we get a few more free minutes or hours during the week, we naturally want to use that time to "catch up."

The problem is that we will never have enough time to review enough résumés to find that perfect job applicant or to check enough emails to completely clear out our inbox. These infinite tasks would easily consume all of our free time if we allowed them to. I don't know about you, but my email never ends. I triage my inbox as best I can, attacking the high-priority items, but there is always a backlog. Zaira's executive assistant sorts her emails for her, which helps, but it is still overwhelming. And if Zaira ever were to get through her emails, there are dozens of discussion threads on Microsoft Teams, WhatsApp, or the business's Facebook page that she could spend countless hours reviewing.

While these tasks are important, they never end. They do not significantly advance the business because they are *sustainment activities*. They help us maintain our current business and lifestyle, but they do not propel us forward to achieve the business, marriage, or life that we truly desire. Sustainment tasks are like treading water; they prevent us from drowning, but they don't get us out of the water. They will not help us achieve the spectacular life that we deserve. If you invest your newfound time and energy into sustainment activities, you are wasting an opportunity.

When you increase your standards and get more energy and time, you need to use that energy for *growth activities*. Instead of spending an extra hour each day checking email, you need to improve some aspect of your life or career. Growth activities include actions like reading and *implementing* lessons from professional development books (like this one); working with a coach, counselor, or mentor; setting goals that push you outside your comfort zone; creating a new marketing campaign; learning a new skill; or investing in a relationship.

I can confidently say that most of the adults I encounter seem to spend most of their energy on sustainment. But when I look at the top 1% of performers in any field, I find that they spend the majority of their time on growth and development. They constantly learn new skills, pursue new passions, experiment with new ideas, seek new mentors, and are thirsty for growth. This should be your goal too.

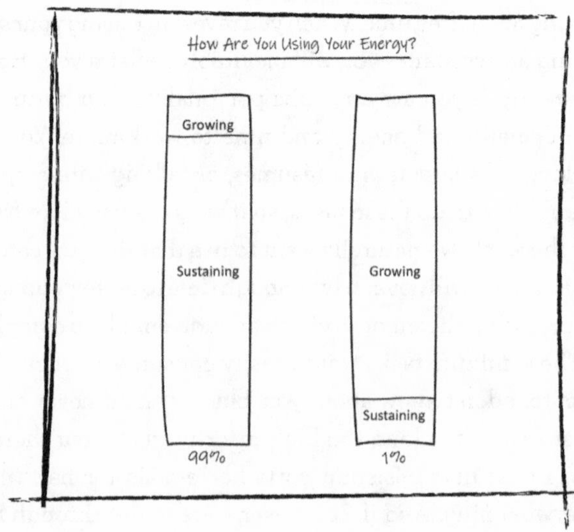

The key difference between a corporate job and entrepreneurship is how growth is measured and rewarded. In corporations, growth is usually measured by *years of experience* and rewarded with *promotions,* while in small businesses, growth is measured by *mastery of skills* and rewarded with *revenue and profit.* These are huge differences that incentivize behavior differently.

Let's first take a look at corporations. A typical large corporation requires two to four years of experience to become a junior manager, ten to fifteen years to become a senior manager, twenty to thirty years to become a director, and thirty to forty years to become a senior vice president. As long as employees perform at least average quality work, they will be competitive for promotion in a few years. They are not incentivized to grow faster than their corporate culture will allow. As a result, most corporate employees spend the majority of their time on sustainment activities and not growth.

As an example, a middle manager can ask their supervisor, "What skills do I need to become a vice president?"

The supervisor may respond, "You need to gain experience in financial management, budgeting, and negotiations."

If that employee was really motivated, he could attend a financial management course at Harvard Business School, learn budgeting directly from a Fortune 500 chief financial officer, and hire the best negotiator in the world to train him. Afterward, he would be a master of profit and loss statements, be able to budget the federal deficit, or could negotiate hostage rescues. He could be the best in the corporation in all three areas and would still need to wait another ten to twenty years before he could become a vice president. The idea of promoting a junior manager directly to senior vice president is unimaginable. In the corporate world, learning mastery may help a manager perform their duties, but ultimately the most assured way to get promoted is to gain experience over time.

In contrast, small business owners like Zaira are rewarded as soon as they can master a task. For example, when Zaira started her business, she had to learn how to manage bookkeeping, accounting, and budgets. She needed to master these skills ASAP so that she could manage her business and avoid debt or trouble with the IRS. Her clients wanted to get their green cards in exchange for their payments, her staff wanted to get their paychecks on the first and fifteenth, and Zaira wanted to avoid failing as a business owner. Her clients or staff did not care if she had *experience* in financial management; as long as the staff got paid and clients got their green cards, everyone was happy. More importantly, the business generated positive revenue and profit, which meant that Zaira could get paid too. Entrepreneurs get financially rewarded for their mastery, which is based on performance, and not for their experience, which is based on time.

Some corporations reward performance with annual bonuses, stock options, and profit-sharing. This is especially true for sales associates and at senior ranks. But those benefits are still a much smaller percentage than small business owners receive. A corporate manager who wins a $5 million contract may be lucky to earn a $15,000 bonus while a lawyer who wins a $5 million settlement could take home $500,000 or more!

A few years ago, Zaira and I attended a three-day intensive public speaking workshop. The training was great and really challenged us to be better public speakers. It was a growth activity that cost us $4,500.

The following weekend, Zaira gave three different immigration seminars throughout Birmingham. That weekend, she had fourteen clients hire the law firm. The average case value was $5,000 each, for a total of $70,000. This was all within one week of her training. Considering that her profit margin is about 20%, that one weekend of speaking led to almost $14,000 in profit—not too bad.

In contrast, I used the skills I learned to give a series of management workshops for my department. My workshop got great reviews and were an outstanding success. I received a great performance review at the end of the year, but that's it. I didn't get an immediate promotion, pay raise, or more stock options. I enjoyed teaching the workshop, which is rewarding in itself, but who had greater incentive to invest $4,500 in public speaking, Zaira or me?

For a business owner like Zaira, it makes financial sense to pay $4,500 to learn a new skill that can generate ten times as much profit. She has a high conversion rate efficiency between self-development investments and profit, but for a corporate employee like me, the juice is not worth the squeeze.

This paradigm repeats itself in many aspects of our lives. Small business owners usually have more incentives to improve and grow than their corporate counterparts.

The same dynamic appears when it comes to hiring help. An entrepreneur who can hire a housecleaner, assistant, or nanny, and then use that time to be more productive, has a much greater incentive to outsource routine tasks than a corporate employee who has a fixed salary. If I hired a housecleaner, personal assistant, and nanny, I would go broke unless I had equivalent growth in my salary.

That is not to say that corporate employees cannot also benefit from hiring help, but the financial justification is more tenuous for fixed-salary employees.

The diagram below shows how this profit feedback can help you achieve self-sustaining growth. The cycle begins with raising your standards—reduce the time you spend on sustainment activities, hire help for routine tasks, and stop doing shit you hate.

If you raise your standards, you will inevitably get more time and energy as a result. The key to increasing profit is to invest this time and energy toward professional growth, not sustainment. After you invest in your own professional development, you will be a more effective leader and can, therefore, deliver greater value to your customers, staff, community, and other stakeholders. Thanks to the Law of Exchange, the more value that you deliver to your stakeholders, the more profit you will earn.

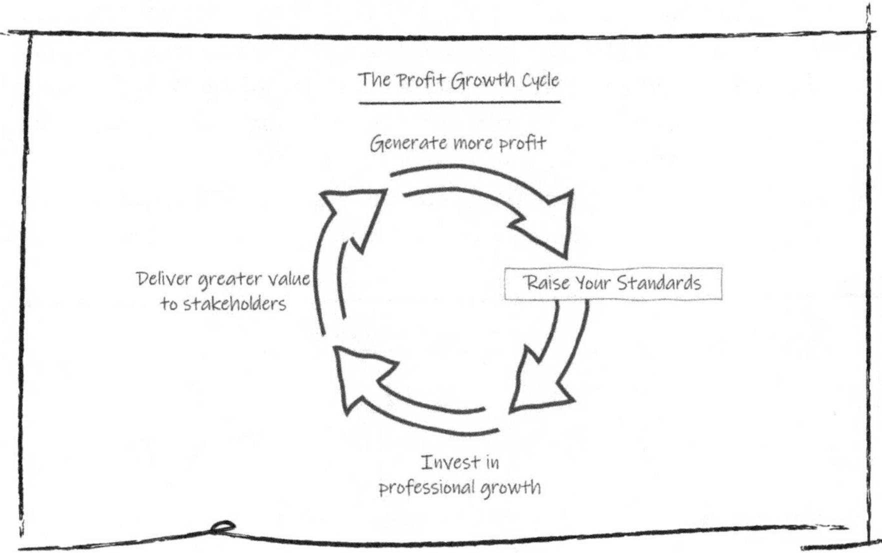

For small business owners, this profit feedback may be almost immediate. For corporate employees, this profit feedback may take a little longer as they wait for end-of-year bonuses or for future promotions. The increases in profits will allow you to reinvest more money into raising your standards even higher, which will allow you to invest even more time and energy into your professional growth.

Investing all of your time and energy into professional development will help you generate more profit, but working relentlessly on your business will not increase your happiness. As you generate more profits and continue to raise your standards, you also need to invest more of your time and energy into your own happiness. Investing in your own happiness means that you stop doing things that make you unhappy: spend more time on personal development, improve your health and mental well-being, pursue hobbies and interests, and focus on being a better person.

Happy people have happy relationships. As you improve yourself, you will develop deeper and more meaningful connections with your friends, coworkers, community, family, children, and spouses. And as you develop stronger connections, they will inspire you to live a more meaningful and purpose-driven life. If you love your clients, you will have a greater drive to help them; if you love your neighbors you will be more inclined to give back to your community; and if you have a stronger relationship with your spouse, you will love him or her more and more with each passing day. Then, you may realize that by raising your own standards, you are raising the standards for everyone around you. This should hopefully inspire you to keep raising your standards.

When this happiness cycle is combined with the profit cycle, it creates *The Profit-Happiness Growth Cycle*. Both the profit and the happiness sides of the cycle start with raising your standards. If you can balance investing in both sides of this cycle, you can create patterns in your life that can help you continuously increase your profits and happiness.

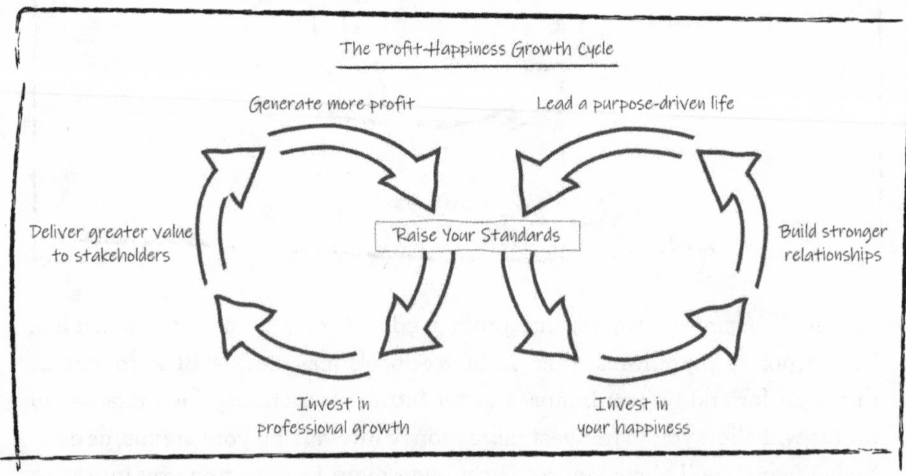

People usually break the cycle when they focus on one side but not the other. For example, I have friends who hired a nanny to help with their children. The nanny relieved them from a lot of time commitments that they would otherwise spend preparing meals or cleaning the house. Instead of investing some of that newfound time into being better parents, they spend all of their free time working. They regularly work at the office until 7 or 8 p.m. every night, which they can only do because their nanny cooks dinner and watches the kids until they get home. They could use that time to build stronger relationships with their children—for example, while the nanny is cooking, they could take the kids to the aquarium—but instead they just give all that free time and energy back to the business.

Happy people have happy relationships. As you improve yourself, you will develop deeper and more meaningful connections.

As an inverse example, I have an attorney friend who got lucky and won a settlement that paid her $50,000. After receiving the settlement, she immediately took a vacation and then bought a new car. Meanwhile, she did not have an assistant, her businesses' growth was stagnant, and she never thought about hiring a business coach. She could have used some of her settlement to boost her profit potential, but instead used all of her one-time settlement for personal happiness, without allotting any of it for professional development.

If you live a first-class lifestyle but do not invest in your professional growth, you will go broke. Conversely, if you invest all of your energy into your business but do not invest in yourself or relationships, then you will have a meaningless life. To build a really fulfilling life, you need to raise your standards and then balance your time between investing in your business and on your happiness.

This sounds easy, but it is actually really hard. Growth is not easy. Zaira describes it like this:

> No business owner who is either at my level or who is further than me on their journey has ever told me that growth comes easy, or without pain, or without hard work. This is actually a conversation that I had very recently with my team.
>
> A lot of our staff want to come to work every day, and they want to

continue to do what they have always done. Everybody wants to be comfortable, but there's no growth in comfort. Growth allows us to implement new ideas and strategies, growth also helps me become wiser as a business owner, and growth helps us get to our goals. But it's freaking hard. When you're growing a business, every quarter is a new level and a new devil. It's hard—it's a gift and a curse.

Sometimes, I just want to take a break too. I want to say, "Hey, we're happy where we are. Let's take a little break on growth for a month or two, and let's just be satisfied not rocking the boat." But that kind of mindset is not going to get us where we actually want to be.

The same is true in my personal life. Actually, it's probably harder to grow personally. I know that I should go to spin class more, read a book once in a while, or go to the spa more often, but there is always so much work to do for the business. I feel like I never have enough time, and usually if it comes down to the business or my personal life, I'm going to spend my time working on the business. This is something that I'm trying to get better at.

LET'S RECAP

- **When you raise your standards, you gain more energy and free time. Resist the urge to waste that time and energy by catching up on work. Instead invest in professional growth and your personal happiness.**
- **Strive to deliver greater value to your stakeholders, which will result in more profit. Simultaneously, invest in your happiness, build strong relationships, and lead a purposeful life. Investing in your business and happiness is the key to constant growth.**
- **Everybody wants to be comfortable, but there's no growth in comfort. If you want to upgrade your life, learn to accept discomfort.**

CHAPTER TWENTY

BONNIE & CLYDE

"Put us together, how they gon' stop both us?" —Jay-Z

In a Medium article titled "Do you Really Need a Cofounder?" entrepreneurs were asked about their experiences running their companies with partners versus alone. I love the answer provided by Maria Andrea Gonzalez, a business owner in Bogotá, Colombia. Maria says:

> What I've come to realize after all these years is that a cofounder is a *must*, not just because he or she brings something new to the table, but because they share your most inner desires. It's the affinity towards the goal in the purest way. This kind of match, where you go deep into arguing about the same thing, where you speak the same language and read each other between the lines, is what gives the ride a whole new level of worthiness. The friction that comes from digging deeper, challenging the other, and questioning the same essential problems is what results in great companies that change the world. There's no fire without friction.[38]

Maria's statement is not only applicable to a business partnership but also applicable to marriage. Speaking the same language, sharing our most inner desires, and helping each other dig deeper are all the same goals that we should desire for our most intimate relationship. Gonzalez's answer is especially important for Alpha Couples because her cofounder is also her husband.

Although it is hard to work with a spouse, some couples have made their partnership an extremely successful cornerstone of their career. For example, Kevin and Julia Hartz cofounded Eventbrite together, Bill and Melinda Gates lead the Gates Foundation, and Chip and Joanna Gaines built a *Fixer-Upper*

---

38 "Do You Really Need a Cofounder?" (2017), *Brocoders*, medium.com.

empire. These couples are incredible examples of how spouses can also be business partners.

Even spouses who don't work full-time together frequently leverage each other for help. Take, for example, Bobbi Brown and Steven Plofker, entrepreneurs who have been married for over thirty years. Bobbi is a titan in the beauty industry. She is the founder of Bobbi Brown Makeup and CEO of Evolution_18. Meanwhile, her husband, Steven, is a successful real estate mogul. Although they each have separate careers, their partnership has had a huge role in their success in each of their respective fields. When asked who helped her get to where she is today, Bobbi replied:

> There's not a chance I would have been successful if I had not met my husband. He has been not just my biggest supporter. He is also my biggest troubleshooter. I could honestly say that we created all of my brands together. He has always been an incredible support system and I could not have done it without him.[39]

Similarly, Steven attributes his success to Bobbi's support. When Steven was considering getting a "real" job, Bobbi told him, "That's the stupidest thing I have ever heard you say." She supported him and gave him the confidence to go to law school and then start his real estate business.

This is the kind of partnership that I want to have with Zaira. I want a partnership where each of us brings new perspectives and insights into the relationship, where we challenge each other to excel, and where we work together to build something impactful and lasting in the realm of family, business, and, ideally, both.

Although this was my personal goal when Zaira and I got married, we were partners in our personal lives, but our partnership ended there. We each had our own separate careers, assets, and liabilities; I had *my* career, *my* real estate, *my* savings, and Zaira had *her* business, and *her* savings. This clear separation of ownership caused a lot of friction in our marriage. We were not in sync.

I remember one of the first times I helped Zaira with her business. Zaira was swamped with work and her receptionist just quit. This was a very important role and put a lot of stress on the team to cover down on the position while it was vacant. Zaira did not have the time to sort through applications and interview candidates, so the position went vacant for weeks.

---

39 Yitzi Weiner (2018). "Life Lessons From a Power Couple: With Bobbi Brown, beauty industry titan, and Steven Plofker, real estate mogul," *Authority Magazine*, medium.com.

After listening to her complain about it every night at dinner for over a month, I volunteered to help out and find a candidate. Over the next few weeks, I screened hundreds of candidates, interviewed about forty, and scheduled the most promising ones for an office call with Zaira. I thought I had a great pool of receptionist candidates, but Zaira's assessments were "nope, nope, nope, nope." She would give me feedback like, "She does not have enough office experience," "I don't like his résumé format," "He was nervous during the interview," "She didn't send a follow-up thank you email," or "She is simply not a good fit."

"This is an entry-level position," I argued with her. "You want a bilingual college graduate with excellent interview skills and seven years of office experience. Those people are not going to apply to be a receptionist at a law firm, and especially not for $12 an hour!"

Out of the approximately forty candidates we interviewed, I would have hired at least five of them, but none passed Zaira's extremely high standards.

"You are losing money. You need to hire someone today," I told her. "If you don't hire someone, I am going to do it for you. When you show up to work on Monday, a new receptionist will be sitting there!"

That really pissed her off.

She gave me a stern warning, "You better not."

I probably overreacted, but I was frustrated. I felt like I was wasting dozens of hours of my life trying to hire someone great, but I lacked any real authority to actually make the decision. Eventually, after the position went vacant for three months, Zaira reluctantly agreed to hire one of my candidates—she quickly became one of the firm's best employees.

Over the next few years, we frequently fought about the law firm. Usually our arguments started because I had a recommendation to improve the business and she refused my advice. A few examples include the time that I tried to launch a social media marketing campaign, but she nitpicked every post and said no so many times that I eventually gave up. In another example, I wanted to expand the firm's market to Florida, but she refused to set up a new office. Over and over, I thought that I had great ideas, but if she disagreed with me, she just shut me down.

In another example, the law firm had a paralegal who did exceptional work but was also disrespectful to teammates and rude to clients. One day, there was a petty office argument after one paralegal ate another paralegal's yogurt. After Zaira spent all day investigating the yogurt incident, interrogating the staff, and stressing about the office drama, I told Zaira, "You need to fire him immediately."

"I can't," she argued. "We need him to do visa cases."

"You can hire someone else. He is toxic. Fire him. Today."

"I'm not going to fire him!"

I knew that the employee would continue to incite office drama and cause stress for Zaira. For weeks, I continued to listen to Zaira complain about the employee almost daily. Every time she complained, I told her to fire him, and she would refuse. A few months later, he quit without notice.

When it came to the law firm, I did not feel like a partner in any way. Instead, I felt like a therapist—my job was to listen to her complain, but I had zero authority to implement solutions. I like helping people, and I especially like helping my wife. For me, listening to her complain without helping her solve the problem was very frustrating.

Furthermore, Zaira's business had huge impacts on our family and relationship. If she made a mistake in the business, she would need to go to Atlanta for weeks at a time to get the ship back on track, or if sales were down, she would need to spend all hours of the nights and weekends making client calls. In worst cases, a poor employee could screw up and cost Zaira her bar license, which could threaten the future of the business.

On the flip side, successful business bets could allow us to have stress-free vacations and extra revenue could help us pay for those trips, remodel the house, or buy a new car. Zaira's business decisions, for better or worse, had a huge impact on our free time, finances, and relationship. The business may have been hers, but it definitely affected both of us. I wanted to help where I could, but Zaira was a very difficult boss to work for.

One evening, while preparing dinner in the kitchen, I asked Zaira, "We are partners, right?"

"Of course," she replied without hesitation as she put two chicken breasts in the air fryer.

"Okay. How can we improve the way we work together as partners?"

I took a sip of wine and then clarified, "For example, how can we work together to make Solano Law Firm better?"

"Well," she said, thoughtfully, "if there is something that I need help with, I can explain to you what needs to get done, and then give you the tools to do it. For example, if I ask for your help in managing the budget, I should explain the policy and procedure that we use and then let you manage the budget."

"I agree with that. Give me a task and let me execute," I said as I prepared to ask her the hard part of the question. "But what about when it goes the other way? What should I do if I need *you* to change something in the business?"

For a moment she looked confused.

I restated the question, "For example, when I told you a few months ago that you needed to fire your paralegal. If I need you to fire someone, what should I do? Could I tell you to fire someone?"

After a brief pause, she said, "No. You don't know how we operate. You can't tell me what to do."

"That's not a partnership." I stood up from my seat at the table. "The scenario you described, where you give me a task to do, and then I do it. That is me working *for you*. If you really think of our marriage as a partnership, then it needs to be a two-way street. We need to make decisions together. And sometimes if I feel really strongly about something, I hope that you would support me even if you disagree, like when I told you to fire that asshole paralegal."

"No!" she snapped. "This is *my* business."

I want a partnership where each of us brings new perspectives and insights into the relationship, where we challenge each other to excel.

There it was. It was *her* business. It wasn't *ours*, it was hers. As long as it was her business, we could never be partners. A partnership generally involves debate, discussion, compromise, equality, and respect. Zaira, who enjoyed a high level of control, may have welcomed my opinions in general, but when it came to the business, she had final say. Partnership felt like a term we used to show our affection without any real significance or implications.

Zaira hates to feel controlled and I knew that my questions would trigger her, but this was a topic that we needed to discuss. *Were we really partners?*

I understand why Zaira felt the way she did. She built her business from nothing, she loved it, and she knew it in and out. She was the boss and sole proprietor. I admit that in the beginning of our relationship, I probably encouraged this view without understanding the long-term effects.

When we first started dating, we discussed a prenuptial agreement. Before we got married, Zaira had her business and I had my rental properties. As young professionals coming into the marriage, we were each moderately successful and wanted to protect the businesses and assets that we worked so hard to build. We did not sign a prenuptial, but we agreed that her business was her premarital property and my rental properties were my property. In other words, we agreed that if we got divorced, neither of us would try to take 50% of the other's business. Since I was previously divorced, this protection strategy made sense to me.

It is ironic that 5,000 years ago, humans invented marriage to accumulate resources between families. Now, in 2020, many couples like Zaira and me enter marriage trying to protect and maintain our individual assets. We get married with implicit or explicit prenuptial agreements that protect our individual property—*this is my business, that is your dog, that is my car, that is your motorcycle*. This is especially prevalent with older and successful professionals, like Zaira and me, who each built our own careers, businesses, and wealth prior to marriage. For couples like us, it is easy to say, "What's mine is yours and yours is mine" but it is much more difficult to actually practice it.

Prior to the Industrial Revolution, it was easy for couples to treat each other as partners because most spouses actually did work together in their family businesses. For example, the husband baked the bread and the wife sold it, but today, with our complex businesses and corporate jobs, it is extremely difficult to really feel and act like true partners.

If I wanted Zaira and me to be an Alpha Couple, I knew that we needed to develop a real partnership in practice, not just in words. We needed to be less like sympathetic roommates and more like Chip and Joanna, Bill and Melinda, and Barack and Michelle. If we wanted to build a powerful marriage, we needed a new way to think about our relationship with our businesses, careers, income, debts, and assets—we needed to be partners.

To improve our partnership, I began to change the way I thought about our relationship. I asked myself questions from a business perspective: "*What are we partners or cofounders of? If we are really partnering in everything, how should we make important decisions? And in what areas of my life I am resistant to partnership?*"

I started to imagine that we had cofounded a company called The Robert & Zaira Solano Corporation, or *The Sol Co* for short. Much like a corporation, a marriage is certified by a legal document that recognizes the entity. In many aspects, we were already authorized to act as a single entity. For example, we can file joint taxes, make important medical decisions for each other, and some lower courts even allow a spouse to appear in court on behalf of the other.

The first step to establishing Sol Co was merging our assets. Each of us entered the marriage with our individual assets and businesses. Although I

To improve our partnership, I began to change the way I thought about our relationship. I asked myself questions from a business perspective: "What are we partners or cofounders of? If we are really partnering in everything, how should we make important decisions? And in what areas of my life I am resistant to partnership?"

worked for a large company, my career could loosely be considered a business; I delivered my services to my company in exchange for pay, similar to how Solano Law Firm delivered legal services to clients in exchange for retainers. Our individual assets included:

- Solano Law Firm
- Zaira's financial assets
- Zaira's real estate
- Robert's career
- Robert's financial assets
- Robert's real estate

When we got married and became partners, the Sol Co became the parent company for *all* of these assets. Now, the Sol Co owns Solano Law Firm, my career, all of our assets, and our properties.

This meant that I needed to treat Zaira as an equal partner when I was making career decisions and that instead of treating my rental properties as mine, I needed to treat them as ours. Our marriage owned everything. It wasn't mine or hers anymore, it is *ours*. This is very difficult for many couples to accept because our society places such a strong emphasis on ownership. As young adults, we take a lot of pride in owning a car, a house, or a business. Our ego, and how we see ourselves as people, is strongly tied to our possessions.

When a couple gets married young, it's easier for them to merge assets because they usually have so few of them. They naturally bring less ego into their relationship. But for a couple like Zaira and me, who each entered the marriage with over half a million dollars in assets and much more in business value, we entered the relationship with a lot of ego tied to our assets, businesses, and careers.

When Zaira snapped at me and said, "This is my business!" that was her ego trying to protect her.

Although I'm using Zaira's business as an example because we worked together frequently on the firm, I got equally defensive when it came to my career, real estate, and money. For example, Zaira wanted me to transfer to South Carolina where she had a lot of clients and the law firm could do very well. I refused because I didn't like the corporate culture in that department of my company, and that was the end of the story. In retrospect, we should have had a serious partnership discussion and made a decision based upon what was best for the marriage's business and not my individual desires.

Eventually, Zaira and I began to work more as partners. It started gradually. At first, we usually separated tasks. When I offered to help Zaira, or when Zaira asked me for help, I began to demand autonomy. For example, if I was tasked to hire a marketing assistant, I told her beforehand that I needed to be able to make the decision on who to hire. I would ask for her opinion and assessment, but I needed hiring authority if that was my task. Similarly, when I was running social media marketing for the firm, I told her that I needed to be able to run campaigns without asking for her approval every time.

Julia Hartz refers to this technique as *divide and conquer.* In 2006, Julia cofounded Eventbrite with her husband, Kevin. Together, they still run the company and have grown it into a global brand with $300 million in annual revenue. She reflected on her initial worry about partnering with her spouse:

> Some of our close friends, who had built a few businesses together, gave us this great advice: "Divide and conquer," they said. "Never work on the same thing at the same time." And that was our golden rule. We just never worked on the same area of the business at the same time. If you're working on the same spreadsheet, you're going to be fighting over the mouse.[40]

This separation of duties also helped Zaira and me, especially when we initially started working together. It also helped us begin to develop business trust with each other, which was the real underlying issue.

Although Zaira and I each had successful careers before we got married, neither of us worked together in any professional sense. Although we trusted each other as lovers, we didn't trust each other as business partners. This kind of trust was much different than trusting each other to babysit the kids, manage household expenses, or provide consoling. This trust takes time, persistence, and intentionality to develop.

As we started to work more frequently together, we also instituted a weekly business lunch. Previously, we always talked about business at dinner, after a long day, when both of us were tired and sometimes grouchy. I would often have a hard time differentiating when Zaira was complaining because she just wanted to vent, or when she was complaining because she actually needed help with something. By meeting for lunch once a week, we could have a much more structured conversation where we discuss which projects each of us were focused on and where we could help.

Zaira still occasionally complains about business over dinner, and I do too for that matter, but our friends Rachel and Scott Baker taught us a great lesson on

---

40 David Gelles (2019). "Julia Hartz Founded Eventbrite with Her Fiancé. Then She Took His Job." *The New York Times.*

how to deal with this. Rachel and Scott are also both entrepreneurs. Rachel owns a home and industrial cleaning service and Scott owns a Mac computer repair shop. When I asked how they unwind at the end of the day, Rachel put it like this:

> One of the things I learned is when he comes home at the end of the day, I tell him, "I just need to get some things off my chest, and I don't want you to fix it. I just want you to listen." So, I tell him and he's like "Okay." I've turned our arguments around by letting him know my state of mind. "Hey, this is where I'm at. Don't fix me."

This strategy has helped Zaira and me immensely. Another tip that Rachel and Scott gave us is the art of positioning when we provide feedback. When Scott provides feedback to Rachel, especially if it is unsolicited feedback, he leads with a positioning statement. His positioning statement goes like this:

> Hey, this is just a piece of advice or a story that is similar to the experience you are having. You do not have to do this. This is just what I have to say and what I'm feeling or receiving right now. I'm just going to communicate it and you do what you want.[41]

The strategy of communicating our expectations and then positioning our response has helped us improve our communication and balance being a sympathetic and caring spouse with being a powerful business partner.

Over time, we have gradually improved our business working relationship. Now, when we do have a conflict about something, we trust each other much more. I can honestly say that in our Alpha Couples book and coaching business, we have been 100% partners. Although I did most of the writing, every idea in this book was jointly developed together. We feel like real partners now, not just in words, but in actual practice.

Our partnership extends beyond just the law firm and this book. We also began to treat our real estate as a partnership. It took a while to transition from the idea of our individual properties to joint properties, but the mindset shift has helped us get financial benefits. Here is an example: When we got married, I owned two properties and Zaira owned one. We each bought our properties with our own savings. My annual interest rates were 3.25% while Zaira's was 4.5%. For three years, Zaira paid her mortgage and I paid mine. Both Zaira and

---

41 Robert & Zaira Solano feat. Rachel and Scott Baker (2019). "Rachel and Scott Baker," *Alpha Couples Podcast, 1.* Available at AlphaCouplesThrive.com/podcast

I felt like the properties were our individual responsibilities. I continued to make extra principal payments to my properties and was on track to pay off my first loan in less than fifteen years.

It takes a lot of time, energy, and trust to let someone else be co-owner of your life's work.

Once we stopped thinking about our real estate as our individual properties, and began to think of them as joint properties, I realized that I should be paying extra principal payments to Zaira's higher interest rate property instead of mine. The Sol Co jointly owned all three properties. It took us a long time to break through our old paradigms of *mine* and *yours*. By paying off Zaira's mortgage before mine, in the long run we will save approximately $25,000 in interest. This is another reason why merged accounts are required for a partnership mindset.

Merging our bank accounts was actually the easy part of establishing the partnership. It was much harder to actually think of each other as partners and treat each other as such. Hardworking, ambitious Alpha personalities usually spend a lot of time working on their businesses. If your spouse does not work with you, it is easy to think that "I invest all of my time and energy into my business, I do all the hard work, therefore I call the shots."

In marriage, partnership is a state of mind that is built on respect, trust, and cooperation. Partnership is not proportional to the amount of work you do, the title you hold, or how much money you contribute. Nor does it require that each partner's name be listed on the company letterhead or articles of incorporation. More than anything, partnership is about how you treat each other.

But in actuality, our spouses also invest a lot of time in our businesses. They travel with us to work conferences, or are left home alone when not. They deal with us working on the laptop in bed, get date night interrupted with work-related text messages, have their sex life decrease because of our work stress, and put up with our work in countless other ways. Even if your spouse never works directly in your business, they almost certainly are investing their time and energy into your business's success. That investment is yet another reason why we should treat our spouses as partners of our businesses. Their investment also gives them the right to question our decisions and hold us accountable when we fail to meet our goals. They deserve the right to be partners through marriage and also through putting up with our shit.

The idea that I am part owner of my wife's law firm because I married her may be a little jarring—this is counter to the way that our modern society is conditioned to think and it flies in the face of the strong independent women narrative that ladies are told—but this kind of shared ownership mentality is exactly the way couples need to think if they truly want to be partners in life.

The same is true for men who may be entrepreneurs if their wife is not. Partnership goes both ways. It is also important to note that for this kind of relationship to work, I inversely needed to treat Zaira as partner of my career, my retirement accounts, my rental properties, my coaching business, and this book.

It takes a lot of time, energy, and trust to let someone else be co-owner of your life's work. Most couples are not 100% partners the day they get married—Zaira and I sure were not. It takes a lot of time to learn how to trust your partner's judgment, to develop a system to manage finances, to resolve decisions that you strongly disagree about, and to really put your marriage ahead of ego.

Some couples may never truly be partners because the level of business and financial acumen between the partners is too wide to overcome. This is why it helps to have similar intellect, education, and experience with our partners, and why it is important to continue to try to grow and develop together both personally and professionally. Equality only works if both partners are truly capable of being equals.

I am confident that the strongest marriages are equal partnerships, which is why we continue to try to be better partners—in all things. More than anything, Zaira and I are committed to the learning and growing process and hope that every year we become better partners for each other.

Today, the organization of the fictional Sol Co looks something like this:

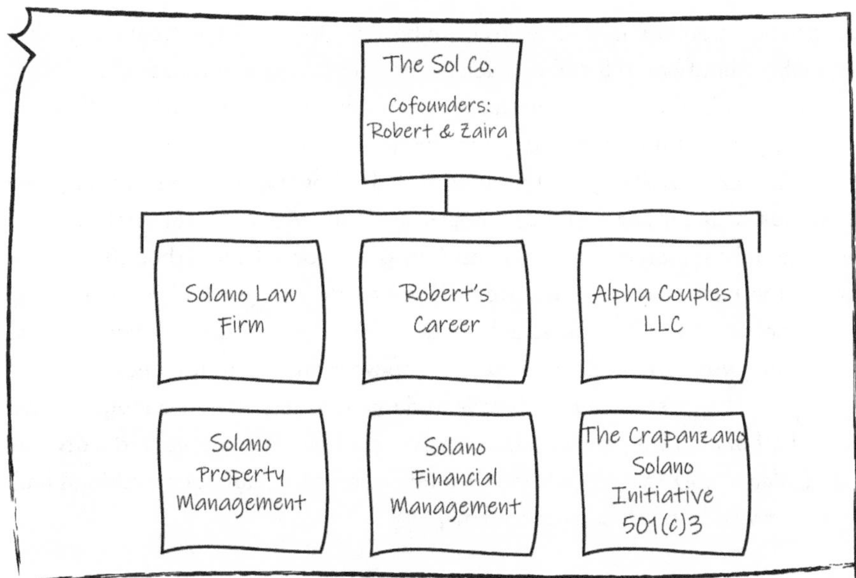

As you may notice, The Sol Co has grown since we started our marriage. Today, it includes Alpha Couples and the Crapanzano-Solano Initiative (our 501(c)3 nonprofit organization).[42]

We jointly manage our rental properties and financial assets. Although we each have our individual roles and responsibilities for each of these organizations, we try as best we can, to improve our partnership as we challenge each other and work together to change the world.

Some people will question this approach and worry, "That means that my husband could take half of everything if we got divorced!"

Stop thinking this way. This isn't a book about getting divorced. This is a book about building a powerful marriage that thrives. If you are worrying about divorce, then you are wasting energy which could be used to build a powerful marriage.

Partnership is a way of framing your marriage. I am not advocating that you list your spouse as 50/50 partner on every single business or asset that you own. On paper, I am the sole proprietor of Alpha Couples and Zaira is the sole

---

42 The Crapanzano-Solano initiative is dedicated to uplifting underprivileged and underrepresented communities throughout the United States and abroad. We currently have two main efforts. The first is providing mentorship and academic scholarships for underrepresented minorities. The second is donating clothing and household supplies to impoverished communities in the Dominican Republic. You can find out more about our initiative or donate by visiting www.robertsolano.com/initiative

proprietor of Solano Law Firm. You can be 100% partners and treat each other as such without being listed on each other's articles of incorporation.

The truth is, that even if you have a prenuptial agreement and are listed as the sole proprietor or owner of your business, properties, and bank accounts, your partner is probably still entitled to half of everything you own anyway! Just look at MacKenzie and Jeff Bezos. Jeff built Amazon from nothing and was the richest man in the world—until he got divorced. Even though he could afford the best lawyers in the world, his ex-wife still got half of everything, a whopping $38 billion. Just accept that your spouse already owns half of everything you own, and then you can stop worrying about divorce.

Ultimately, we should already love and respect our partners enough to give them half of anything anyway. If Zaira ever decided that she wanted a divorce *(God, please no!),* I would, without hesitation, give her half of everything I had.

In her wedding vows, Zaira told me,

> I promise to be your partner in crime as we foster and cherish a relationship of equality, knowing that together we will build a life far better than either one of us could imagine alone.

Without actually committing any crimes, I plan to take her up on that offer and reciprocate in kind.

LET'S RECAP

- **Marriage is very similar to a business partnership. By supporting each other's goals, troubleshooting ideas, and challenging each other to dig deeper, you can create a powerful relationship that can change the world.**
- **True partnership should include all aspects of your personal lives, finances, and business.**
- **Ego and distrust are the biggest inhibitors to partnership. You and your partner can develop trust through intentional business discussions, shared financial responsibilities, developing common goals, and open communication.**

CHAPTER TWENTY-ONE

VENUS VS. MARS

"Shawty like Pac, me Big Poppa." —Jay-Z

Zaira travels almost every week and is often up late in bed booking flights. She enjoys arranging her travel at the end of the day because completing the small task of booking a flight or making a hotel reservation gives her a sense of accomplishment to finish her day.

While she enjoys booking travel in bed, this habit frustrates the hell out of me. I constantly tell her that working in bed late at night is unhealthy, that her assistant should book travel for her, and that it interrupts our Netflix and chill time.

"Next month I'm flying to Atlanta on Tuesday the 17th," she said as she sat in bed with her laptop. "Do you think I should fly back on Friday, or stay through the weekend and fly back on Monday the 23rd?"

It was after 11 p.m. and we were in bed. "I don't know," I said as I watched an episode of *Lost in Space*. "Does it look like I'm calendaring right now?"

She huffed and continued to scroll through flight options.

I had work the next day and wanted to go to sleep. I planned to turn the TV off as soon as Zaira was done working so that we could go to sleep together at the same time. After another ten minutes passed without any indication that she would be done soon, I told her, "Zaira, it's almost midnight. Shut off the laptop and go to sleep."

"Soon," she continued to click away. "I just need to book this flight."

On the television, the robot chimed, *"Danger, Will Robinson."*

I knew that her trip was still three weeks away and told her, "The flight will still be there tomorrow. Go to bed."

After giving her this advice twice, she started ignoring me.

I knew that I would not be able to fall asleep with her next to me on the laptop. It was now after midnight and she was still working, "Zaira! Go to fucking bed!"

"Danger, Will Robinson. Danger. Danger."

I should have listened to the robot.

"You don't need to curse," she said as she got out of bed with her laptop and stormed to the guest bedroom.

I finished my episode of *Lost in Space* and then went to sleep. When I woke up a few hours later to go to the bathroom, I noticed that her side of the bed was still empty. I walked over to the guest bedroom and found her asleep, with the nightstand lights still on, her laptop opened on the bed, and drool coming from her sideways mouth. I suspected that instead of going to sleep after she booked the flight, she proceeded to work until she passed out. I turned the lights off for her, put the laptop on the nightstand, and then went back to sleep in our bed.

Almost all couples occasionally get into arguments and disagreements; Zaira and I are no different. What makes Zaira and me a little unique, and what we share with many professional and entrepreneurial couples, is that we are both type A—ambitious, goal-oriented, conscientious, and driven.[43]

Knowing what personality type someone is helps us understand their behavior, reactions, values, and priorities. Similarly, if you know your own personality type and that of your partner, you'll have an easier time understanding why you two do have disagreements when you do.

You probably already know if you are a type A or type B personality, but if

---

43 Meyer Friedman & Ray Rosenman (1959). "Association of Specific Overt Behaviour Pattern with Blood and Cardiovascular Findings: Blood Cholesterol Level, Blood Clotting Time, Incidence of Acrus Senilis, and Clinical Coronary Artery Disease," *Journal of the American Medical Association.*

Although we view type A personalities as ambitious, driven, and goal-oriented, it is interesting to note that the term was originally used to describe work behaviors that lead to heart attacks. *Type A* personality traits is a term coined by Drs. Friedman and Rosenman in the 1950s. The history of the term is this: Friedman and Rosenman worked together as cardiologists. One day, they got the fabric on the chairs in their waiting room replaced and the upholsterer brought to their attention that the chairs were unusually worn on the forward edge of the seat. Friedman and Rosenman speculated that the wear pattern had to do with the personalities of the clients who suffered from heart disease. Intrigued by this observation, they conducted a study where they divided professionals into different groups based upon their work behaviors. Group A members were selected based upon their "intense, sustained drive for achievement and as being continually involved in competition and deadlines, both at work and in their avocations." While group B members had the opposite characteristics. Group A people were quite literally people who spent most of their lives on the edge of their seats. After studying these type A and type B personalities for over eight years, Friedman and Rosenman found that "clinical coronary artery disease was seven times more frequent in group A than in group B...." (Bad news for type A personalities like Zaira and me.)

you are unsure or want to assess your other personality dimensions, you can take a quick and easy personality assessment at alphacouplesthrive.com/test. 

It is important for you to understand your personality traits because our traits affect our reactions to different environments, events, and feelings. For example, an introvert may get nervous in large crowds, a neurotic person may get anxiety from unfortunate news, and an open-minded person may easily upset in a room of conservatives.

Usually, we are attracted to people with similar personalities to ourselves. Usually this isn't bad and this natural attraction works out great. For example, a very open-minded couple would be happy to go to Burning Man, an introverted couple might be happy to stay at home on a Friday playing board games, and an agreeable couple would never disagree with their partner's restaurant selection. But when it comes to Alpha Couples—almost always made up of two ambitious, self-disciplined, goal-oriented people— they usually butt heads in predictable ways.

To begin, Alphas are career-driven people. It is not uncommon for an Alpha to make their career a priority over their relationships and personal lives—this is especially true during the early stages of a relationship. Some couples will be fortunate and have careers that do not impact their relationship, but as is the case with Zaira and me, many professional and entrepreneur couples will make career choices that definitely will impact their relationship.

In an Alpha Couple relationship, our marriage can experience a lot of friction and tension if we ask our spouse to make sacrifices to their careers. The same is true if our spouse asks us to make sacrifices for our careers.

Another challenge with Alpha Couple relationships is that we tend to be perfectionists and workaholics who are more susceptible to burnout and work-related exhaustion. This is why type A personalities, especially men, have a higher risk of cardiovascular disease. As a couple, these traits can lead to serious relationship and health issues if left unchecked.

A final challenge that Alpha Couples face is that both Alphas like to be in control, and that's not always possible. Alpha personalities take pleasure, to some degree, in their stress. This is why Zaira consistently works past midnight, enjoys booking her own travel, and hates when I tell her what to do. Here are some other things that upset type A people:

- Receiving criticism
- Failure
- Disorganization

- Poor performance
- Little attention to detail
- Changes to plans
- Coming up short of goals

Although these would upset many types of people, they make type A people abnormally upset. In fact, they can make a type A person so upset that they trigger the person's physiological fight-or-flight response. And, between two people like us, a vicious cycle can start. Zaira triggered me by staying up late and working. My fight-or-flight response was activated, and I chose fight: "Go to fucking bed!" This, in turn, triggered her fight-or-flight response—she chose flight.

The first step in avoiding marriage-destroying arguments is to recognize when we get triggered.

When we get triggered, a few interesting things happen in our bodies. First, our heart rate elevates, our muscles tense up, and our senses become heightened. In our brain, our prefrontal cortex—the part of the brain responsible for rational thought—begins to shut down. Decision-making shifts to our limbic system, the area at the base of our brain responsible for primordial instincts like fight or flight. These physiological changes prepare our mind and body to fight or run. Although something like feeling out of control does not present the same physical threat as a tiger, our bodies' physiological response to the two scenarios is nearly the same.

Another characteristic of my personality that exacerbates our arguments is that I hate feeling undervalued. I could explain at least ten scientifically documented reasons why working on her laptop, in bed, at midnight was unhealthy for Zaira and our relationship. I have explained some of these reasons to her before, but she once again ignored my professional advice. Her ignoring my advice made me feel unappreciated and disrespected—she wounded my ego by ignoring my advice. As our conversation continued, and she persisted to ignore me, my prefrontal cortex also shut down and my fight-or-flight response took over. I chose to fight and continued to raise my tone, and then began cursing (fighting), until she escaped to the guest room (flight).

Situations where both partners trigger each other, like this late-night argument with Zaira, are the worst-case scenarios for our relationships. These arguments are more likely to spin out of control and hurt our marriages. In these types of arguments, many of us resort to unhealthy behaviors. For example, I got triggered and cursed at Zaira; Zaira got triggered and worked to the point of passing out. Similarly, I know other people who get triggered and then smoke a pack of cigarettes, open a bottle of Johnny Walker, go to the strip club, throw stuff, punch the wall, or start biting their nails. Whether we bottle our emotions, or release our rage, none of these fight-or-flight habits are healthy and, if left unchecked, they can destroy our marriages.

Although conflict resolution is a very complex discussion that needs a whole book, here are a few lessons that have helped Zaira and me.

The first step in avoiding marriage-destroying arguments is to recognize when we get triggered. When in fight-or-flight mode, it is difficult to self-evaluate, therefore I found it useful to ask Zaira to help me identify my triggers.

When we were levelheaded, far removed from any arguments, I asked Zaira, "What triggers me? What really makes me upset? What causes most of our arguments?"

By asking her these questions and then discussing them with clear heads, we were able to identify that I hate to feel undervalued, underappreciated, or unloved. On the other hand, Zaira hates to feel controlled or demeaned.

Now, when a disagreement begins to devolve into an argument, we try to identify when we see each other get triggered. As our arguments heat up, we pause and tell each other, "I think I'm triggering you. Should we take a pause?" or "I'm getting triggered. Can we talk about this after dinner?"

On many occasions, a small statement like this has helped us take a step back, recompose ourselves, and either finish the conversation rationally, or save it for a different time.

Another technique that we learned from Sara Blakely and Jesse Itzler is to slow dance when upset. When Sara and Jesse get into an argument, they stop, take a pause, and slow dance. They don't have music, they just take a moment, stop arguing, and dance.

I call this technique *grounding*. Even if you don't dance, sometimes just the physical act of holding each other for a moment can dramatically diffuse an argument. It's like electricity. During an argument, we develop polar opposite energies. Those energies build and build and if left unchecked they can result in destructive lightning. The simple strategy of physically holding each other grounds out those energies.

Another healthy behavior that we began practicing is evaluating our physiological states. When I notice one of us getting triggered, I ask myself: *Are either of us tired, exhausted, stressed, hungry, sick, or is Zaira PMSing?*

Ladies, I'm sorry. I know a lot of you get upset if we blame mood swings on your menstrual cycle, but this does, in fact, affect most females' feelings and emotions. But men, you are not immune to this either. We also experience irritable male syndrome (IMS) as our testosterone and cortisol levels change. IMS is not as noticeable as PMS, nor does it occur on a monthly schedule, but it does happen to men, especially as their testosterone levels drop later in life.

It is no surprise that most of our arguments occur late at night, after a long workday, and on empty stomachs. If Zaira or I recognize that we are irritable for any of these physiological reasons, we try to avoid the argument and approach the subject again when we are well rested, fed, and stress-free.

It's as simple as saying, "Babe, it's late at night, we've each had a long day at work, and we had a really light dinner. Can we save this discussion for tomorrow morning? After breakfast, I promise that I will listen to what you have to say."

Delaying an argument until the next morning has resolved over 90% of our relationship conflict. Most of the time we realize how stupid the argument was in the first place and never bring it up again. We have learned that going to sleep angry is much better for our marriage than duking it out before bed.

If you would like to explore conflict resolution even further, I recommend the book *The Seven Principles for Making Marriage Work* by John Gottman and Nan Silver. John and Nan have studied thousands of couples and in their book they share the habits that can destroy a marriage and tips to avoid them.  If you would like a full list of my favorite relationship books, you can also check out my recommended reading list at www.robertsolano.com/relationship-books.

LET'S RECAP

- Alpha couples are usually type A personalities. These characteristics—ambitiousness, perfectionism, workaholism, etc.—make them more susceptible to burnout and work-related exhaustion.
- Alphas usually have predictable emotional triggers. A relationship can turn ugly when both partners get triggered at the same time.
- Avoid arguing when you are tired, hungry, stressed, or in a poor physiological state. Delaying an argument for the next morning can save your relationship.

CHAPTER TWENTY-TWO

BREAK UP TO MAKE UP

"You and me, havin sex, after an argument, that shit's the best." —Jay-Z

Whether your car, your house, or your marriage, if you want it to last for a while, it requires maintenance.

In many ways, marriage is like a car. When we are dating, we take the new Porsche for a test ride. We take it for a spin around the block, and maybe the dealer even lets us take the car home for the night. We fall in love with the sunroof, chrome rims, stereo system, heated seats, and leather interior. The next day, we go to the dealer with our checkbook in hand and a few hours later we drive off the lot with our brand-new Porsche. The first few weeks, we love our new car. We wash it every week and we avoid parking under any trees for fear that a falling acorn would dent the hood.

But four years later, we start to neglect our car. We forget to change the oil, we drive around with worn windshield wipers, the leather seats are beginning to look worn, and the car skids a little in the rain because the tires are worn out. Yep, after a few years we start to consider trading our Porsche in for a newer model. We blame the car and say that we don't like it because it is old, but in reality, the car is performing poorly because of our own negligence. For years, we forgot to give the car proper maintenance and now we hold that against it.

If we took care of the car and changed the oil regularly, replaced the tires, and got her detailed once in a while, the car would have been in excellent condition for another five to ten years. With really good maintenance, the car could have become a classic.

Similarly, there are certain things that we can do ourselves to maintain our marriage. We can schedule date nights, take vacations together, or renew our vows, but eventually, all marriages need to see a mechanic.

Zaira and I began seeing a marriage counselor before we got married and continue to periodically see a counselor today. When we first began seeing a counselor, it was because we had relationship trouble. While we were dating in Atlanta, we broke up for a few months. At the time, I was still recovering from my divorce and felt like I was getting rushed into another marriage. I was afraid that Zaira would give me an ultimatum that we needed to get engaged if I wanted her to move. I felt like I was losing control and getting rushed into marriage, so I dumped her. This was my fight-or-flight response.

Eventually, I realized my mistake and begged for her forgiveness. Zaira took me back, but only on the condition that we saw a counselor. The counselor helped us communicate openly with each other in a way that was difficult to do otherwise. The counselor asked us questions and gave us exercises to help draw out our buried emotions and feelings, and she helped us discuss those emotions in a safe, nonthreatening environment.

Usually, we schedule four to six sessions once every two years or so. We try to schedule our counseling sessions regardless of whether our marriage is going well or has trouble. Sometimes the car needs a tune up, not because it's broken, but just because it needs some tweaking. On many occasions, a marriage counselor helped us identify and talk through areas of conflict in our relationship that neither of us were consciously aware of, but that nonetheless caused tension. One such topic area was with trying to get pregnant.

When we got married, we agreed to try to get pregnant as soon as possible, but for the first three years of our marriage, life events made that goal very difficult. At first, we had frequent travel to Mexico and the Dominican Republic during the Zika outbreak. After each visit to these places, we cautiously waited three months before trying to get pregnant. Then, Zaira broke her foot and needed monthly X-rays for six months. During this time, her doctor recommended she wait until after the X-rays before getting pregnant. In retrospect, I am not sure how sound that advice was, but we erred on the side of caution. Besides the Zika concerns and X-rays, our individual travel also occasionally impacted our pregnancy chances—it was hard to get pregnant during ovulation when we were not in the same state. When we were clear of Zika and X-rays, we tried to time our sex to get pregnant. We had sex every other day during ovulation. Still, month after month, nothing happened.

Getting pregnant was our goal as a couple, but three years after agreeing to start a family, we were no closer to getting pregnant. Over time, we each developed a huge amount of emotional baggage. We rarely acknowledged or discussed our feelings about pregnancy and infertility. We never argued about it, but we didn't really talk about it either. Our marriage counselor helped shine a light on those issues and communicate more productively.

Seeing a marriage counselor was like we took the car in for a tune-up, and the mechanic said, "It's a good thing you came in when you did because your brake line was leaking. Another hundred miles, and you could have gotten into a serious accident!"

As I write this, in year four of our marriage, Zaira and I continue to try to get pregnant and are preparing for in vitro fertilization (IVF). Our marriage counselor has helped us confront and discuss our emotions surrounding pregnancy in constructive ways, and we are a much stronger couple because of it.

Other couples frequently experience similar marital tension around topics such as:

- Caring for elderly parents
- Raising a child
- Financial management
- Excessive alcohol or drug use
- Issues with health or illness
- Work-related stress

It's foolish to think that we could understand, discuss, or resolve these issues without professional help. This is why every married couple should periodically see a marriage counselor. Importantly, since we usually are blind to our issues until they become too big to handle, you should schedule marriage counseling sessions even when it feels like your relationship is going great. Periodic visits to a counselor are an excellent environment to air the dirty laundry before these issues fester and ruin your marriage.

Zaira and I also enjoy attending a couples retreat about once a year. A couples retreat is a unique vacation-like package that combines couples counseling, coaching, relationship workshops, and other partnership-building activities. Usually these retreats are three-day weekend getaways, but some may be a full week or more. Couples retreats are no substitute for marriage counseling and will not fix a marriage in crisis, but if combined with other relationship-building activities, a couples retreat is a great way to strengthen a marriage. Zaira and I host our three-day Executive Couples Getaway once per quarter, but there are certainly many other options. You can find out more about our Executive Couples Getaway by visiting alphacouplesthrive.com/getaway.

It is important to note that marriage counselors are different from marriage coaches. Marriage counselors are licensed professionals who require a certain level of education and certification. They are usually licensed in specific states and have to comply with various state policies and regulatory guidance.

Marriage counselors typically charge by the hour—usually between $50–$300, and sometimes, health insurance or employer benefits will cover the cost of counseling.

In contrast to marriage counselors, anyone could be a coach. There are certainly coach education and certification programs. For example, there are prestigious programs at business schools like Georgetown University and there are different certification levels from organizations like the International Coach Federation. On the other end of the spectrum, there are janky $49 online programs that certify coaches as soon as their credit card payment clears. Some of the best coaches are uncertified, and some of the most certified coaches are mediocre at best. When it comes to coaches, there is a huge spectrum of bad, good, and world-class.

The biggest difference between a counselor and a coach is that a counselor is focused on the past or present while a coach is focused on the future. A counselor helps you deal with your emotional baggage, improve your communication, and strengthen your resilience so that you can have optimal mental health and a healthy relationship. In contrast, a coach is focused toward your future as a couple.

I am a coach. My goal is to meet my clients wherever they are in their life, and then help them achieve their goals. I help people with their business, professional, and personal goals. I am an expert in organizational behavior, leadership, and goal setting, but I am not a licensed counselor, nor am I an expert in conflict resolution, sex therapy, or behavior disorders. The difference between a counselor and coach is subtle, but the two roles should not be confused. Although some marriage counselors are also marriage coaches, they serve different and distinct purposes.

Here is a summary of the difference between counselors and coaches:

Marriage Counselor	Marriage Coach
Certified education and experience requirements. Regulated by state agencies. Counselors must be licensed.	Optional certifications and education. Not regulated by states.
Usually a general practitioner. Focused on conflict resolution, communication, and mental health.	Focused on helping clients achieve future goals.
Charge by the hour, usually $50-$300 per hour.	Usually charge by the product, can be $99 for online training, or over $100,000 for a yearlong program.
May be covered by insurance or employer benefits.	Not covered.
Can be certified to deal with different behavior conditions, such as clinical depression, bipolar disorder, or post-traumatic stress disorder.	Not certified.

Like any professional service, the quality of marriage counselors and coaches varies greatly—some are terrible, and some are phenomenal. If you have never seen a counselor or coach, I recommend that you start with a marriage counselor.

Many couples are hesitant to share with their friends that they are seeing a marriage counselor. This is because marriage counseling is taboo for many social groups. I have observed this to be especially true for Black and Latino communities, like the ones that Zaira and I grew up in. I think this taboo exists because these communities have a strong sense of pride and privacy. They think that family business should be kept within the family and that a married couple should be able to figure out their own problems. These cultures believe that troubled partners should turn to their parents or older aunts and uncles for help, not an outside expensive professional. I hope that more people learn to understand and appreciate the help of marriage counselors.

When Zaira and I moved to Tampa, we needed to find a new marriage counselor. We asked our Facebook friends for help and posted, "Hey, married friends, anyone have any recommendations for a great marriage counselor near Tampa? No issues, we just like to see one for periodic maintenance. Thanks." In addition to asking our Facebook friends for recommendations, we also Googled local marriage counselors. The search results for a city like Tampa were overwhelming.

When we look for a new marriage counselor, we treat it like a job interview. We start by reviewing their website and online reviews, then call their office.

Here are some examples of questions that we ask the counselor or receptionist:

- What kind of counseling services do you provide?
- Does your office specialize in any areas?
- Could you tell more about your background and experience in marriage counseling?
- Do you have a lot of experience counseling professional or entrepreneur couples?
- How long are sessions and what is the recommended frequency?
- Could we schedule sessions in the evening, on weekends, or via video calls?
- What are the rates per session?
- Does your office accept any insurance providers?

Zaira and I learned that many counselors are general therapists. They will counsel anyone who comes through the door. In one day, they may counsel someone with severe depression, another couple on the brink of divorce, and someone else with anger management issues. We will make occasional exceptions for a great counselor, but in general, we prefer counselors who specialize in couples therapy.

The biggest difference between a counselor and a coach is that a counselor is focused on the past or present while a coach is focused on the future.

We schedule an initial counseling session with two or three different counselors before we settle on one. When we looked for a counselor in Florida, we had three bad experiences before we found our regular counselor. First, we met a marriage coach. Our initial free video consultation with her was great, but her yearlong coaching program cost $100,000, which was incredibly outside of our price range. Then we met a local marriage counselor for an hour-long session.

She talked almost the entire time and barely let us say anything. The next marriage counselor we met was almost the exact opposite. She let us talk the entire time and barely offered any help or guidance. Finally, we met a marriage counselor who was just right. She gently steers our conversations, provides Zaira and me equal opportunities to express ourselves, and offered tips and advice along the way. As an added bonus, the cost of our sessions was covered by my employer benefits.

A common mistake that couples make is going to a counselor when they need to settle an argument, or when they want to fix their partner. Even Michelle Obama admitted this when she shared, "I was one of those wives who thought, 'I'm taking you to marriage counseling so you can be fixed, Barack Obama.' "[44]

If you want to break a tie, I recommend you play rock, paper, scissors as Sara Blakely and Jesse Itzler do when they have a disagreement. A marriage counselor will rarely side with one partner or the other and instead of trying to fix your partner, a good counselor will usually turn the mirror on you.

As a final thought on marriage counselors, many inexperienced couples treat marriage counseling like going to the emergency room. They don't visit the physician until they have something wrong such as back pain, migraines, broken hip, or type 2 diabetes. If you get diagnosed with type 2 diabetes, a doctor can prescribe medicine to improve your quality of life, but you will have permanent limitations from the disease.

Similarly, many couples never visit a marriage counselor until they are preparing for divorce. At this point in a relationship, a marriage counselor can usually diagnose your relationship problem and provide some treatment to reduce the intensity of arguments, but the relationship may never be as strong as it was before the breaking point. Most couples who only see a counselor when they are already considering divorce do end up getting divorced. This is why some counselors will not see couples considering divorce—by that point, couples are going to the emergency room and it is usually too late.

Instead, you should think of marriage counselors or coaches like personal trainers. Ideally, we hire personal trainers before we have injuries or illnesses. Trainers can help us live a happy and healthy life and maintain that life once we achieve our goals. They can give us meaningful, actionable, and practical advice, diets, and training strategies to help us live a healthy life and hopefully prevent an injury before it happens.

Similarly, we should see a marriage counselor or coach while our marriage is

---

44 Michelle Obama (2018), *The Tonight Show Starring Jimmy Fallon*.

healthy. A good counselor can give us tips, advice, and exercises to maintain a healthy and happy relationship—marriage counseling is best used as preventive medicine. You need to condition your marriage the same way you condition your body, and a professional counselor is usually the best way to do that.

Most couples reading this are probably looking for tips on how they can work better with their spouse, how they can increase their wealth, how they can spice up their sex life, or how they can be like Jay-Z and Beyoncé. Marriage counseling may not be the sexiest topic, but strong communication and conflict management are the foundation of any powerful marriage. In your marriage, counseling and coaching are preventative maintenance tools that can prevent the wheels from falling off.

Zaira and I had a hard time finding a good marriage coach. As busy executives and entrepreneurs, it was difficult to find someone that could understand our unique personalities. Fortunately, we were able to find a few phenomenal marriage coaches who understand couples like us. We have partnered with these coaches and developed a coaching program to help other executive and entrepreneur couples.

If you are a boss couple, and want to build a powerful marriage, visit www.alphacouplesthrive.com/coaching

LET'S RECAP

- Seeking a marriage counselor or coach is a sign of your commitment to each other and not a sign that your relationship is in trouble.
- Couples should periodically see a marriage counselor even when they think their marriage is going great. There is always room to improve communication and it helps to have a third party identify any trouble areas in your relationship before they lead to conflict.
- Marriage counselors, coaches, and couples retreats serve different purposes. Your marriage can benefit from a combination of all three.

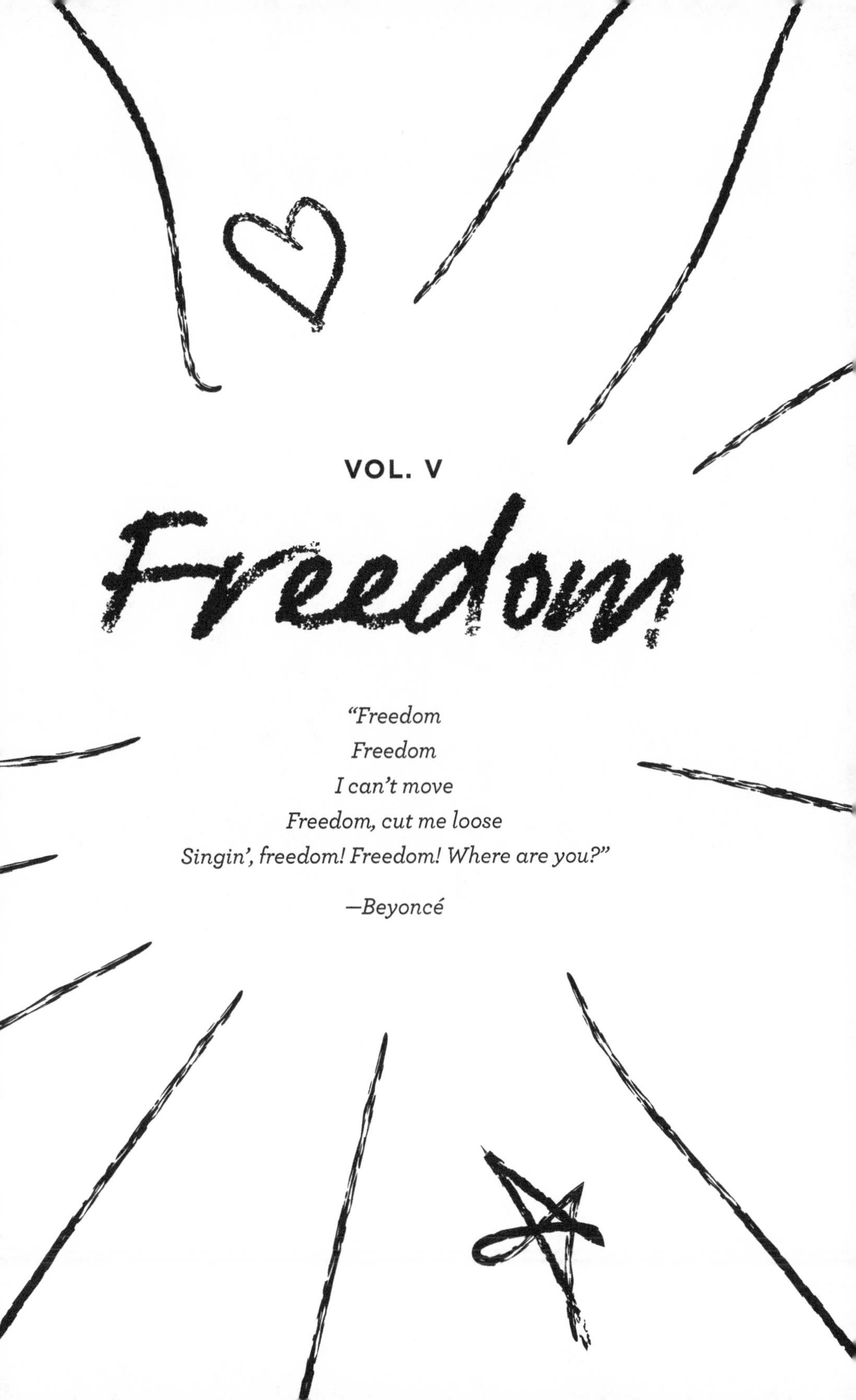

VOL. V

Freedom

"Freedom
Freedom
I can't move
Freedom, cut me loose
Singin', freedom! Freedom! Where are you?"

—Beyoncé

CHAPTER TWENTY-THREE

LOVEHAPPY

"Long way to go, but we'll work it." —The Carters

Occasionally, Zaira and I rent a power boat, invite some friends over, and then cruise up to one of the secluded beaches near Clearwater, Florida. We have always enjoyed these day trips and a few years ago I got an idea. Instead of these short trips, we could take a longer trip on a sailboat in the Caribbean.

At first, it was only an idea. I didn't know anything about sailboats, but it seemed like a great experience. I searched Google for "sailboat, Caribbean, friends" and found a photo that I liked. The photo was of a sailboat, anchored in emerald water, with four sun-kissed people in bathing suits and bikinis. The two guys on the boat were chatting and smiling while one lady sunbathed and the other dived into the magnificently clear water. I wanted to experience whatever those people were experiencing.

The photo invoked feelings of relaxation, warmth, seclusion, friendship, and fun. I showed Zaira the photo and told her that we should make it a goal to go sailing with friends in the Caribbean. She agreed that it was a good idea. We weren't sure how we would get there, but we knew that we wanted to be there. I framed the photo and hung it on the wall outside my bedroom. It was one of the first photos of my *vision wall.*

When Zaira and I moved from Orlando to Tampa, we bought a house a half mile from the local marina, which offered free sailing lessons every Thursday night. Free sailing lessons seemed like a perfect first step toward our sailing goals.

We were excited to learn to sail, but then life happened. I worked late every Thursday, and on the few days that I did get home early, Zaira was out of town on work. Every few months, Zaira and I discussed our goal to go sailing, but we never went. We always had a good reason why we needed to delay sailing for another week or month. I walked by that sailing photo every morning and every night for two years and never touched a sailboat. *So much for a vision wall,* I thought.

Almost all of us have our own sailboats. Some of us want to take a trip to Europe, others want to move to a new city, start a business, or have children. It seems like there are always things that prevent us from pursuing our goals—"a Europe trip is too expensive," "I'm too busy to take a vacation," "finding a job in a new city is too hard," or "we'll try to get pregnant after we have more money saved up." Usually these excuses are based in reality, but they are still limiting beliefs.

Whether we realize it or not, most of the goals that we aspire to in life require us to move outside our comfort zones. Whether our goals are learning how to sail, moving to a new city, or raising a family, each of these activities represents something new and something a bit risky.

Our unconscious hates new things. It preferers the safety and security of repeating the same habits day after day. Our subconscious has an uncanny ability to deceive us. By merely shifting our focus it can change our logical decision-making process and trick us into believing that a trip to Europe is too expensive, that a new city has unacceptably high crime rates, or that the weather is too cold for sailing. In most cases, these beliefs are false—a trip to Europe can be relatively cheap, every city has high and low crime areas, and we can sail in a wide range of weather conditions.

Change is required for growth, but our subconscious is incredibly adept at preventing change. This, in turn, limits our growth. For two years, my subconscious prevented me from sailing the ocean. Instead, I sailed over excuse after excuse.

One particularly despicable tactic of my subconscious was selective memory. Usually, while relaxing over the weekend, I would remember my wish to go to sailing. But whenever Thursday approached, I would forget about the free lessons. I always seemed to remember sailing when there was nothing I could do about it—for example, when I was away for work travel or when it was Thursday and I had to work late.

Another master tactic that my brain used to prevent me from sailing was shifting responsibility to Zaira. I told myself that Zaira and I set this goal together, therefore, if she was out of town, I needed to wait for a different week when Zaira would be home and available to sail together. When I shifted responsibility to her, I could postpone my goal guilt-free.

One day, I looked at the photo on my vision wall that was mocking me and, in the words of William Ernest Henley, said, "Enough is enough. 'I am the master of my fate. I am the captain of my soul!' I need to go sailing."

I searched the internet and found three local sailing companies. I called each of them and asked, "Do you have any sailing lessons this weekend?"

The first company did not answer their phone, the second company emailed me a class schedule—the next available class was in six weeks—and I left a voicemail for the third company.

Later that night, the third company called me back and the receptionist told me, "Yes, we have one spot available for a sailing lesson this weekend. It costs..."

"It's okay," I cut her off. "Sign me up. Can I give you my credit card now?"

Two days later, I was on a boat learning the basics of tacking, jibs, helms, and bowline knots. A few weeks later, Zaira also attended a basic sailing class. We spent the rest of the summer learning how to sail together and spent plenty of fun and enjoyable days cruising around Tampa Bay.

That experience, and others like it, have taught me the importance of a vision wall. My vision wall technique is a cousin to the vision board, which are typically collages where people post motivational quotes and images that are intended to help them achieve their goal through the Law of Attraction.

For most of my life, I thought that vision boards were cheesy tactics of campy self-help gurus and life coaches. The first person I ever met with a vision board was an old roommate. At the time, he worked in an entry-level position like me, but in his spare time he was part of one of those sketchy pyramid schemes that promised to make people rich. He sold products like electronic accessories, but his main goal was to recruit other participants to join the pyramid scheme. In his room, he had a vision board with a photo of a G-6 Gulfstream jet and sticky notes with quotes like, "Get rich or die trying," and "The dream is free. The hustle is sold separately." Considering that my friend was in an entry-level position and barely sold a dozen cell phone chargers each month, I could not see how his little vision board was going to attract a G-6 jet. Fifteen years later, I look back and think that my roommate may have been on to something.

What I eventually realized is that vision boards or vision walls can be a great goal-setting technique. Instead of relying on the Law of Attraction, Zaira and I use our vision wall to set goals and then actively take steps to advance toward those goals. We skip the photos of jets and mansions, and instead have photos of goals that we hope to achieve within the next five years. Each photo on our vision wall represents a specific goal for our family, home, work, or other area of our life. We think that anything more than five years in the future is a dream, and not a goal, which is why we do not have photos of Gulfstream jets or Lamborghinis. We call it a vision wall instead of a vision board because it takes up an entire wall in our house.

Ultimately, our vision wall is a way for us to work together toward intentional goals. This is critically important for your relationship regardless of which visioning technique you use. Will Smith described it like this:

> If you don't have a purpose for your relationship, if you don't have a place that you're going, something that you want to accomplish, something that you want to do, you can really get lost in the murk of the journey... There has to be a vision.

Will's amazing wife, Jada Pinkett, also added,

> We're two big beings that came together, and I had my vision and he had his. So, we had to join it [our visions]. [45]

Today, Zaira and I develop our vision wall together; we update it every two or three years, which usually coincides with when we move to a new house or city. We start by each searching the internet for photos that represent our dream house, our ideal businesses, future family, dream vacations, or other parts of our ideal life. We save those photos and then, together, pick out about ten that we both agree most represent our ideal life together. We print them as large glossy photos and frame them in the center of our foyer outside of our bedroom. In the middle, we put a photo of us from our wedding day and a quote. The current quote is from Anaïs Nin: "Life shrinks or expands in proportion to one's courage."

Most people who walk by our vision wall think that it is merely a really nice set of photos from our past vacations. Until they inevitably ask something like, "That photo of the elephants is awesome. Did you go on a safari or something?"

"No, but one of our goals within the next two years is to see elephants in the wild in Africa."

Even our wedding photo in the middle of the wall is a goal: Every day we are married we want to be even more in love than we were on our wedding day.

Creating the vision wall helped us in many ways. To begin, it forced us to take our dreams and turn them into something tangible. Ideas become more powerful when we articulate them in writing, photos, art, or speech.

The vision wall process also forces Zaira and me to communicate our dreams and share them with each other. If we disagree about something, we can talk through our disagreement and try to set goals that we both agree on. For example, when I wanted to live in the countryside, but she wanted to live in the city, we talked about our differences and tried to come up with a middle ground. We brainstormed options like having a house in a city with enough

45 Will and Jada Pinkett Smith (2010). *Oprah.*

property for a vegetable garden or having a house in the countryside while keeping a small condo in the city.

Whether we realize it or not, most of the goals that we aspire to in life require us to move outside our comfort zones.

The vision wall process also forced us to prioritize our goals. This is one area that I failed at when I began my wall with the sailing photo. Although I had started the vision wall, I made excuse after excuse as to why I could not go sailing. Now, instead of just a jumble of photos, Zaira and I prioritize the desires from our vision wall and they become joint goals.

The real secret of our vision wall is our quarterly calendar meeting. Once a quarter, Zaira and I spend a full day going over our calendar for the upcoming year. We always start this day by getting brunch together and discussing our vision wall. We ask each other how we are progressing on our vision and then set milestones to help achieve our goals. For example, in preparation for launching Alpha Couples—the book, couples retreats, and coaching services—we set various milestones on when we would hire an editor, hire a marketing assistant, host a couples retreat, and launch the book. In summary, during our quarterly calendar meetings we review our goals and then set milestones and deadlines to achieve those goals.

Our vision wall also helps us make decisions faster and with less energy. One of our goals was to spend Christmas in Hawaii. I admit that this was originally one of my individual goals. She wanted to visit Hawaii for the first time but did not have a preference for the time of year. I explained to Zaira how amazing Hawaii was, and how Christmas was the perfect time to visit because there would be perfect weather and ideal surf. After we discussed it and she agreed to it, it became a joint goal and got on our vision wall.

During one of our calendar meetings, I turned to Zaira and asked, "Are we going to spend Christmas in Hawaii this year?"

Zaira hesitated and replied, "Some of my family is thinking about going to Dominican Republic this Christmas."

Christmas in Hawaii was on our vision wall—going to Dominican Republic was not. I replied, "It's been our goal to spend Christmas in Hawaii. We can go to Dominican Republic with your family for Thanksgiving, or they can visit us in Hawaii. Hawaii has been on our wall for over a year."

"Okay, you're right," she replied. "Let's go to Hawaii."

At that moment, we reviewed our calendar and picked a good window around the holiday. Then, I turned to our assistant, who was at the calendar meeting with us, and told her, "Please research ticket options for us to go to Hawaii from December 22 to January 5."

A few days later, our assistant came back to us with flight and hotel options. We selected the flights and within a week we had a Hawaiian Christmas vacation booked—another example of how an assistant decreases the activation energy required for change.

Even after assigning our assistant this task, we almost talked ourselves out of the trip. We told ourselves excuses like "the flights to Hawaii and the hotels were really expensive, especially around Christmas," "our parents and cousins would be disappointed if we did not spend the holidays with them," "Dominican Republic is a much cheaper alternative," "spending the holidays with family is really important," and "the flights from Florida to the Dominican Republic are much shorter."

There were dozens of excuses that we could have made to postpone Hawaii, but we agreed that following our vision wall was more important. We decided to ignore our subconscious fears and fully submit to our vision wall. Those excuses were tools that our subconscious fed us to try and keep us in our comfort zone. It is well intentioned—it's trying to protect us—but it's not actually helpful. By submitting to our vision wall and making decisions quickly, we disarmed our subconscious' most powerful weapons.

Hawaii turned out to be one of the best trips we have ever taken. We absolutely loved every day in the islands and look forward to returning. I actually began writing this book during that incredible vacation. Decision-making becomes incredibly easy and less stressful when you set a vision and stick to that goal.

Goal-setting theory is very common in leadership psychology and organizational behavior studies. In business, we teach that goals should be Specific, Measurable, Achievable, Realistic and Time-oriented (SMART). There are certainly some instances in our marriages when it makes sense to have SMART goals. However, when trying to work toward our vision wall goals, SMART can actually hold us back. In particular, measurable, achievable, and realistic assessments are tools that our subconscious can use to trick us into keeping us in our comfort zone.

Instead of SMART goals, I recommend that you SEE your goals. When it comes to your vision wall, goals should be Specific, Exceptional, and Emotional (SEE).

Specific: Your goal should be a specific experience or event in time that you can clearly imagine and visualize. In visualizing your specific experience, you should be able to describe it using your senses. For example, if your goal is to go to Hawaii, where in Hawaii do you want to go? What will you do when you get there? How will it feel when you are at that place?

Specific goals also give you a clear measure of success. Simply landing in Hawaii is not a good goal. There is nothing particular amazing about the airport besides the tourist in floral shirts and orchid lei necklaces. Specific goals give you a clear target that you can aspire toward and a sense of accomplishment when you do finally find yourself drinking a mai tai while watching the sunset on the North Shore.

Exceptional: Your goal should also be exceptional and take you outside of your normal routine or comfort levels. It should be something so far beyond your normal routine that the memory will be seared into your mind for decades to come. For example, one of my goals is to see a magnificent herd of elephants in the wild. There are very few places in the world where this goal is achievable. In order to make this goal happen, I will need to fly around the world to South Africa, then I will need to spend a half day or more traveling deep into the nature reservations where these elephants roam. The experience is so far beyond my normal routine that it challenges my imagination.

The exceptional aspect of your goals will help you become more accustomed to pushing yourself outside of your comfort zone. Even while on vacation, your subconscious will constantly fight to keep you in your comfort zone. This is why so many tourists go to vacations in foreign countries and rarely leave the hotel property. Sitting at the pool of a Marriott Courtyard in Hawaii is not exceptionally different than sitting at the pool of a Marriott Courtyard in Orlando. Exceptional goals should push you outside of your normal comfort zone, which is an important aspect of growth.

Emotional: You should be able to describe how your specific and exceptional goals will make you feel when you do finally experience them. For example, drinking a mai tai while watching the Hawaiian sunset would make me feel peaceful and warm. Watching elephants roam across the Sahara would make me feel awestruck and humble.

The emotional aspect of SEEing your goal will precondition your subconscious to feel those feelings when you do finally achieve your goal. Imagining emotional experiences beforehand also increases the magnitude of those emotional experiences. If you imagine that taking a sunset walk with your wife will make you feel more in love, then you will actually feel more in love when you do eventually take a sunset walk with your wife.

As an added benefit, imagining future emotional experiences will trick your brain into feeling those emotions today. This is because our subconscious has a very difficult time separating imagined emotions from experienced emotions. So, if you imagine that walking on the beach with your wife will make you feel love and happiness, the simple act of imagining that emotion will help you feel more in love with your spouse and happier today.

Decision-making becomes incredibly easy and less stressful when you set a vision and stick to that goal.

Although most of my examples were related to vacations, the same principles apply to other aspects of our life—for instance, getting a new car, launching a business, or growing a garden.

For Zaira and me, our vision wall is the epicenter of our goals. Although we are very happy with our current life, our vision wall reminds us that there are more opportunities to enjoy life even more. By setting goals and then actively and aggressively pursuing those goals, we are constantly challenging ourselves to live a happier, more rewarding, and more love-filled life.

After learning how to sail, Zaira and I still had a photo of a sailboat on our vision wall. Although we enjoyed sailing around Tampa Bay, it was not the crystal-clear water and lazy sunbathing that we envisioned. Then, one day I received an email from our sailing school. The subject was, "Announcing Sail Greece," a seven-day sailing trip around the Aegean Sea.

We previously imagined sailing in the Caribbean, not the Mediterranean, but the flyer for the sailing trip contained a photo of a sailboat that looked just like the sailboat on my vision wall. I forwarded the email to Zaira. "What do you think?"

A few minutes later, she replied, "Let's do it."

I immediately replied to the school's administrator, "Sign us up! Our assistant will call you and provide our credit card info. This looks great! Thank you."

I cc'd our assistant and he called her the following day to provide our info. Within twenty-four hours we were signed up for a seven-day sailing trip in Greece—we had no clue what we were getting into.

Most people would spend weeks or years researching and planning a trip like that before they pulled the trigger. Collectively, Zaira and I spent less than sixty seconds deciding to take a trip to Europe. From the flyer, it appeared that the trip was exactly the kind of experience that we imagined in our vison wall. Fortunately, we received the announcement from our sailing school, which was a trusted source. We had to do it regardless of distance, logistics, or cost—coincidently, it was actually relatively cheap.

Our assistant registered us for the trip and arranged our flight and travel plans. A few months later, we flew from Tampa to Athens and had an amazing week aboard a sailboat in the Aegean Sea. The trip was phenomenal and one of the most memorable trips of our life.

The second day on the boat we anchored for some afternoon swimming in emerald clear water. I stood on the deck of the boat chatting with the captain, as one of the ladies sunbathed, and Zaira jumped into the water. Our goal was specific, exceptional, and emotional—and I knew then and there that we had achieved it all.

LET'S RECAP

- A vision is necessary to live an exceptional, fulfilling, and joyful life. A vision wall is a great tool and can help you transform your vision into specific, exceptional, and emotional goals.
- A vision can improve your decision-making processes. It allows you to say yes to opportunities and no to the distractions and self-doubt. A vision can help you trick your subconscious—when your subconscious wants to hold you back in your comfortable current life, a vision can help you overcome the fear, anxiety, and self-sabotaging that prevents growth.
- I recommend you SEE your goals: They should be Specific, Exceptional, and Emotional.
- A shared vision is a compass that can ensure that you and your spouse are headed in the same direction.

CHAPTER TWENTY-FOUR

ME, MYSELF, AND I

"I took a vow that from now on I'm gon' be my own best friend." —Beyoncé

My divorce devastated me and left a hole in my heart. For a long time afterward, I felt unworthy of love. Even after I met Zaira and fell in love, I still had a lot of residual hurt from my previous marriage. I thought that falling in love again would help me overcome that pain. I expected Zaira to make me happy.

I thought that the purpose of falling in love was to make our partners happy and for them to make us happy in return. It sounds innocent enough, but this actually caused some trouble in our relationship. Since I expected Zaira to make me happy, I took it personally when she didn't. Likewise, I wanted to make Zaira happy and kicked myself when I couldn't.

When I moved to Orlando, I had to learn a new program and negotiate a multimillion-dollar contract almost immediately after starting my new job. At the same time, I had a lot of work for my Ph.D. studies that kept me up late each night. It was a very stressful time in my life.

When I came home from a hectic day at the office, I wished that Zaira would be there to hold it down. I imagined that she would rub my shoulders, relax with me over dinner, and help me decompress. When she was out of town in Atlanta for half the week, I felt resentful.

I also beat myself up when I couldn't offer her the same. There was one particular instance I remember when Zaira was stressed out with work and life. I bought her a bouquet of stargazer lilies, I cooked a romantic dinner for us, I listened to her vent about work, and afterward I even cleaned up the kitchen. I thought I did everything right to help her relax and make her happy, except that after dinner I found her in the bedroom crying. She was still overwhelmed with stress and I felt like I failed as a partner.

It is your individual responsibility to make yourself happy. It is not your spouse's, child's, or friend's job.

It's silly, I know, but I am not alone. Many of us have small areas in our lives where we expect our spouse to make us happy and other areas where we try extra hard to make our spouses happy. I was struggling with this in my life when, once again, Will and Jada Pinkett Smith came through with solid relationship advice. In his Instagram story, he said:

> Me and Jada were reflecting about love, and I asked her, I said, what does she think was one of the biggest revelations that she had about love. She said, "You cannot make a person happy." And I thought that was a real deep idea. You can make a person smile, you can make a person feel good, you can make a person laugh, but whether or not a person is happy, is deeply and totally and utterly out of your control... her happiness was her responsibility and my happiness was my responsibility. And we decided that we were going to find our individual, internal, private, separate joy, and then we were going to present ourselves to the relationship and to each other, already happy. Not coming to each other, begging with our empty cups out, demanding that she fills my cup, and demanding that she meet my needs. It's unfair, it's kind of unrealistic, and can be destructive, to place the responsibility for your happiness on anybody, other than yourself.[46]

"You cannot make another person happy." This statement blew my mind.

For so long, I tried to make my previous girlfriends, ex-wife, and now Zaira happy. Similarly, I expected my lover to make me happy in return. After this revelation, I made a commitment to take more responsibility for my own happiness and to let Zaira take responsibility for hers.

Here's an example: I generally dislike going to the mall with Zaira. When we do go to the mall together, it takes me thirty minutes or less to look through the men's departments at Nordstrom's or Banana Republic. For the other three hours, I follow Zaira around as she drags me between Chanel, Sephora,

46 Will Smith (@willsmith) (2018). Instagram.

Anthropologie, and every other chick store. During these trips, I spend an incredible amount of time sitting outside of dressing rooms, watching shopping bags, and scrolling through my phone. I go to the mall because I want to make Zaira happy, but I hate it. After three hours in the mall, I almost always end up grumpy and argumentative.

Eventually, I took Will's advice to heart and stopped going to the mall with her. I realized that it was not my responsibility to make Zaira happy. If she wanted to go to the mall, she needed to be happy with or without me. I understand that she wants to spend time with me, but sacrificing my happiness for hers is unfair, unrealistic, and unsustainable.

Zaira will still ask me to go to the mall with her. On a Saturday morning she will say, "Babe, can you come to the mall with me today?"

Sometimes I will go to the mall with her, but usually, I reply, "No, I really don't want to and I have other things to do today, but have fun."

She makes a pouty face, sometimes she will even give me a hug, and then says, "But it would make me really happy."

Ever since I shared Will Smith's video with her, I reply with the same line, "Your happiness is your responsibility and my happiness is my responsibility."

She walks away with a grumpy face and then goes to the mall and returns four hours later, very happy, and with three or four shopping bags.

While she is at the mall, I stay at home by myself and write, exercise, or run my separate errands. After Zaira does return from the mall, we usually order in some pizza and drink wine, and she tells me about her day and tries on her clothes for me. We are both more relaxed and happy, and still spend quality time together. Our quality time after the mall is usually even happier and more enjoyable than it would be if I went to the mall with her.

It is your individual responsibility to make yourself happy. It is not your spouse's, child's, or friend's job. For me, skipping a trip to the mall when I didn't need to shop was one small technique to make myself happier.

LET'S RECAP

- Your happiness is your responsibility, not your husband's or wife's. If you are unhappy, you need to figure out a way to make yourself happy without relying on your spouse.
- Your spouse's happiness is their responsibility. Although you should want to make your spouse happy, it is ultimately their responsibility to make themselves happy. You should avoid the habit of making yourself unhappy in favor of your spouse's happiness.

CHAPTER TWENTY-FIVE

NIGGAS IN PARIS

"Ball so hard, got a broke clock, Rollies that don't tick tock." —*Jay-Z*

Let's dive a little deeper into the research and discover what makes people happy.

First of all, the good news is that marriage is positively correlated to health, wealth, and happiness, so if you are married and reading this book, you are already ahead of your single peers. Even better, if you are having a healthy sexual relationship with your partner and have sex at least once a week, you may be able to increase your happiness even more.[47]

Money also makes you happier, with a few caveats. Research shows that very wealthy people are generally happier and more satisfied in life than average-wealth people, especially if they use their wealth to help other people. The caveat to this is that wealthy people are only happier if they earned their wealth themselves. Unearned wealth—for example, money received through a trust fund—is actually a negative predictor of wealth.[48] [49]

Even if you are not very wealthy, you may be able to boost your happiness with as little as $40. Numerous studies show that spending money to reclaim time can make you happier. In 2017, a group of researchers in Vancouver put this theory to the test. They recruited participants and over two consecutive weekends, they gave each person $40 on the first weekend and another $40 the following weekend. On one weekend participants were instructed to spend the money on material purchases (such as buying clothes or accessories) and on

---

47 Zhiming Cheng & Russel Smyth (2014). "Sex and Happiness," *Journal of Economic Behavior & Organization.*

48 Donnelly, Zheng, Haisley, & Norton (2018). "The Amount and Source of Millionaire's Wealth (Moderately) Predict Their Happiness," *Personality and Social Psychology Bulletin.*

49 Elizabeth Dunn, Lara Aknin, & Michael Norton (2014). "Prosocial Spending and Happiness: Using Money to Benefit Others Pays Off." *Current Directions in Psychological Science.*

the other weekend they were instructed to spend the money on time-saving services (such as hiring someone to do chores around the house). Participants were counterbalanced so half made material purchases first and the other half made time-savings purchases. The results were that the participants reported that they were happier and less stressed when they spent the money on time-savings services versus material purchases. [50]

This research was a clear win for time-saving services and supports my previous recommendation that you should spend more money on hiring assistants, housekeepers, gardeners, nannies, and any other services that could help you reclaim time.

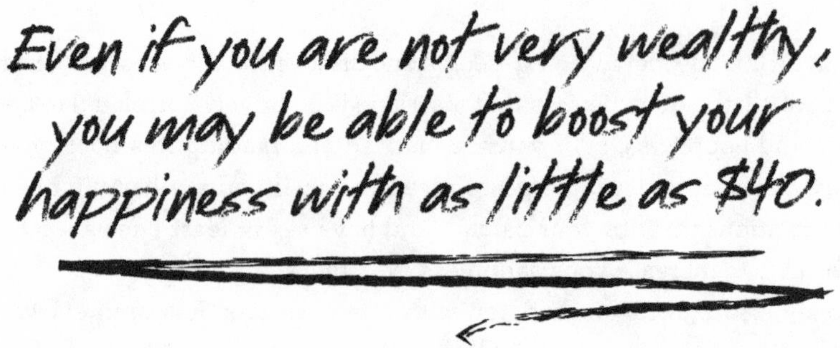
Even if you are not very wealthy, you may be able to boost your happiness with as little as $40.

The challenge, as the previous researchers soon found out, is that people are rarely inclined to spend their money on time-saving services. When given the option, most people opt to spend their money on shopping and material items instead. The same researchers from earlier asked a different group of working-class adults how they would spend an unexpected $40 bonus. Only 2% of the group said that they would spend the money on a time-saving service. This research shows that people may not understand or appreciate just how much time-saving services can actually improve their happiness.

In order to understand happiness a little more, I conducted a survey. I asked 1,000 people, "What makes you happy?" The anonymous survey was an open-ended short answer and the responses ranged from a few words to a few sentences. Here is a graphic showing some common responses. The results were insightful: [51]

---

50 Whillians, Dunn, Smeets, Bekkers, Norton (2017). "Buying Time Promotes Happiness," Proceeding of the National Academy of Sciences (114).

51 Survey conducted through Amazon Mechanical Turk in April 2020.

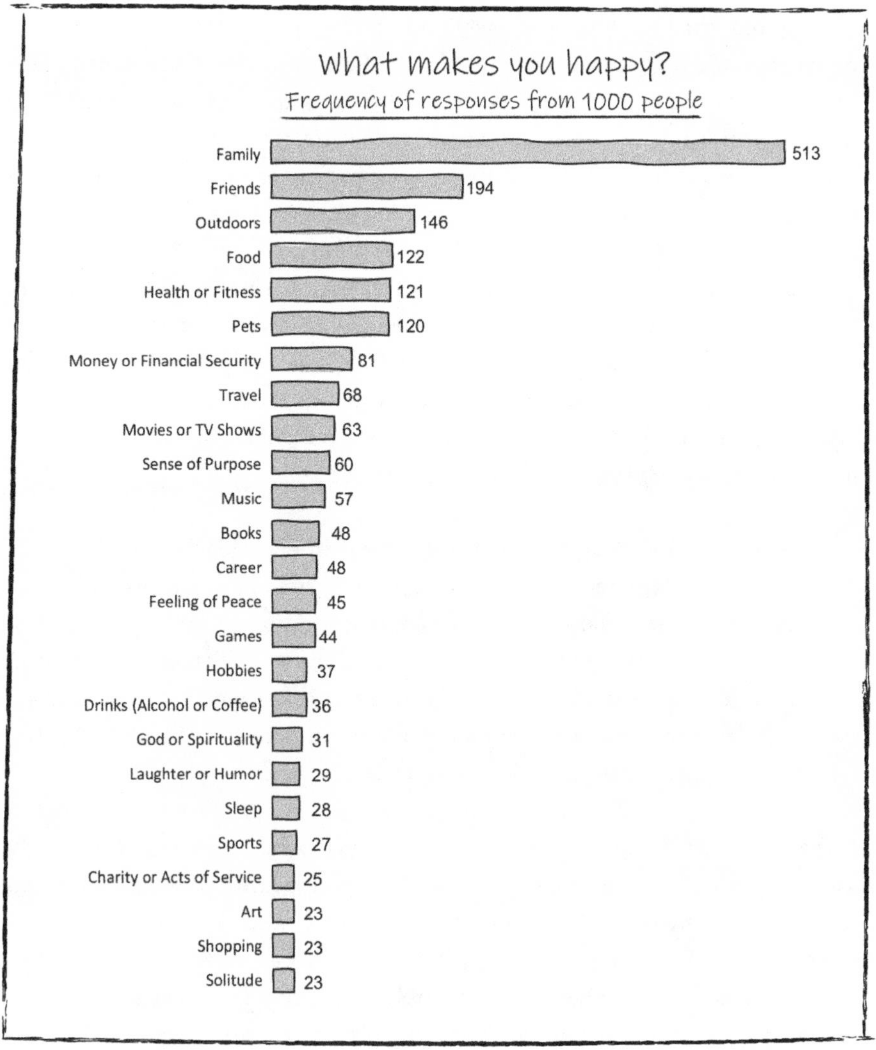

Note that family tops the list with a majority (51%) of people listing those relationships with loved ones as something that makes them happy. Of these 513 responses, 15% specifically mentioned their spouse or partner and 12% mentioned their children. It is also interesting to note that alcohol or coffee (3.6%) was mentioned more frequently than God (3.1%), which is quite funny (2.9%). Items that did not make top 25 but were still intriguing include dancing (eight responses), cars (six responses), and handbags (one response)—this last place category is a contentious topic in the Solano household.

I'm sharing all this research about happiness because so many of us spend most of our lives working endlessly and chasing paper. When we do finally make good money, we rush out and buy the Rolex watches, Gucci belts, Louis Vuitton bags, or Manolo Blahniks. While a good career, financial security, and luxuries can bring us some happiness, we get much, much more happiness when we use our money to help others, invest in time-saving services, eat great food, focus on our health and fitness, and spend more time outdoors with our family, children, significant other, friends, and pets.

I'm not saying that you shouldn't buy nice things once in a while, but the luxury items will not make you as happy as you would be if you used your money to create memorable experiences with your friends and family. This is a particular point of contention between myself, Zaira, and many of our female friends.

A few years ago, I shared a video on my Instagram of Zaira and me kayaking in Weeki Wachee Springs in Florida. In the post I said:

> People are most happy when they invest in experiences. That's one of the reasons why me and Zaira always try to get out, see something new, try something different. Lots of people want a fancy car or nice pair of shoes or something like that, but research shows that when you invest in experiences—that is what brings you the most happiness and joy in life.
>
> Zaira wants me to buy her a Louis Vuitton purse, but I really want her to be happy, so I took her kayaking instead.

Although I was teasing her, Zaira gave me a lot of grief afterward and apparently a lot of her friends agreed. Dozens of friends responded with comments like, "An LV purse is an investment that you can give to your children," "She works hard, she deserves it," and "You can go kayaking AND buy a Louis Vuitton purse."

Unfortunately, research shows that purchasing luxury items has a very short-lived improvement to our happiness. An example is when we upgrade our iPhones. The first day or two that we have a new phone, we have elevated happiness hormones, but after a week, we return to our regular happiness setpoint.

In contrast, our family, friends, experiences, health, pets, careers, and financial security have a much greater and longer-lasting positive effects on our happiness. It is no wonder that shopping and material items like purses or cars were the least frequently cited items in my survey. Dollar for dollar, investing in relationships, activities, and experiences has a much higher happiness ROI than purchasing material goods.

For example, imagine the difference between spending $2,000 on a luxury, like a nice purse or watch, versus spending $2,000 on a vacation.

A couple of years ago, Zaira and I took a weekend getaway to a beachfront house in Cocoa Beach. It was a *nearcation*—only forty-five minutes away from our home in Orlando. Every morning we had coffee and breakfast on the balcony overlooking the waves, we spent hours napping on the beach, and had sex every day. The trip also coincided with the launch of a SpaceX Falcon Heavy rocket. The launch pads at Cape Canaveral were only a few miles away and we were able to hear and see the launch from our balcony.

Imagine our awe and amazement as we toasted champagne together, felt the rumble of nine Merlin 1D liquid oxygen rocket engines, and watched mankind's largest rocket lift into space. Later that same night, we went for a walk on the beach and watched a giant 500-pound sea turtle make its way up the sand, dig a nest, and lay its eggs before it returned to the sea. We sat on the beach, only about 15 feet away from this creature and watched one of the most amazing miracles of life. The entire trip, one of the most memorable of our lives, cost about $2,000, less than a Louis Vuitton purse or Cartier watch. I could never imagine that any material item could bring us as much joy and happiness as that weekend did.

The magic of enjoyable experiences is that they bring happiness whenever we remember them. Even while writing this chapter, I was flooded with the warm memory of that great weekend with Zaira. Likewise, I have those same memories whenever I see photos from that trip, discuss it with Zaira, or think about Cocoa Beach. The added benefit is that since I shared the experience with Zaira, the memory connects us deeper to each other and that connection gets reinforced whenever we think about our time together.

Shared experiences are the foundation for long-term growth in a marriage. Instead of trying to make ourselves happy through material purchases, we prefer to invest in memorable experiences that we would both enjoy, for example Sunday at the Ritz-Carlton spa, a picnic at St. Pete beach, an Andrea Bocelli concert, or a vacation to Hawaii. For long-term happiness, to truly live an emotionally rich and rewarding life, spend more money and energy investing in experiences with friends and family rather than material possessions.

I'm not an ascetic, though. Luxury items can be a nice treat once in a while. Frequently, luxury items and collectibles are a work of art. Furthermore, if you want to upgrade your life in all aspects, you should desire to surround yourself with possessions of higher quality. When it comes to luxury items, the key is to balance your investments in material possessions with investments in experiences and time-saving activities. Additionally, there are some techniques you can implement to increase your happiness ROI from material possessions.

One technique is that, whenever you have your heart set on buying a luxury item, link that purchase to an experience. For example, if you want a new Louis Vuitton purse, make a goal to buy the purse after you get a promotion at work; or if you want a Porsche, set a goal to buy the car after your firm breaks $1 million a year in revenue. In this way, you can use the purchase to motivate you toward your goal and when you think about that car or purse in the future, it will be linked to the experience of getting promoted or reaching a revenue milestone.

Another technique to increase the happiness ROI of material items is to purchase items in conjunction with a new experience. The goal is to create a memory link between that purchase and an enjoyable experience. Here is an example: While Zaira and I were on our honeymoon in Italy, we rented a sporty Italian convertible. A few days after starting our honeymoon, I purchased a pair of $500 Italian driving loafers. Now, when I think about those shoes, I think about the three weeks we spent in Italy, zipping around switchbacks with our top down in the Tuscany hillsides. That experience is much more visceral and memorable than if I simply went to the local outlet mall and bought a pair of shoes, and the shoes bring me a lot more happiness as a result.

When it comes to purchasing luxury items with our personal expense accounts, Zaira and I spend money on whatever we want, without judgement. I would never stop Zaira from buying a designer purse with her personal account. If she asks my opinion, I will give it, but generally I encourage her to spend her money on things that she thinks will make her happy, whatever they may be. Sometimes, though, on the rare occasion that I do go to the mall with her, we will pass a designer store, she'll look at a $10,000 Hermès purse and joke, "You could buy me that for my birthday."

I smile and reply, "I can buy you a purse or we can go to Paris. Which would you prefer?"

The magic of enjoyable experiences is that they bring happiness whenever we remember them.

LET'S RECAP

- Investing in time-saving services such as hiring an assistant, housekeeper, landscaper, or nanny will probably make you happier than buying material items.
- To be happier, spend more time with family, friends, and pets, and spend more time outdoors, eating great food, and being healthy.
- If you want to buy a luxury item, link that item to accomplishing a positive goal or other memorable experience.
- Shared experiences with our spouses trigger positive emotions whenever we remember those great experiences. Investing in experiences as a couple creates a deeper emotional connection with our spouse.

CHAPTER TWENTY-SIX

BLUE

"Each day I feel so blessed to be looking at you." —Beyoncé

In my survey of 1,000 people, family was the thing that people most frequently listed as making them happy. But why? What is it about those relationships that bring us joy?

Zaira and I are DINKs—dual income, no kids—so I understand the limitations of my perspective. In a later chapter, I will be interviewing parents about their experience, but in this chapter, I wanted to share our experiences as a couple who is trying to start a family.

Years before Zaira and I were married, we raised a child together. Sometimes misfortune falls on good people, and when that happened to Zaira's cousin, his daughter Giselle needed a home. For nine months, Zaira and I had parental custody of a precious and unruly three-year-old.

Although Zaira was her legal custodian, we shared parenting duties. When Giselle moved in with us, we made a small bedroom for her, decorated it with Disney princesses, took her to her first day of preschool, taught her how to use the potty, dealt with her temper tantrums in the middle of a grocery store, and experienced how drastically a child will impair a young couple's sex life. Raising her was a rewarding experience, but also very challenging.

Giselle came into our life shortly before I graduated from Georgia Tech. We raised her for six months while we were in Atlanta, and then for another three months while Zaira and I were separated between Atlanta and Orlando. We were already stressed with a long-distance relationship and challenging work and school schedules, which made it probably the worst time in our relationship to get thrown into parenthood.

When Zaira was in Atlanta, she would drop Giselle off at day care in the morning. Then, in the afternoon, she would pick her up and bring her to the office to play in the conference room while she finished her work. When they flew to Orlando, Zaira would work from home as Giselle watched *Peppa Pig* on YouTube or played with our dogs. After a few months of traveling back and forth, we began to look for a second day care in Orlando. It was a challenging nine months, but we made it work—just barely.

We were just getting our sea legs, and were even considering adopting Giselle, when her dad got back on his feet and she was able to return home.

On social media, when I post photos from a weekend at the Ritz-Carlton or a trip to Italy, a frustrated parent will comment things like, "Enjoy it now. Wait until you have children."

I know it can be very difficult and expensive to travel with children or to enjoy some of the other luxuries that DINKs take for granted. However, I also know it is possible to have two successful careers, travel, *and* have children because many of our friends do it every day. On dozens of occasions, Zaira and I have traveled to some exotic location or business workshop with our executive friends or CEOs and spent a wonderful day relaxing at the pool, the beach, or conference with our friends and their children. It requires a lot more logistical planning to travel with children, but it is possible. Life after children is never the same, but that is the nature of any growth and change.

Obviously, we found our time with Giselle rewarding, because on top of considering adopting her, we have now been trying to get pregnant for over three years. The first two years, we had sex whenever we felt like it and hoped that nature would work itself out. The third year, we took an active approach and began scheduling our lovemaking sessions around ovulation windows, trying various positions to help the sperm reach the egg, taking ovulation urine tests, and wearing smart watches to predict the best time to have sex—those did not work either. Now, we are meeting with fertility specialist, getting specialized tests, taking hormones, and once a month I'm going to doctors' offices to make a deposit in the cup.

Nothing is more frustrating than getting test results showing that everything is normal and the doctor telling you that you are in the unexplained category. Soon we will move onto the next step of trying in vitro fertilization.

For most of our lives, Zaira and I cautiously waited to have children. For over thirty-eight years—or at least since I lost my virginity—I've been trying to *avoid* getting a girl pregnant. Now, when we actually want to get pregnant, it is not as easy as we would have expected.

It has been a frustrating process. Both of us had always wanted to be parents for a very long time, even before we met and fell in love. Now, the possibility that we may be infertile challenges our sense of self-identity. While going through our struggle, we have met dozens of other couples who have shared their own fertility challenges, losses, and victories.

Gabrielle Union and Dwyane Wade had a similar struggle before they got pregnant. The Hollywood star describes it like this: "For three years, my body has been a prisoner of trying to get pregnant—I've either been about to go into an IVF cycle, in the middle of an IVF cycle, or coming out of an IVF cycle."[52]

Kim Kardashian and Kanye West, Sarah Jessica Parker and Matthew Broderick, Mark Zuckerberg and Priscilla Chan, Hugh Jackman and Deborra-Lee Furness... these are just a few of the high-profile couples that have admitted to fertility or pregnancy challenges. There are millions of parents who struggle with infertility.

Life after children is never the same, but that is the nature of any growth and change.

Infertility and miscarriages are much more prevalent than a casual observer may think. This is one of the reasons I get incredibly frustrated when someone offers unsolicited pregnancy advice. For example, usually our *abuela* asks us, "When am I going to have grandchildren?"

I'm sorry, Abuela. We all can't get pregnant at nineteen like you and Poppa.

While other professionals tell us things like, "You guys are young. Don't rush to have kids."

Don't rush? Don't rush!?! Do you know how many thousands of dollars I'm spending on these tests and procedures—which, I should add, are not covered by insurance. This baby needs to come ASAP!

As Afro-Latinos, Zaira and I get the "don't rush" comment a lot. When people meet us, they think that we are in our twenties. This is a gift but frequently leads to people underestimating our age or experience—a particular challenge for minorities in professional settings. I know *Black don't crack*, but I'll be 40 years old in just over a year. I'm not a young stallion anymore. Although professional couples are getting married later in life, and humans are living longer, our fertility window has not lengthened proportionally. Infertility will continue to be a rising concern as couples delay marriage and childbirth in lieu of career and financial goals.

---

52 Sarah Grossbart (2020). "How Gabrielle Union and Dwyane Wade Become One of Hollywood's Biggest Success Stories," *ENews!*

Most couples will tell you that there is never a perfect time to get pregnant.

Giving unsolicited pregnancy advice is a very precarious practice because you never know who is in a silent battle. Even a very young person may have emotional trauma surrounding pregnancy. For example, I have a twenty-one-year-old sister who experienced preeclampsia in the eighth month of her pregnancy. Preeclampsia is the same condition Beyoncé had when she gave birth to her twins.

My nephew died a few minutes after the emergency C-section. During the operation, my sister lost most of her blood and her heart flatlined. For the next week, she was in a coma as we patiently waited and prayed for her recovery. Strangers who see her as a young girl and tell her "Don't be in a rush to get pregnant" have no clue how much post-traumatic stress she carries.

Of course, some couples seem to get pregnant the first time they even think about having sex. At one point while Zaira and I were trying to get pregnant, I had no less than three of my other sisters all pregnant, at the same time—life seems unfair sometimes.

Most couples will tell you that there is never a perfect time to get pregnant. You will never feel like you are prepared, you can always be more financially stable, you can always be in better health beforehand, and you will always hope that your relationship was stronger. If you are dual career professionals like Zaira and me, your career and business can be another excuse to delay getting pregnant. Although some of these excuses are valid, many of them are not.

Although Zaira and I have not had children yet, many parents have told me how much they have grown spiritually after having children. Beyoncé, who had multiple miscarriages before giving birth to her first child, Blue Ivy, and then her twins, Sir and Rumi, expresses the feeling like this:

> Having miscarriages taught me that I had to mother myself before I could be a mother to someone else. Then I had Blue, and the quest for my purpose became so much deeper. I died and was reborn in my relationship, and the quest for self became even stronger. It's difficult for me to go backward. Being "number one" was no longer my priority. My true win is creating art and a legacy that will live far beyond me. That's fulfilling.

For many parents, having children changes their professional priorities—family becomes a greater priority than career—but as Beyoncé shows, you can continue to slay while *also* being a parent. I know that parenthood is not for everyone, but parenthood does not need to feel like a sacrifice to your career, finances, or happiness. Instead, it can be a catalyst for growth and learning.[53]

Speaking for myself, I realize now that many of the reasons that I used to rationalize delaying pregnancy, either with Zaira or in my previous marriage, was merely my subconscious trying to protect me from change. Change requires growth, and growth can be very uncomfortable. When faced with change, our subconscious is a master at using rational arguments to persuade us to avoid change. Sometimes it makes sense to delay getting pregnant, but other times it does not. Personally, I wish that Zaira and I began taking a more deliberate approach to pregnancy sooner. The fact is, if you want to have kids, start earlier than you think you should because it will never be the perfect time, and it might take longer than you expect.

LET'S RECAP

- Infertility and miscarriages are more prevalent than most people think, and the likelihood of these obstacles become more prevalent as people get older. This will challenge many aspiring parents as professionals wait longer in life to get married and start a family.
- There is rarely a perfect time to get pregnant. You will never feel prepared and you will probably never have a great window of opportunity during your career, but being a parent can be emotionally and spiritually rewarding on a higher level.
- Getting pregnant and being a parent can be a catalyst for spiritual growth. Although you should not rush into getting pregnant, it is important to understand that discomfort is required for any type of growth.

53 "For Beyoncé, Creativity Is the Ultimate Power" (2019), *Elle*.

CHAPTER TWENTY-SEVEN

HALO

"May God bless and keep you always." —Beyoncé

If the idea of having children while managing two careers seems overwhelming, imagine how my parents felt. Victor and Dorothy, or Vic and Dot for short, have been married for fifty-six years. In addition to each working long careers, they also served as foster parents from 1970 through the 1990s. They have raised over 70 children—that's seven-zero!

Their children varied greatly in age, with some being infants and others being young adults. While serving as foster parents, they opened their home to an unimaginable number of children, many who had unique challenges. For example, many children were previously abused or sexually assaulted, some had learning disabilities, some were autistic. They had an infant foster child who was addicted to crack cocaine and born with AIDS, one teenage girl came to them pregnant, and they even legally adopted a deceased infant who was found in a dumpster just so that they could give her a proper funeral.[54]

At the peak, Vic and Dot had thirteen children living in their home at the same time. Some children stayed with them a few days or a few weeks, some a few years, and some never left. In addition to their foster children, they have two biological daughters and adopted three other children, myself included. It is clear why many of Vic and Dot's friends and family call them "miracle workers" or "saints."

I can personally attest to their generous spirit and open hearts. They adopted me when I was a very young child, and I lived with them and my other adopted and foster siblings until I left for college.

I am incredibly excited to share my interview with my parents, not just because of our relationship, but because they are definitely an Alpha Couple.

---

54 Lisa Saunder (2006). "The Nameless Dead," *Outlook Student Press, 39*. Copy available at www.robertsolano.com/hope-grace

Although they may not be as professionally successful as other couples in this book, they have accomplished feats that would seem impossible to most couples, and they have done it together.

When I was trying to gain a parenting perspective, I could not think of any other couple with as much unique experience and breadth in the subject as my mom and dad. Here are some excerpts from the interview Zaira and I did with our parents.

> **Robert:** How'd you get into adoption and foster care?

> **Vic:** We started in 1970. We took in a young Hispanic boy from the Bronx, New York, and then Angelo came. Angelo was seven years old. And from then it just took off like wildfire, just from one child to another child. I came from nine brothers and sisters, and I was used to a large family. I don't know what inspired us. I can't tell you that it was an inspiration, or a God-centered thing, but it just happened, and we just carried on for over twenty years. We're still carrying on in the year 2020 with three grandchildren living with us. A four-year-old, a six-year-old, and a sixteen-year-old—they live with us. And of course, our two daughters live with us as well. I'm assuming that other people have done what we've done too. I don't know.

I love my parents' humility. I am fairly certain that raising seventy children is an extremely rare occurrence and I highly doubt that any foster family has as unique and special of a story as Vic and Dot.

> **Robert:** Lots of times we grow up and we have this idea of what a family looks like, and sometimes it's very difficult for us to imagine a life other than the *Leave It to Beaver* sitcom. What was that first step for you guys? Did it make you nervous? Did it make you uncomfortable? How'd you get over that first step?

> **Dot:** Well, honestly and truthfully, growing up in the Bronx in an Italian Irish neighborhood, I had never been involved with Hispanic or Blacks or anything. My father couldn't understand why we would think of taking strange children into our home. And then when we were planning on adopting, he was like, "You can't do that. What are you gonna do with these poor children? Dah dah dah dah." But then after a while, it just became part of us. You know.

My parents, with the exception of the foster children, were a normal middle-class family. They both grew up in New York City in the 1940s and '50s. After they married, they moved to upstate New York, where we lived in a typical 2,200-square-foot single-family suburban home. My dad worked in construction as a concrete and brick mason and my mother worked as a clerk at the Rockland Community College registrar's office. Before my brother Angelo, their first foster child was twelve when he first came to the house. At the time, their two biological daughters were two and four years old.

Robert: How did you manage to have two careers, thirteen kids, and not go crazy?

Dot: We have no friends.

Everyone laughs.

Vic: At the time, Liz and Donna were a little older and most of the kids were going to school. Moms [that's what Vic calls Dot] didn't go to her job until about quarter after eight, and all the children basically were all bused to school. Moms got out of work early and I worked at construction and would be home by three thirty or four.

The thirteen children, they weren't with us that long, no more than a year. And then at the end of that thirteen-kid period, we probably zoomed down to about seven or eight. I don't use the word "luck," I use the word "blessings" and "fortunate," and God and Jesus and all the saints must've been with us because it did work out.

Robert: Your faith guided you versus having a plan. It sounds like you didn't necessarily have a plan on how you were going to accomplish it.

Dot: No.

Vic: Social Services system would call us on the phone, "Could you take in another child?" "Okay, bring 'em over." They would call back three weeks later, "We've got two children. Could you take them in?" "Okay. Bring 'em over." And it just was like, they brought 'em over and we accepted 'em. We accepted all kinds: Hispanics, Black, mentally handicapped children, anxiety, children who were raped by their parents, et cetera. And everybody just came, and we accepted it. No plan.

I should point out that my parents are White; my dad is Italian and my mom is Irish. I am biologically Black Latino, Dominican and Puerto Rican. I identify as Black, Dominican, Puerto Rican, Italian, and Irish. My other adopted siblings, not my biological siblings, are also Latino. Vic and Dot's other foster children were all races, but predominantly either Black, Latino, or White.

Robert: Zena was mentally handicapped; that's really hard for a lot of parents. How did you guys get through that and how did it not demotivate you from helping other children?

Vic: Zena came to us when she was twenty years old. She had an IQ of approximately 18, and she was bent over hunchbacked, she drooled, and she couldn't talk. When she came to us she couldn't comb her hair, she couldn't take a bath, she didn't know how to wash—nothing.

In the beginning we just had her on the weekends, and then it was a week, and then she came to live with us permanently five years. Somewhere along the way we taught her how to comb her hair, how to take a bath, how to stand up. She stopped sniffling, she stopped drooling, she started to talk, she went to school, and so on. Believe it or not, she did a lot of things that were exciting and we enjoyed it. She was an amazing child and we really had a great time with her.

Dot: She didn't like "Muther."

Vic: She didn't like Mommy. She loved me. She was my friend.

Dot: "No like Muther. Make me sweep. Made me make samwich. No like you."

Vic and Dot start laughing and smiling at the memories of their special foster child. I also smile and chuckle. As a child, I remember her living with us until about the time I was five years old. Although she was severely handicapped, I vividly remember her incredibly happy demeanor, beaming smile, and loud cackling laughter. She will always have a special place in our hearts.

Regrettably, our family lost contact with her after she returned to the state's custody—such was the way with many foster children before the age of email and Facebook. Today, she would be in her sixties.

Social Services system would call us on the phone, "Could you take in another child??" "Okay, bring 'em over." They would call back three weeks later, "We've got two children. Could you take them in?" "Okay. Bring 'em over."

Zaira: Mom, you didn't give up your career. You continued to work during most of the time that you had all these children at the house. You only retired much later in life for medical reasons. But lots of people, especially women, feel like they need to quit their job or put their careers on hold in order to be a better mother. What message would you have for women in that situation or that are thinking that they can't be a mother and also have a career?

Dot: Well I think that's the new modern thing, but we're all not together all day long. Children go to school, come home; children go out and play. It's the time that you're spending with your family at home—dinnertime, TV time, playtime—that matters.

You have to set a rule. In our house, as you know, everybody sits down together for dinner. And then after dinner we all used to talk, "How was your day? What did you do at school today?" You've got to give them quality time. Even if you have thirteen kids, at least one time during the day, all fifteen of you have to sit down, break bread together, discuss your day, throw the food at one another, whatever it is, but you have to be together. So, if I worked, they were in school, and even if they were home, I had a person that I trusted to take care of the babies and that's how I did it.

Robert: A lot of professional couples these days are waiting later in life to get married. After they get married, they're waiting later in life to have children because they want to either reach a certain point in their career first, or save up enough money, or buy a house before they have children. And so, what's the right time to have children?

Dot: There is no right time.

Vic: I agree on that.

Dot: Especially today, you all have such high bills. You're all professionals, you all have good jobs, but each individual, it depends on what you want from life, 'cause you're all older. I mean, you're not in your early twenties, like we were. You're all older, so you've been places as you travel, you've seen stuff.

Vic and Dot got married shortly after Dot turned twenty years old. A year later, in 1965, Dot gave birth to her first daughter at twenty-one years old.

Vic: I'd like to add a little bit to that. We bought our first house for $20,000! We put $500 down. Just think what I just said—$500 down! Today, that buys you a gallon of milk, two steaks, and maybe a pork chop. These days you buy a $200,000 house and that's approximately $40,000 down. How many people in their early twenties have $40,000 laying around?

So, financially, it's a lot more difficult to start a family in your twenties, but biologically it's more difficult to start a family in your thirties... and by the time they're eighteen you're sixty!

Robert: What makes you happy?

Dot: Well, for me it's trying to make Vic happy, which sometimes I do, sometimes I don't. But the main thing is my children. I'm getting older and my children are getting older. They are constantly showering me with love and respect. They all married lovely spouses who loved me as much as I love them.

Robert: What about you, Dad?

Vic: Linguini and white clam sauce on a Friday night!

Everyone laughs again. Dad loves cooking and makes a delicious linguini and clam sauce.

The first thing is there's no such thing as 50/50. Whoever told you that is wrong because it isn't. It's <u>fight your battles</u>. If it's something small to you, you say, "Eh, the hell with it. Whatever, I'll give in," but if there's something you feel really strongly about that your significant other is not allowing, you have to buck it.

Vic: But no. Lots of things make me happy. I'll tell you what—that all the guys: our children, and their wives, and their family members—they're all in good condition. They're all healthy and you know what's good about it? We all talk... And all our guys, they correspond with each other and that's rewarding.

And I'm happy that we're healthy. We really are. Even though Moms is not feeling good, but basically, what she's been through in the last ten years—

My parents are both in their eighties. My dad is very healthy for his age, despite having bad knees from a lifetime of cement work. My mother is currently cancer-free, but she is still recovering from bladder cancer and lung cancer.

Vic: I know people don't talk about it much these days, they don't emphasize it much these days, and I'm not an over fanatic religious person, even though I do a lot of things, and my guys telling me that I'm weird, but that's okay.

Faith in God, I think, is an important happy solution to life. Faith.

Faith. It's a key word. If you have that, my God, you can do wonders in life, you can. Faith is the key. It's an important thing in life. If you have that, you'll be very successful, and I think that's what kept me and Dot together.

I know you probably have a lot of friends that are in the situations, you know, where they both work, they have two children, or one child, or no children, and they find it difficult. It is, but it can be done. We're not miracle workers, but maybe then we are, I don't know. Maybe God gave us the miracle call. I can't say that.

I'm not saying everything was a bed of roses. I think youse understand that. There was occasions when it erupted. I won't go into too many details about some of the things that happened, but they did. We did have eruptions, but we also had a lot of pleasantries and that was a key factor, and we remember them, and we talk about them. We still talk about them. We still talk about Zena and et cetera.

Robert: If I asked you what's your favorite memory in life, what pops in your head?

Vic: I'm going to explain that question to you because I've heard that quite a few times in my life, and it's the thing people ask the most as you get older, "What do you miss?"

And Robert, if I have to list the things I missed in life or the memories in life, it would take us probably three or four days. Do I miss my first-grade teacher? Do I miss the first little girl that I liked? Do I miss all my friends? Do I miss all my coworkers? Do I miss all my Marine buddies? Do I miss all those things? It's the same thing with memories, Robert. The memories are huge. I mean, I can't give one that's a specific.

The memories that I spent in the streets, on Freeman Street? I had terrific times playing marbles in the streets.

Do I miss all my coworkers? I want to tell you right now, I'm just going to deviate a little bit—I had the best job in the world. Nobody who is reading this and who is a professional will ever have a job like I had. Nobody wants to go into the construction business except Vic Crapanzano and a few of my friends.

I had an unbelievable life of fifty years in the concrete construction business. I had a life of freedom!

I came and chose, and went where I went, when I wanted to, how I wanted to, why I wanted to. If I didn't like the job at five after eight in the morning, I walked off the job, went home, I ate breakfast, lunch, and dinner, and I went to another job the next day. If I didn't like the foreman, I quit. If I didn't like the superintendent, I quit, and I go to another job the next day.

That's a memory I can't forget. My fifty years as a mason. It was the most extraordinary life. I worked on probably, and I'm not exaggerating, over 5,000 different jobs. I worked on the original World Trade Center in 1965. I worked on many, many huge historical buildings, and hospitals, and museums, and art centers, and things, or the Guggenheim Museum in New York—I worked on that. I worked at the Museum of Art in New York.

The same sentiment my dad expressed about coming and going from jobs as he pleased is the same reason why Zaira started her business. Although society rarely thinks of blue-collar construction workers as entrepreneurs, my dad definitely had the freedom and flexibility that so many young entrepreneurs today desire. My dad was his own boss.

Robert: What advice do you have to give to other young couples who are just beginning their marriage?

Dot: Okay. The first thing is there's no such thing as 50/50. Whoever told you that is wrong because it isn't. It's *fight your battles*. If it's something small to you, you say, "Eh, the hell with it. Whatever, I'll give in," but if there's something you feel really strongly about that your significant other is not allowing, you have to buck it. Other than that, life is too short. You have to weigh, which is more important—fighting all the time or moving on?

Vic: As for me, I'd say just be happy as much as possible. Be friendly, not too negative. Don't be too picky. Don't be too mean and vindictive. Try to be liberal as much as possible. Remember the anniversaries, remember the birthdays. Those are important issues. We celebrated my birthday last week, and the kids sang "Happy Birthday" to me, and we had a candle, and we had a little cake. In fact, I made a homemade cake. I'm eighty-two and we're still doing that. So, do those things. They are important. And just be as friendly as possible and as patient as possible. Be patient, don't be angry, and be forgiving.

Dot: Say sorry sometimes.

Vic: Em, yeah...

Dot: "Em, em, em, yeah." You're eighty-two years old and have never said, "I'm sorry about that."

Vic: [*Laughs*] It's true. It's just that some of those things are still left to me from the old days. I should say, "I'm sorry," more. Sometimes I do, but it's rare. Moms is always asking me, "Do you love me?" And I know I don't say it enough. But she knows that I do, because I like to shop for her—*I love you.* I love to cook—I'm telling her I love her. I do the dishes—I love you. I wash the floors—I love you. That's the way I show it. You don't have to express it in words but show it in the details. If your wife says, "The kitchen needs to be painted," paint the kitchen, even if it takes you a year. You know what I mean?

Today, Vic and Dot, my mom and dad, are in their eighties and retired. They still live in upstate New York, in a modest 2,000-square-foot home with their two daughters, three grandchildren, and a pit bull.

Throughout this book, most of the Alpha Couples referenced have been celebrities, millionaires, and executives. They are couples that many people know and can relate to, but as my parents show, you do not need to be a pair of corporate executives or hip-hop legends to be an Alpha Couple. Even a modest middle-class couple can accomplish extraordinary feats with the help of a powerful marriage.

Alpha Couples don't need to be entrepreneurs or executives in the traditional sense of the words; sometimes even a blue-collar construction worker and an office clerk can have more freedom and family happiness than a wealthy Fortune 500 executive.

LET'S RECAP

- If you have faith, you can do wonders. When you begin your journey, you may not know how you will manage dual careers or how you will support a large family, but if you want it, go for it. Have faith that you will figure out a way to make it work.
- Set rules on when you will spend uninterrupted time with your family and spouse. For example, make evening dinner an important time to connect as a family.
- If you want your marriage to last for over fifty years, shop for your wife, cook for her, do the dishes, and paint the kitchen once in a while.... Oh, and have a lot of kids.

CHAPTER TWENTY-EIGHT

SOON YOU'LL UNDERSTAND

"...this whole life we made together." —Jay-Z

For years, Zaira and I felt like outliers. We had two successful careers, we owned multiple businesses together, we traveled all the time, we worked incredibly hard, we enjoyed a spectacular life, and most importantly, we were partners in all things. When we shared stories about work or posted videos on social media, our friends frequently comment things like, "You're such a power couple." I'm not sure what really made us a power couple, but I felt like we were somehow abnormal.

In contrast, it seemed like most of our friends and family lived happily in the suburbs and were content with the man's career being a priority while the woman was the homemaker. While there is nothing wrong with the traditional suburban family model, if that is what both partners desire, my relationship with Zaira has never been traditional. Compound this with the observation that we are one the few successful couples of color in our professional circles, and it was enough to make us think that we were either a very unnatural anomaly or that such a partnership surely should not exist.

When I began writing this book, I originally planned to call it *The Power Couple Handbook*. I began researching other couples to understand if Zaira and I were really anomalies, or if there were other couples like us. If there were others, I hoped that I could learn from them so that Zaira and I could divorce-proof our marriage.

As I began my research, my initial challenge was that I had a hard time defining what makes a power couple a power couple. I admired Barack and Michelle Obama for their intellect, charisma, and leadership; I admired Bill and Melinda Gates for their dedication to philanthropy; I admired Ellen DeGeneres and Portia de Rossi for being courageously open about their sexual orientation and relationship; and I admired Prince Harry and Meghan Markle for going against the traditional royal status quo. While those couples get a lot of attention, and are incredibly successful by the media's standards, there are other lesser known couples that I equally admire, like my parents.

I had a hard time identifying a set of criteria that distinguished one power couple from another. So, I asked Zaira for help, "What does power mean to you?"

After thinking for a moment, Zaira replied, "Choice." I asked her to elaborate. She continued, "Power is the freedom to decide what you want to do and when you want to do it. It's the ability to hop on a flight and travel around the world, or to be able to buy a pair of shoes without worrying about the price, or to be able to decide if you want to work or not," she explained, "It's the freedom to choose."

Before I talked to her about this, I was thinking about power in the traditional sense—influence, social status, strength, wealth, fame, authority. In these traditional norms, the couples I admired were all incredibly different; my working-class parents were incredibly different than Prince Harry and Meghan Markle. Then I realized that what all of these couples shared was that they all made decisions that were incredibly different than societal norms. In other words, they allowed themselves an abnormal amount of freedom.

Instead of using their wealth to only indulge in jets and yachts, Bill and Melinda Gates established the Gates Foundation and dedicated their lives and wealth to helping less fortunate people, which is very uncommon among the ultra-wealthy.

Similarly, my parents dedicated their lives to raising foster children, which is very uncommon for most middle-class couples. Although the Gateses and the Crapanzanos live in extremely different circumstances, they share their courage in pursuit of nontraditional paths—that is *real* power.

It is easy to look at these couples and admire everything they accomplished, but when they first started their journeys, I am sure that most of them were incredibly stressed, anxious, and scared. In cases like my parents, they had family members who discouraged them and told them, "You can't do that," yet they did it anyway.

If I were in their shoes, I am not sure if I would be able to make the same decisions that they did. A few times throughout this book, I discussed the power of our subconscious in keeping us comfortable and preventing us from change and growth. All of these couples seemed to have overcome that obstacle in order to get to where they are today. That is the kind of freedom that I want Zaira and myself to have. Whether Zaira and I decide to start a new business together, adopt ten children, or travel around the world in a sailboat, I want us to have the freedom to choose our own destinies, and that is ultimately what this book is about.

I thought it important to start fresh with this book, which is why I use the term Alpha Couples instead of power couples. The term power couple is a weighted term and carries preconceived ideas about business success, financial wealth, and fame or notoriety. Was my ethological assessment of Alpha Couples in nature 100% correct?—probably not. There are thousands of species of animals, each has unique societal behaviors, and even within each species, behaviors vary greatly between packs. Furthermore, many of the more intelligent animal species have such complex societal behaviors that I could not adequately discuss them without distracting from the rest of the book. This is why I intentionally avoided discussing our closest primate cousins, the bonobo and chimpanzee. None of us can ever truly explain the love or mating instinct between a pair of alpha wolves, horses, or bonobos.[55]

The only way that we can ever break free and live the life that we truly deserve is if we stop tolerating the things that make us unhappy.

We also cannot fully explain how couples viewed or treated each other before humans began recording history, which was only about 5,000 years ago. When it comes to relationships, we can only hypothesize why our ancestors behaved the way they did, but it is difficult to draw any definitive conclusions. Human behavior is always changing and that is the real lesson I learned while examining our ancestors. Change is the only thing that we can be 100% certain about.

Today's traditional concepts of love and marriage are merely a blip in the 200,000 years of our existence. The 1950s *Leave It to Beaver* family is fictional; there's no long-term evidence or science that supports the idea that our marriages should be patriarchal. To the contrary, history and nature lean more toward egalitarian relationships.

All this means that we can create our own definition of marriage and be very

---

55 For further reading about primates, I recommend *Bonobo: The Forgotten Ape* by Frans de Waal and Frans Lanting, and *Chimpanzee Politics: Power and Sex among Apes*, also by Frans de Waal.

happy doing so. This realization gave me a tremendous amount of freedom to choose how I wanted my marriage to look. This led Zaira and me to try our nontraditional intercity marriage. I admit we were generally unhappy during this early period of our relationship—not with each other, but with our circumstances—and at times I asked myself, "Is this it? Are we going to be flying red-eye Spirit flights back and forth from Orlando to Atlanta for the rest of our lives?"

I think a lot of couples ask themselves the same thing—"*Is this it?*" Remember, change is the only thing you can be sure of. You're not stuck.

If power is the freedom to choose, you should choose happiness, you should choose love.

The only way that we can ever break free and live the life that we truly deserve is if we stop tolerating the things that make us unhappy. We need to stop doing the shit we hate just because it costs a little money or because our friends, family, or parents will doubt us. The absolute only way that we can build a rich and rewarding life is if we do fewer of the things we hate and more of the things we love. Unfortunately, the thing that holds so many of us back from upgrading our lives is money.

To increase your financial wealth, you've got to establish a good relationship with money. A healthy relationship with money can support a healthy marriage while an unhealthy relationship with money can destroy a marriage.

When we can learn to balance our investments with an abundance mindset, and when we can trust our spouse with money, we can build greater trust and confidence in our relationship and ourselves. In this way, I hope I have shown how wealth, happiness, and a strong relationship are all intertwined with one another; this is the essence of partnership.

Many couples say things like, "I could never work with my spouse," but if you can unlock this superpower ability, your relationship can grow incredibly strong. This is why each section of this book begins with a lyric from a Beyoncé or Jay-Z song. Beyoncé and Jay-Z are each incredible artists and businesspeople on their own, but as a combined duo, their strength is even greater. They are nearly royalty.

Power is, after all, the freedom to choose happiness. I can use language like a *powerful marriage, fulfilling career, loving family,* or *extraordinary life,* but ultimately what they all have in common is happiness—a happy marriage, a happy career, a happy family, and a happy life.

It is no surprise that when I asked my father for couples advice, the first thing that came to his mind was "Be happy." It's a choice.

Earlier, I argued that you need more than love for a marriage to be successful. Although your marriage needs more than love to be successful, if you give a lot of love *in several areas of your life*, you might find your marriage extremely successful.

What does love have to do with happiness? Well, everything!

On the happiness scale, love is the highest level of happiness. If you aggressively try to raise your standards on the happiness scale, you will find yourself doing more things you love, and less thing you don't love.

A very happy life is synonymous with a love-filled life and the derivative of this is that a love-filled life will lead to a love-filled marriage. All aspects of your life will rise together once you choose happiness. Not the kind of happiness you get from money or shopping—instead, the kind of happiness you get from deep connections with other people, helping your customers and community, sharing memorable experiences with people you care about, and, most importantly, from loving yourself.

If power is the freedom to choose, you should choose happiness, you should choose love.

In the same way that happiness looks different for everyone, every couple must also define for themselves what it means to be an Alpha Couple.

For Zaira and me, we became an Alpha Couple when our relationship with ourselves and one another allowed us to express all of our love, joy, and abilities for one another as well as for our community, clients, staff, friends, and family. Our relationship with ourselves and one another is the center from which all love emanates to positively affect those around us. We communicate well with each other, support each other's physical and spiritual health, and maintain a great sexual relationship. These strengths help us build a family legacy, steward a beautiful environment, and be leaders in our community, businesses, and family. A love-filled life leads to a love-filled relationship and vice versa.

Ultimately, when I think of Alpha Couples, I return to the painting that hangs above our bed: two strong, wild, and powerful horses. These free creatures sprint through the world together, side by side, as equals. They live an intense life, enjoying their freedom and each other. They are fully present, focused, and engaged. They live fearlessly and blissfully, and that is our goal as an Alpha Couple.

Every couple must define for themselves what it means to be an Alpha Couple.

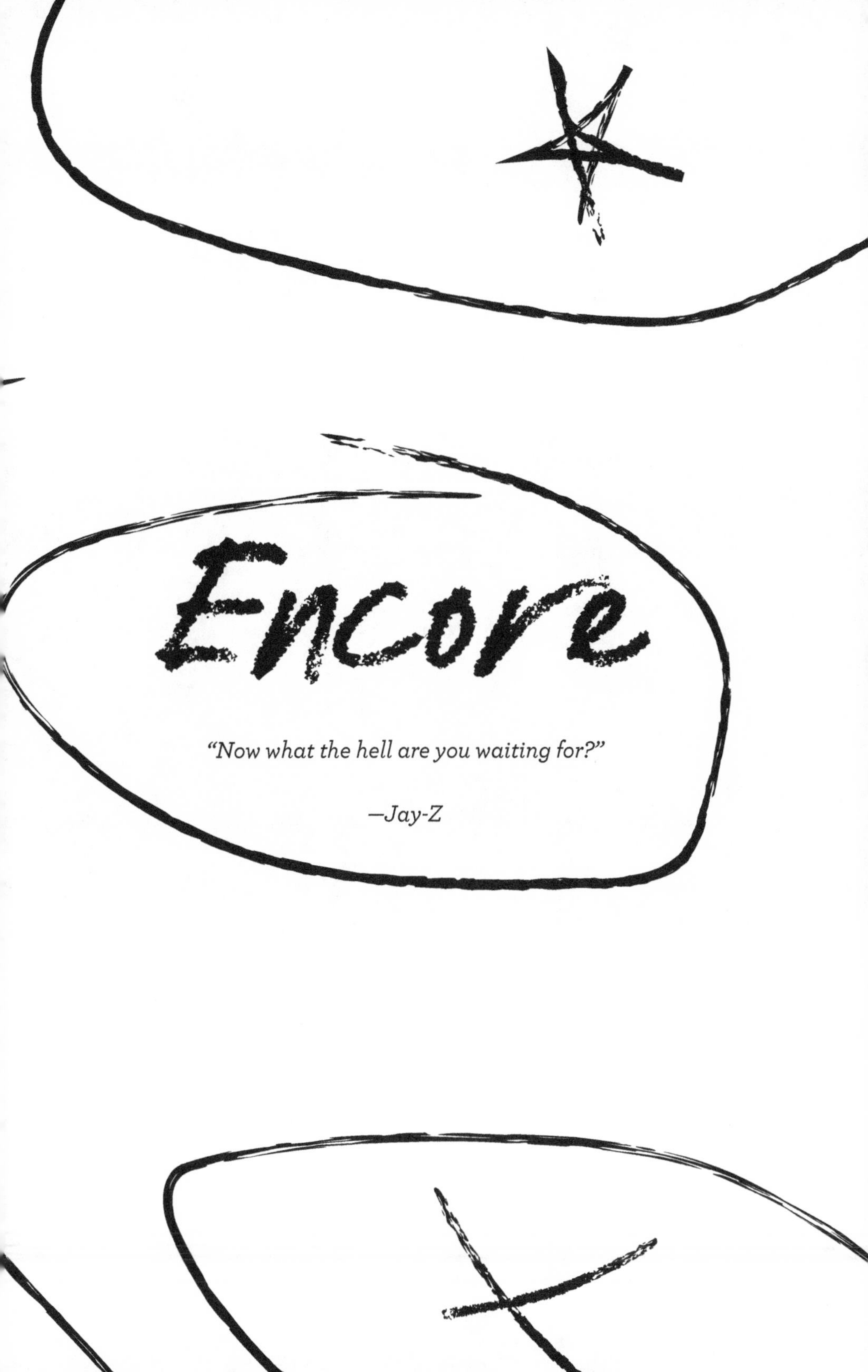

Encore

"Now what the hell are you waiting for?"

—Jay-Z

THANK YOU

"Hold your applause, this is your song not mine." —Jay-Z

There are so many people I need to thank for helping me on my journey. To begin, thank you, reader. I am not perfect. I have my flaws. Thank you for temporarily overlooking them and joining me on this exploration. I only hope that my experiences may help you in some way or another.

If you found something useful, or if you have any questions, I would love to connect. Please visit www.robertsolano.com to find my social media handles and latest news, or you can text me at +1 (202) 933-1501. Thank you for your support. I really could not do this without all of you.

Next up, thank you to my parents, my Dads and Moms, for teaching me the value of love, altruism, sacrifice, and hard work. To my in-laws, thank you for raising an amazing woman. To my many brothers and sisters, aunts and uncles, nieces and nephews, and cousins. I am so blessed to have such a large family. I wish I could thank all of you by name, but if I did the list would be well over 70 names long! In my survey, a majority of people said that family brings them happiness and I completely agree—thank you all.

To the many Alpha Couples who have been a huge part of our lives, in particular Alberto and Nadia, Angus and Jen, and Neera and Vijay—thank you for being examples of amazing couples that Zaira and I can aspire toward. To the handful of coaches and counselors who have helped us over the years, especially Ale and Rjon, David, and Kristen. Thanks for your services; you were expensive, but worth it. To my mentors and supervisors who have helped me through school and my career: John, who helped me get into West Point; Mark, my sponsor at the academy; all my brothers of Alpha Phi Alpha fraternity; and the many others that have helped me succeed. Thank you for your advice, support, and guidance through the years.

To all the soldiers, sailors, airmen, and Marines. Thank you. May God bless you and keep you safe. To the hundreds of students, coworkers, teammates, and friends whom I have worked with throughout the years—if I have accomplished anything it is through the strength of a team. Thank you. To the civil rights activists, past and present, who fight social injustice. Thank you for paving the way for me and future generations. Black lives matter.

Thank you. May God bless you.

To the literary team helping me from Raab & Co.—Josh, Amélie, Cathy, Andrew, and Jackie—if this publication is a success, you have played a huge role in that. I had a dream to design a book that felt like a record album. Thank you for turning that dream into a reality.

Above all others, thank you to my beautiful and amazing wife, Zaira. Sending you a drunk message late at night in 2013 was one of the best decisions I have ever made. Thank you for giving me a chance, and then after I fucked up and dumped you, thanks for giving me a second chance. I love sharing my life with you and am looking forward to many more happy years and decades.

In 2018, I set a goal to write a professional development book. Unfortunately, I did not have a particular topic or focus area. In order to home in my topic, I began blogging and vlogging. I wrote a few different articles and filmed a short video every day for 365 days of the year. Without fail, the videos and blogs that got the most attention and responses were always the ones that included appearances or discussions about Zaira and our personal or working relationship. That small observation led me to the realization that the topics in this book were critically important to other professional couples like Zaira and myself. I also realized that by writing and researching about entrepreneurial couples, I could also potentially learn lessons to improve my own relationship. From there I set out to write this book and I am extremely grateful to Zaira for supporting me on this journey and for letting me share our story honestly and fully.

Zaira is actually quite a private person. When she reviewed an earlier version of the book, her response was, "Holy shit, there's a lot of information about me in this book that I don't want to share with the world." When I asked her if she would be cool with this book, her response was, "I'm just going to pretend like anybody that reads this doesn't know me. Whoever reads this will be in some distant world and I'll never meet them. That's how I get through this."

Well, Zaira, thank you. Thank you for allowing me to share our story, but more importantly, thank you for inspiring me to be a better man, for always having my back, for loving me with all your heart, for sharing your world with me, for putting up with my crazy ideas, for balancing me, for working so hard to support our family, and for having a generous and giving heart. *Te amo, todos los siempres.*

Lead with Love,

Robert Solano

P.S. I'm serious. If you have any questions or comments about this book or anything else, send me a text. Your feedback and support means a lot to me. I also love helping dreamers, hustlers, and entrepreneurs. If you ever have a question about business, relationships, or life, I'd be happy to give you my thoughts or opinions. Hit me up at +1 (202) 933-1501. I look forward to connecting.

CPSIA information can be obtained
at www.ICGtesting.com
Printed in the USA
BVHW030918230820
587087BV00001B/1/J

9 781735 346809